Rural and Small-Town America

SOCIOLOGY IN THE TWENTY-FIRST CENTURY

Edited by John Iceland, Pennsylvania State University

This series introduces students to a range of sociological issues of broad interest in the United States today and addresses topics such as race, immigration, gender, the family, education, and social inequality. Each work has a similar structure and approach as follows:

- introduction to the topic's importance in contemporary society
- overview of conceptual issues
- review of empirical research including demographic data
- cross-national comparisons
- discussion of policy debates

These course books highlight findings from current, rigorous research and include personal narratives to illustrate major themes in an accessible manner. The similarity in approach across the series allows instructors to assign them as a featured or supplementary book in various courses.

1. *A Portrait of America: The Demographic Perspective*, by John Iceland

2. *Race and Ethnicity in America*, by John Iceland

3. *Education in America*, by Kimberly A. Goyette

4. *Families in America*, by Susan L. Brown

5. *Population Health in America*, by Robert A. Hummer and Erin R. Hamilton

6. *Religion in America*, by Lisa D. Pearce and Claire Chipman Gilliland

7. *Diversity and the Transition to Adulthood in America*, by Phoebe Ho, Hyunjoon Park, and Grace Kao

8. *Aging in America*, by Deborah Carr

9. *Rural and Small-Town America: Context, Composition, and Complexities*, by Tim Slack and Shannon M. Monnat

Rural and Small-Town America

CONTEXT, COMPOSITION, AND COMPLEXITIES

Tim Slack and
Shannon M. Monnat

UNIVERSITY OF CALIFORNIA PRESS

University of California Press
Oakland, California

© 2024 by Tim Slack and Shannon M. Monnat

Library of Congress Cataloging-in-Publication Data

Names: Slack, Tim, author. | Monnat, Shannon M., author.
Title: Rural and small-town America : context, composition, and
complexities / Tim Slack and Shannon M. Monnat.
Other titles: Sociology in the 21st century (University of California
Press) ; 9.
Description: Oakland, California : University of California Press,
[2024] | Series: Sociology in the twenty-first century ; 9 | Includes
bibliographical references and index.
Identifiers: LCCN 2024003613 (print) | LCCN 2024003614 (ebook) |
ISBN 9780520401129 (cloth) | ISBN 9780520401136 (paperback) |
ISBN 9780520401150 (epub)
Subjects: LCSH: Small cities—United States. | United States—Rural
conditions—20th century. | United States—Rural conditions—
21st century.
Classification: LCC HN59.2 .S58225 2024 (print) | LCC HN59.2 (ebook) |
DDC 307.72—dc23/eng/20240313
LC record available at https://lccn.loc.gov/2024003613
LC ebook record available at https://lccn.loc.gov/2024003614

33 32 31 30 29 28 27 26 25 24
10 9 8 7 6 5 4 3 2 1

To Dryden, New York, and Gueydan, Louisiana,
two small towns that have played big roles in my life.

—Tim Slack

To my rural hometown, Lowville, New York.

—Shannon Monnat

Contents

List of Illustrations		ix
Acknowledgments		xi
	Introduction	1
1.	Rural Population Change	17
2.	Rural Economies and Livelihoods	35
3.	Rural Ethnoracial Diversity and Inequities	61
4.	Rural Population Health and Health Disparities	95
5.	Rural Politics and Policies	125
	Conclusion	145
	Notes	153
	References	167
	Index	205

Illustrations

FIGURES

1. Census urban and rural areas in the 2020s   11

2. Metro and nonmetro counties in the 2020s   12

3. Population change by metro and nonmetro status, 2000–2020   26

4. Nonmetro population change, 2010–2020   27

5. Median nonmetro population change by level of natural amenities, 1970–2015   29

6. Percent farm population and rural population as a share of overall U.S. population, 1900–2000   38

7. Percent manufacturing sector share of private nonfarm jobs and earnings in metro and nonmetro areas, 2001–2020   40

8. Farming-, mining-, and manufacturing-dependent counties   44

9. Percent underemployed in metro and nonmetro areas, 1968–2017   47

ix

ILLUSTRATIONS

10. Percent poor in metro and nonmetro areas, 1959–2019   48

11. Persistent poverty counties   49

12. Nonmetro population, 2020, and population change by race and Hispanic origin, 1990–2020   66

13. Nonmetro population under age 18 and age 18+ by race and Hispanic origin, 2020   68

14. Foreign-born population totals and population share in nonmetro counties, 1890–2020   69

15. Ethnoracial composition of the nonmetro population, 2016–2020   72

16. Mortality rates by metro status for males and females, 1980–2020   98

17. Mortality rates from the leading causes of death by metro status, 2020   100

18. Mortality rates by metro status, 1999–2020   102

19. Mortality rates for nonmetro counties, 2017–2019   106

20. COVID-19 mortality rates for metro and nonmetro counties   120

21. Percent of votes for the Republican presidential candidate in metro and nonmetro areas, 1976–2020   129

22. Average state policy liberalism scores among more and less urbanized states, 1970–2014   135

TABLES

1. Rural-Urban Continuum Codes in the 2020s   14

2. Percent of Households Engaging in Informal Work by Type and Residence   56

3. Economic Well-Being by Ethnoracial Group in Nonmetro and Metro Counties, 2016–2020   88

Acknowledgments

We would like to extend our tremendous gratitude to the many people who contributed to the development of this book. While two of us authored it, seeing this project to completion was very much a team effort.

Special thanks to John Iceland (series editor) for his invitation to contribute to the excellent collection of books in the Sociology in the Twenty-First Century series. We owe John a debt of gratitude for all his input and patience along the way. Many thanks are also due to Naomi Schneider (executive editor) and colleagues at the University of California Press for their steady guidance and technical expertise in moving us through the process from a prospectus to a completed book.

This work benefited immensely from the critical feedback of mentors, colleagues, and friends, including Leif Jensen, Brian Thiede, Ken Johnson, Dan Lichter, Linda Lobao, John Cromartie, Don Albrecht, Sarah Low, Katherine Curtis, Jessica Schad, Danielle Rhubart, Richelle Winkler, and Shaun Golding. We are also thankful for the technical and intellectual assistance of Yue Sun, Xue Zhang, and KayLynn Larrison.

In addition, we want to thank several organizations and communities of scholars that supported this project. The small but dedicated group of rural demographers who make up the Rural Population Research Network, a USDA-supported multistate research project on the causes and consequences of demographic change in rural America, have been a special source of inspiration and encouragement. Thanks also to the Rural Sociological Society and the Interdisciplinary Network on Rural Population Health and Aging (funded by the National Institute on Aging, R24-AG065159) for facilitating communities of scholarship focused on rural social and demographic issues. Tim acknowledges the support of LSU's Department of Sociology and College of Humanities and Social Sciences, and Shannon acknowledges the support of Syracuse University's Maxwell School of Citizenship and Public Affairs, Center for Policy Research, Lerner Center for Public Health Promotion and Population Health, and Department of Sociology.

Finally, we are grateful for the love and support provided by our families, and for the small communities that have endowed us with an abiding concern for rural America throughout our careers. Tim thanks Tracey Rizzuto and Spencer, Reya, Steve, Susie, and Juli Slack, Dryden, New York (2020 pop. 1,887), and Gueydan, Louisiana (2020 pop. 1,165). Shannon thanks William Schaab, Paul and Christina Monnat, Michelle Monnat, and Lowville, New York (2020 pop. 3,272).

We are indebted to you all. Any shortcomings are our own.

Introduction

> In the domain of rural sociology, even slight acquaintance with the facts destroys commonly held opinion.
>
> —Henri Lefebvre

The contemporary United States is mainly an urban society. Most Americans reside in cities or their surrounding suburbs, and metropolitan areas are our centers for economic activity and mass media. As a nation, the result is that where we live and work, and how the media portrays society, is decidedly urban centric. Modern American sociology also reflects this tendency, taking urban life as its disproportionate focus. So why in this context should we pay attention to rural areas and sociological issues therein? What sociological lessons are there to learn from focusing on social, economic, and demographic changes in, and the problems and prospects facing, rural America?

These questions provide the guideposts for this book. Our central argument is that there is much to learn about rural America, and that doing so can help us to better understand the United States as a whole. While smaller than urban America, rural population numbers remain substantial. In 2020 roughly 14 to 20 percent of the U.S. population lived in rural areas (depending on the definition of

2   INTRODUCTION

rural). That translates into between about 46 and 66 million people. Those are not small numbers.[1] They are larger than the population of any single state in the country (e.g., California, the most populous, was home to under 40 million in 2020) or the number of people in most ethnoracial groups nationally (e.g., Black people represented 12.4 percent of the U.S. population or 41.1 million in 2020, and Asian and American Indian numbers were smaller).[2] In addition, rural America accounts for 70 percent or more of the nation's land area and holds most of its natural resources (e.g., minerals, timber, water, and fertile land) and natural amenities (e.g., open country, forests, lakes and rivers, mountains, and canyons).[3] It also supplies disproportionate shares of the country's food, energy inputs, and military personnel. And there is no denying the continued cultural relevance of rural people, places, and things, whether to our food-ways, music, or politics. In fact, despite common notions casting rural and urban as separate spaces, the rural-urban continuum is more socially and economically integrated and interdependent today than ever before.[4] For all these reasons and many more that we cover throughout this book, gaining a better understanding of contemporary rural and small-town America is an important endeavor.

This is an inherently transdisciplinary project that welcomes readers from across the social sciences—including sociology, demography, geography, economics, and political science—as well as those with interests in policy, practice, and social issues in general. While at times we invoke sociology as our home discipline, our aim is for this volume to appeal to a much broader readership.

HISTORICAL PERSPECTIVES ON RURALITY IN AMERICA

It is important to begin a historical account of rurality in America by acknowledging that prior to European colonization, millions of diverse peoples were already settled throughout what would later become the United States. Over millennia, complex societies and cultures had risen and fallen and evolved across the landscape. The idea that European settlers discovered a vast, uninhabited wilderness upon their arrival is a myth and misunderstanding, the product of a Eurocentric framing of American history.[5] Indeed, the very terms *American Indian* and *Native American* are rooted in the arrival of Europeans in the 15th century.[6] Although this book concentrates on rural population changes and challenges in the contemporary United States, we should be clear that the territory's social demographic story began long before the inception of the nation.

A history better known to most Americans is that over the course of the 17th and early 18th centuries, Britain established 13 colonies along what is now the eastern seaboard United States. The economies of the colonies varied regionally but were mostly focused on agriculture and the harvest of natural resources for export back to Britain. Agriculture in the southern colonies centered on large plantations reliant on the labor of enslaved people to produce cash crops like cotton and tobacco, while the northern colonies were primarily organized around smaller family farms. In the late 18th century, the colonists revolted against the British in the American Revolutionary War (1775–1783), issuing the Declaration of Independence on July 4, 1776. After independence, the social and spatial composition of the U.S. population continued to evolve. This process included people of European and African descent, the latter both free and enslaved, as well as the acquisition of territory previously settled and governed by other nations (e.g., France, Mexico, and Indigenous peoples).

Early American society was mostly rural. As of 1790, there were just six communities in the United States with a population over 8,000 residents, and these places were home to only about 3 percent of the nation's population.[7] Most Americans at the time lived in open country settings and small villages where people's livelihoods revolved around farming and natural resources (e.g., logging and hunting). However, in the late 19th to early 20th centuries, the U.S. population underwent major changes associated with the Industrial

4   INTRODUCTION

Revolution, which corresponded with rapid shifts in immigration from abroad and internal migration to fuel urbanization. As industrialization pulled people from farms to factories and from the countryside to cities, the character of American life was radically transformed. By the middle of the 20th century, most Americans were living in metropolitan settings.[8]

The significance of this transformation—and parallel developments in western Europe—was not lost on early sociologists. Indeed, rural-urban social change and associated challenges were a central concern for sociologists from the birth of the discipline. For example, much of the scholarship of Émile Durkheim (1858–1917), a founding figure in sociology, was devoted to the question of how social solidarity could be maintained as society moved from rural-agrarian to urban-industrial forms of social organization. Durkheim introduced the concepts of *mechanical* and *organic solidarity* to help understand this process.[9] Mechanical solidarity characterized social relations in traditional, small, and undifferentiated societies, where collective bonds were maintained by shared values and beliefs and the widespread performance of similar activities in daily life (e.g., farming and churchgoing). Organic solidarity, he argued, emerged as societies grew larger, more differentiated, and increasingly complex. In these contexts, collective bonds were forged based on people's specialization in the division of labor and related interdependencies. That is, people filled many more types of jobs, but as a result depended more upon one another to get by. Instead of sewing their own clothes, growing their own food, and building their own furniture, they hired a tailor and a carpenter and bought their food at the market. According to Durkheim, it was organic solidarity that would provide the social glue in modern urban society.

Similarly, Ferdinand Tönnies (1855–1936), another prominent early sociologist, developed the concepts of *gemeinschaft* and *gesellschaft* to understand the sociological implications of the rural to urban transition.[10] Tönnies contended that traditional rural societies were characterized by gemeinschaft, a context in which social relationships were governed by the bonds of kinship, religion, and direct interpersonal interaction. In contrast, modern urban society was distinguished by gesellschaft, a milieu in which people's connections were more impersonal, indirect, and rationally directed toward economic and transactional ends. In short, both Durkheim and Tönnies saw the transformation from rural to urban life as fundamentally altering the nature of social relations.

The pioneers of American sociology also engaged rurality. W. E. B. Du Bois (1868–1963), a founder of sociology in the United States, directed much of his scholarship toward changes in rural communities and the structure of agriculture, with a special focus on implications for Black people.[11] While perhaps better known for his groundbreaking research on urban Black populations, Du Bois's empirical studies at the turn of the 20th century concentrated on rural Black communities in the South undergoing social and economic transformations amid the agrarian-industrial transition. His work documented the experience of rural Black people whose lives had been characterized by plantation enslavement and the subsequent fall of that system, many of whom would be part of the Great Migration to northern cities in the coming decades (1910s–1970s).[12] *The Philadelphia Negro*, among Du Bois's most famous studies, was in part about the trials of urbanization among the growing number of Black people who had undertaken that journey.[13]

Pitirim Sorokin (1889–1968), another leading voice in early American sociology, also devoted a great deal of research to understanding rural and urban social organization from a comparative perspective.[14] And between 1919 and 1953, the U.S. Department of Agriculture (USDA) housed the Division of Farm Population and Rural Life, led by sociologists Charles Galpin (1864–1947) and Carl Taylor (1884–1975). Dedicated to studying the social structure of rural America and related public policy, the office was the first in the federal government to pursue sociological research.[15]

While the focus of this book is on contemporary rural and small-town America, the point here is that thinking about social change

6   INTRODUCTION

across the rural-urban continuum, and related problems and prospects, has deep roots in sociology. Thus, this book contributes to a vein of sociological scholarship that, while often overshadowed by urban concerns today, traces back to the foundations of the discipline.

STRUCTURE OF THE BOOK

The goal of this book is to paint a social demographic portrait of rural and small-town America, with an emphasis on changes and challenges. In doing so, we provide a social scientific basis for thinking about geographic space and rurality as axes of inequality. Today we are inundated with misinformation and opinions masquerading as facts. The use of a social scientific approach helps us to arrive at more reliable and valid conclusions about the social world. It does not mean we will all agree on the importance of these facts or how best to address existing challenges. But it does allow us to begin conversations on contemporary issues from an empirically informed point of departure.

A narrative tool we use throughout the book is *myths* and *misunderstandings* about rural America. This lens encourages us to grapple with the ways conventional wisdom about rural America is often inaccurate or oversimplified. Here are some examples:

Aren't all rural communities shrinking and fading away? Although it is true that urbanization is a dominant demographic trend, the population of rural America remains significant in size and social and economic influence. Moreover, if we rely on measures that define rural as some combination of small population size and low population density, places that experience sustained population growth only remain rural for so long before they transition to being urban.[16] Sometimes the absence of consistent population growth is cast as a social problem. But if that is the case, it implicates rurality itself.

Isn't rural synonymous with farming? Although agriculture is a vital industry, it represents only a small share of the contemporary rural labor force (less than 10 percent even in completely rural counties).[17] Services and manufacturing are the two largest employment sectors in rural America. Indeed, trends toward deindustrialization have been quite painful for many small communities where manufacturing jobs have long been a mainstay. It is one thing for a factory to shut down in a thriving and diversified metropolis, but quite another when it is the main employer in town.

Didn't a "rural revolt" lead to the election of President Donald Trump? Although it is true that the rural vote disproportionately went to Trump in 2016, rural voters have been increasingly voting Republican for decades. The 2016 (and subsequent 2020) Republican vote shares in rural counties were consistent with a trend that predated Trump. In fact, it was changes in voting patterns in a few small and medium-sized Rust Belt cities that tipped the vote in Trump's favor in 2016.[18] Rural America is also not a political monolith. For example, rural areas with substantial Black, Hispanic, and Native American populations, and places with economies driven by natural amenity recreation, often vote in the Democratic column.

This sample highlights one of the book's primary objectives: unpacking myths and misunderstandings about rural America by confronting the empirical evidence from the social sciences.

The chapter outline is as follows. In chapter 1 we focus on population change in rural America. We describe how three major demographic processes—fertility, mortality, and migration—have contributed to rural-urban population transformations, including instances of "rural rebounds" when social forces coincided to reverse the prevailing trend of urbanization. The chapter also deals with how depopulation, amenity in-migration, youth out-migration, aging, and ethnoracial shifts are reshaping rural America.

Chapter 2 examines how the economy of rural America has changed over time and the implications of these changes. Issues related to economic diversity and industrial sector dependence are covered, as well as the impacts of globalization and deindustrialization. We also explore concerns regarding poverty and underemployment. Last, we

8 INTRODUCTION

discuss participation in informal work—economic activities undertaken outside the regulatory framework of the state—and the role of the social safety net in rural America.

Chapter 3 covers issues related to rural racial and ethnic diversity. Here, we emphasize that rural America has always been more ethnoracially diverse than is commonly assumed, and it is trending toward increasing diversity over time. However, *where* this is happening is highly uneven. The chapter attends to the experiences of a variety of minoritized rural ethnoracial groups, including American Indian people and the special consideration of reservations; Black people and the special consideration of the rural South; Hispanic people and the special consideration of "traditional" and "new destination" settlement patterns; and Asian people, who though comprising a small share of the overall U.S. rural population have a long history of settlement in some parts of rural America. The connection between minoritized rural ethnoracial groups and persistent poverty regions, the latter introduced in chapter 2, also receives attention. Questions around ethnoracial inequities and their roots in historical and contemporary racism guide the chapter.

Chapter 4 addresses rural-urban population health disparities. The chapter covers geographic disparities in various health indicators (e.g., life expectancy and chronic disease prevalence) as well as the "rural mortality penalty" (i.e., mortality rates are higher and life expectancy is lower in rural than urban areas). In addition, we examine the drug overdose epidemic and the COVID-19 pandemic, the impacts of which have varied significantly between rural and urban areas but also across different types of rural places. A point of emphasis in the chapter is the role of upstream determinants of health and mortality disparities, such as political and economic structures.

Chapter 5 turns to a discussion of rural politics and policies. We describe the political tendencies of rural America, including attention to elements of the contemporary rural-urban political divide, but also highlight that the rural United States is not politically monolithic. In addition, we cover the conceptual question of policies that focus on people and others that focus on places (i.e., person-versus place-based policy). A guiding concern in this chapter is how policies can address not only *who* and *what* but *where*.

Finally, in the conclusion we summarize the book's major themes and what they portend for the future of rural America.

This by no means represents an exhaustive account of the changes and challenges facing rural America. For example, one issue to which we do not devote a stand-alone chapter is the environment. That said, environmental concerns are woven throughout the topics covered, including how the environment interfaces with population change (e.g., natural amenity migration), how people make a living (e.g., agriculture and natural resource extraction), where different groups are located (e.g., Black people in the rural South), environmental contributions to health disparities (e.g., exposure to toxins and natural disasters), and major policy questions of the day (e.g., climate change). Other issues one might point to being absent from our chapter outline are housing and crime. However, to address every problem and prospect in rural America is beyond the scope of this (and maybe any) book. Instead, we provide a sample of topics that we hope will pique readers' interest and encourage critical thinking about rural people and places in contemporary America.

WHAT IS RURAL?

At this point it is imperative to ask a seemingly simple question: *What is rural?* Rural, of course, is a concept with which most of us are familiar. We all have ideas about what rural is that flow from our own lived experiences. But our lived experiences are extraordinarily varied, and therefore so are our images of rural places. These subjective interpretations are vitally important from a sociological perspective because they hold implications for meaning making and identity.[19] They shape the ideas we draw on to make sense of the

10 INTRODUCTION

world around us and our place in it. However, given the social demographic thrust of this book, our presentation primarily relies on definitions of rural as a geographic location. In the following we outline the major methods used by social scientists and policymakers to define rural in the United States: namely, the official U.S. definitions of urban-rural and metropolitan-nonmetropolitan.[20] While we often use the terms *rural* and *nonmetropolitan* interchangeably to make our writing more accessible (a frequent practice among rural sociologists), it is important to remain mindful of the distinctions. It is also important to recognize that these definitions do not capture all sociocultural aspects of rurality, an issue we elaborate in the following.

Urban-Rural

The official federal definition of urban-rural comes from the U.S. Census Bureau. Drawing on data from the decennial census, in the 2020s urban areas are defined as densely developed territory encompassing residential, commercial, and other nonresidential land uses. Each urban area must include at least 2,000 housing units or at least 5,000 people.[21] Urban areas are often incorporated places but do not necessarily conform to official municipal boundaries. Rather, they are clusters of settled territory like one might observe on the landscape from an airplane. Rural areas are then defined as the residual: all places not defined as urban. The Census Bureau makes these designations after each decennial census, and they stand for a decade. In fact, the definition of urban areas outlined here is a change from the previous population minimum of 2,500 people, which had been in place from the 1910s through the 2010s. Given the timing of this change, many of the statistics we report in this book rely on the previous definition of urban-rural.

Figure 1 is a map of rural and urban areas based on the definition for the 2020s. It is easy to observe areas many of us commonly think of as urban: the corridor spanning from Boston to Washington, D.C.,

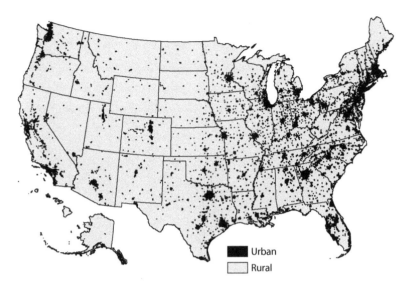

Figure 1. Census urban and rural areas in the 2020s. *Note*: Incorporated places and census-designated places are the units of analysis. *Source*: U.S. Census Bureau, 2023a.

in the East; Seattle, San Francisco, and Los Angeles in the West; and cities like Chicago, Atlanta, Dallas, and Houston. It is also notable that the vast majority of the land area of the United States fits the rural definition. This space was home to about 66 million people, or one in five Americans, in 2020.[22]

Metropolitan-Nonmetropolitan

More widely used in rural sociology and demography (including in this book) is the official federal definition of metropolitan (metro) and nonmetropolitan (nonmetro) areas, a designation made by the U.S. Office of Management and Budget (OMB). Conceptually, this definition is focused on population size, density, and economic integration. The units of analysis are counties and equivalent entities (i.e., places comparable to counties but called by different names,

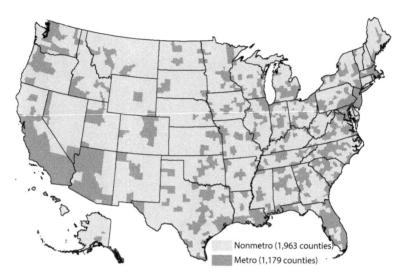

Figure 2. Metro and nonmetro counties in the 2020s. *Note*: Counties are the unit of analysis. *Source*: U.S. Census Bureau, 2023b.

such as parishes, boroughs, districts, and independent cities). The boundaries of county lines have the advantage of being relatively stable, allowing for more consistent comparisons over time. They are also typically significant for local politics and public administration.

Based on census data, in the 2020s metro areas are defined as counties with at least one urban area of 50,000 or more population, plus adjacent counties exhibiting a high degree of social and economic integration with the core as measured by commuting ties.[23] Nonmetro areas are then defined as the residual: counties not fitting the metro definition. Like the Census Bureau approach, the OMB designations are made after each decennial census and stand for a decade. Unless otherwise indicated, in subsequent chapters our focus is primarily on nonmetro populations and places (i.e., counties).

Figure 2 is a map of metro and nonmetro counties in the 2020s. Again, recognizable population centers are evident, notably along the East and West Coasts, but also in the interior of the country. In the 2020s, roughly three in five (62 percent) U.S. counties are defined as nonmetro, while two in five (38 percent) are defined as metro. Nonmetro counties account for most of the nation's land area and in 2020 were home to 46 million people, or 14 percent of the American population. Nonmetro areas can be further subdivided into micropolitan (micro) and noncore areas. Micro counties are centered on urban areas of at least 10,000 but less than 50,000 population and related commuting patterns (like the metro definition), while noncore counties are all the remaining nonmetro areas (i.e., those not micro).

Rural-Urban Continuum

While the official urban-rural and metro-nonmetro definitions provide two-category classification schemes that are useful for comparative purposes, most people recognize that rural-urban space is more of a continuum than it is two discrete categories. Places can be more or less rural and more or less urban. A useful measure produced by the USDA Economic Research Service is the Rural-Urban Continuum Codes (RUCC). The RUCC combines the urban-rural and metro-nonmetro categorizations to create a nine-category measure that considers population size, degree of urbanization, and metro adjacency to characterize counties. Table 1 shows the RUCC categories, ranging from counties in metro areas with a population of over one million to counties that are completely rural and not adjacent to a metro area. The advantage of the RUCC is that it acknowledges greater variation across rural-urban space than do the two-category approaches.

Complexities in Categories

As demonstrated by the RUCC, the official measures of urban-rural and metro-nonmetro are not mutually exclusive. Both metro and nonmetro counties can be home to rural and urban places. In fact, during the 2010s over half (54 percent) of Americans living in rural

Table 1 Rural-Urban Continuum Codes in the 2020s

Code	Description
	Metro counties
1	Counties in metro areas of 1 million population or more
2	Counties in metro areas of 250,000 to 1 million population
3	Counties in metro areas of fewer than 250,000 population
	Nonmetro counties
4	Urban population of 20,000 or more, adjacent to a metro area
5	Urban population of 20,000 or more, not adjacent to a metro area
6	Urban population of 5,000 to 20,000, adjacent to a metro area
7	Urban population of 5,000 to 20,000, not adjacent to a metro area
8	Urban population of fewer than 5,000, adjacent to a metro area
9	Urban population of fewer than 5,000, not adjacent to a metro area

SOURCE: U.S. Department of Agriculture, 2024.
NOTE: Counties are the unit of analysis.

areas also resided in metro counties.[24] In addition, because both the urban-rural and metro-nonmetro classifications are updated after each decennial census, the places included in these categories change over time. Some nonmetro areas experience population growth and become metro, some urban areas experience population loss and become rural, and so on.[25]

It is also important to realize that any approach to categorization (in the social sciences and beyond) masks diversity. Just because things are grouped together in a category does not mean they are the same in all respects. For example, nonmetro areas may be like one another regarding certain aspects of population size and density, but they may be quite different in other ways (e.g., the types of people who live there, political attitudes, or the ways folks make a living). Rural areas are not a monolith.

INTRODUCTION 15

A final caveat is that while social scientists rely on various categorizations of rural and urban space that might suggest separation or apartness, technological advancements and other forms of change in society mean that rural and urban spaces are increasingly socially and economically interconnected. While we use categorization to help us make sense of information, rural and urban spaces are really relational to, as opposed to separate from, one another. This fact is demonstrated every day in the ways rural and urban spaces are connected by people's daily travels, the trade of goods and services, and flows of information and capital. Rural-urban boundaries are spanned and blurred constantly by people commuting to work, shopping, and ferrying children to activities, not to mention interacting on the internet.

All of this said, categorization is critical to our ability to process information. If everything in the world around us was treated as being unique or one of a kind, we would have too great a cognitive load to make sense of it all. Thus, categorization is fundamental to how we think, analyze information, and engage in decision-making. We could not author a book about rural America without categories defining what rural is and is not. These categories are needed for both conducting social science and crafting public policy. In short, the issue is not that standard rural-urban categorizations are not useful—they are critical. Rather, the point is to be aware of what measures do and do not capture and how our conclusions about demographic and social phenomena might vary depending on which definition we use.

CONCLUSION

The goal of this book is to paint a social scientific portrait of rural and small-town America, and the problems and prospects therein, using a social demographic change and challenges perspective. Attention to social issues in the United States tends to be decidedly urban centric. With this book we aim to provide a counterweight, emphasizing how what happens in rural America matters for the entire nation. We approach this task by holding up myths and misunderstandings to the empirical evidence from the social sciences to gain a greater understanding of the context, composition, and complexities of rural America.

1 Rural Population Change

A story in the *Washington Post* in 2019 provided the following account of population change in the state of Wyoming during recent decades:

> Many [rural areas] followed a trajectory similar to Lincoln County, Wyo., home of Kemmerer, the "Fossil Fish Capital of the World." Once a thriving mining town where retailer James Cash Penney opened his first store, Kemmerer is reeling. The owner of a nearby coal mine went bankrupt, and a potential sale fell through last month.
>
> Even before the mine faltered, Lincoln County's population growth slowed dramatically [over time, according to] data from the Census Bureau. Contrast that with Wyoming's two metro areas, Cheyenne and Casper, which added more people than the rest of the state combined.
>
> Both of Wyoming's fast-growing metro areas were once defined as rural areas. But because they grew, they no longer count as rural America in the official statistics.[1]

This account illustrates the varied population trajectories—gain and loss—that are continuously unfolding across rural and

18   CHAPTER 1

small-town America.[2] As indicated in the news story, shifts in population affect a defining characteristic of rural communities. Given that rural is defined by small population size and low population density, the gain or loss of population determines whether a community disappears, stays rural, or becomes urban.[3] On the one hand, sustained population loss can threaten the very existence of communities. On the other hand, sustained population growth can put a community over the urban threshold. Additionally, population gain is often viewed as an important driver of economic development, based on the assumption that stagnant or declining populations undermine prospects for economic growth. In short, population change is a central challenge for rural communities.

The goal of this chapter is to describe major population trends in the rural United States. First, we describe trends in urbanization. Second, we outline changes in the three components of population change—fertility, mortality, and migration—and the implications for rural-urban demographic shifts. Third, we look beyond the effects of population size to consider trends in the population composition of rural America, with a focus on changes in the age structure and ethnoracial makeup of places.

URBANIZATION

As described in the introduction, the United States has transitioned from a rural agrarian colony to a majority urban society over the last two and a half centuries. The urbanization of the U.S. population has corresponded with an increase in the number of urban centers and the share of the country's territory classified as urban. In some contexts, these trends have given rise to "urban sprawl," as the footprints of cities have expanded into rural areas once on their periphery.[4]

While urbanization stands as a dominant demographic trend in the United States, it is important to underline two caveats that contribute to myths and misunderstandings. First, the process of urbanization has not been linear or even unidirectional over time. In the 1970s and again in the 1990s, nonmetro areas experienced greater population growth than metro areas and were net receivers of in-migrants from urban areas, periods referred to as "rural rebounds."[5] Second, places themselves shift between rural and urban status, both from rural to urban and from urban to rural, as populations increase and decrease. For example, several counties that were classified as nonmetro in the 2010s had cities that surpassed the 50,000 population threshold in the 2020 Census and were thus reclassified as metro, including Gallatin County, Montana (home to Bozeman). This illustrates how the United States can lose nonmetro population not because of actual population decline, but instead due to nonmetro population growth that triggers the reclassification of a county to metro. While most reclassified counties each decade shift from nonmetro to metro, there are often also counties that are reclassified from metro to nonmetro as they experience population loss or deconcentration (or lose commuting connections to urban cores). An example following the 2020 Census was Jefferson County, Arkansas (home to Pine Bluff).

The fact that rural places are reclassified as urban once they gain a large enough population highlights an important consideration: many of the people and places classified as urban today were once rural, often quite recently. Between 1960 and 2017, about one-quarter of all nonmetro counties were reclassified as metro, transferring nearly 70 million people between county types. In fact, essentially all growth in the metro share of the U.S. population over this period was driven by nonmetro-to-metro reclassification, rather than growth in preexisting metro counties themselves.[6]

These dynamics have important implications for our understanding of rural society and communities, because the rural places that urbanized were often the most "successful" in terms of population growth and correlated socioeconomic outcomes. In other words, the process of "selecting into" the urban United States means that the places and populations classified as rural represent a moving target

20   CHAPTER 1

from decade to decade, one that is likely to be disproportionately disadvantaged over time relative to urban and urbanizing comparison groups.[7] It is a myth and misunderstanding that all rural areas are characterized by population loss and economic malaise. Many rural areas are socially and economically vibrant and growing. But if that growth is sustained, at a certain point they will be reclassified as urban. Keeping this fact in mind is critical for understanding many of the social and economic trends described in this book.

POPULATION GAIN AND LOSS

The main components of population change are fertility (births), mortality (deaths), and migration (people moving from place to place). All demographic shifts can be explained by changes in one or more of these three factors. In this section, we describe trends and differentials in fertility, mortality, and migration in the rural and urban United States and implications for population change overall.

Natural Change

Natural change refers to the difference between the number of births and deaths in a population during a given period. When the outcome of that difference is positive, a population is said to be experiencing *natural increase* (i.e., growth due to more births than deaths). When the outcome of that difference is negative, a population is said to be experiencing *natural decrease* (i.e., decline due to more deaths than births). Whether a population is experiencing natural increase or decrease then plays a critical role in determining overall population change (alongside migration, which we discuss in the next section).

FERTILITY

The total fertility rate (TFR) provides a summary measure of the average number of births among women over their lifetimes.

Research has shown that the rural TFR is consistently higher compared to urban areas of the United States, though women have been having fewer babies in both contexts over time. Between 2007 and 2017, the TFR for women in nonmetro areas declined from 2.21 to 1.95, compared with declines of 2.11 to 1.78 and 2.10 to 1.71 among women in small and large metro counties, respectively.[8] In other words, the TFR has remained higher, and recently has declined less, in rural than urban areas. This reality reflects a range of sociodemographic and cultural differences between places.

We highlight three such factors here. First, rural women and their partners tend to have lower levels of education and income than their urban counterparts, and greater educational attainment and higher incomes are associated with lower fertility. For example, in 2020, 20.7 percent of adults in nonmetro counties had a college degree or higher, and 24.2 percent had a personal income under $25,000, compared to 35.0 percent and 17.4 percent in metro areas, respectively.[9] Second, rural women are more likely to begin having children at younger ages than their urban counterparts. To illustrate, in 2017 the mean age at first birth for women in nonmetro areas was 24.5 years, more than three years younger than women in large metro areas (27.7 years).[10] Third, cultural differences between rural and urban areas encourage higher fertility in the former. For instance, rural residents are more likely than their urban counterparts to participate in organized religion, which is often associated with pronatalist sentiment.[11]

However, while individual rural women tend to have more children than their urban counterparts (i.e., higher rural TFR), it is also the case that births are less prevalent in rural areas overall. A major reason for this is that the age structures of rural and urban populations differ. Rural areas are more likely to be home to a greater share of older people and thus a smaller share of women of reproductive age.[12] As a result of an older age structure, rural births tend to be less common overall even though the rural TFR is higher.[13]

MORTALITY

Until recently, the rural United States had seen widespread improvements in life expectancy.[14] From 1999 to 2009, both rural and urban counties experienced robust improvements in life expectancy, though urban life expectancy increased by 1.2 years more among women and 0.86 year more among men compared to their rural counterparts. But while urban counties continued to experience modest life expectancy increases from 2010 to 2019, rural counties experienced absolute declines (−0.20 year for women and −0.30 year for men). As of 2019, life expectancy at age 25 (the average number of additional years a person could expect to live after reaching 25) was 55.6 among women and 50.8 among men in rural areas, compared to 58.1 among women and 53.4 among men in urban areas, differences of 2.5 years and 2.6 years, respectively.[15]

These differences in life expectancy reflect what demographers call the "rural mortality penalty" (i.e., shorter lives for people living in rural places).[16] The rural mortality penalty first emerged in the 1980s for males and the 1990s for females and has grown since that time. In addition to overall mortality, rural populations also face disadvantages in many specific domains of health, as evident in age- and cause-specific death rates. Rural populations face a higher risk of premature death at all ages than do their urban counterparts. And the same is true for most specific causes of death, including cancer, heart disease, respiratory disease, diabetes, alcohol-related diseases, and suicide.[17] The COVID-19 pandemic has recently contributed to the disparity as well, due to higher rates of death from the disease in rural areas.[18]

Despite the overall rural mortality penalty, rural areas are not homogenous in this respect. Mortality trends over the last decade or so have been especially worrisome in rural Appalachia, New England, the south Atlantic, and parts of the South-Central United States. Meanwhile, trends have been more favorable in the rural mid-Atlantic, mountain, and Pacific regions.[19] These within-rural mortality differences, and the major determinants of population health that drive them, are described in more detail in chapter 4.

Like fertility, mortality rates are also influenced by the local age structure. Not only are rural residents subject to higher mortality at all ages, but the older population found in rural areas puts additional upward pressure on mortality rates. When combined with lower numbers of births, higher mortality makes natural decrease (more deaths than births) a likely scenario in many parts of rural America. To this point, from 2010 to 2019, most (54 percent) nonmetro counties experienced natural decrease, compared to only about one-quarter (24 percent) of metro counties.[20]

Net Migration

In addition to births and deaths, populations change due to migration. *Net migration* refers to the difference between the number of in-migrants (people moving in) and out-migrants (people moving out) during a given period. Thus, positive net migration occurs when more people move in than out, and negative net migration occurs when more people move out than in. Demographers have tracked patterns of net migration in rural America for decades, and they point to three important conclusions.[21]

The first is that rural counties are characterized by lower net migration than urban counties. During the decade spanning 2010 to 2020, the nonmetro United States witnessed a net migration loss of 510,000 people (–1.1 percent). Only one-third of nonmetro counties had net migration gains over the period. In contrast, metro areas saw a net migration gain of over 4 percent during the same timeframe.[22] Historically, migration has tended to contribute to population growth primarily in rural communities that are adjacent to urban centers—places most likely to eventually be integrated into metro areas (i.e., suburbs and exurbs)—while it has tended to be a source of population loss for more remote rural communities.[23] However, between 2010 and 2020, nonmetro areas saw negative net

24   CHAPTER 1

migration regardless of their adjacency to metro areas, albeit with the most remote rural counties experiencing the greatest relative migration losses.[24]

A second conclusion is that rural communities commonly experience high rates of out-migration among young adults. Since the 1950s, the core counties of metro areas have consistently benefited from in-migration among adults in their 20s, while suburban counties have attracted family-age adults (30–49) and their children. In contrast, nonmetro areas have lost younger adults but seen a net increase in those at older ages (60–74).[25] The implication is that rural counties are most likely to lose—and least likely to gain—people in their prime years for gaining education, being employed, and having children. These dynamics represent an important demographic and economic disadvantage for rural communities, including the loss of potential local workers, business owners, and taxpayers, as well as the vibrancy and future promise of children. Further, this process is selective in terms of educational attainment, with more highly educated young adults being more likely to leave in search of opportunity elsewhere, a circumstance that has been termed rural "brain drain."[26]

Last, migration in rural counties is heterogeneous. While national averages provide important insights into the demographic changes across the overall rural population, they mask considerable diversity in the conditions and trends characterizing smaller subsets of counties. To illustrate this diversity, we can identify four types of counties with different migration patterns. Most consistent with national trends are rural counties experiencing *youth out-migration* and the associated brain drain noted previously.[27] Additionally, rural *retirement destinations* are places characterized by stable or growing populations driven by the in-migration of retirement-age individuals and, in some cases, streams of working-age adults employed in sectors that support the new population of retirees (e.g., health care).[28] Relatedly, rural *amenity destinations* are places characterized by stable or growing populations driven by streams of in-migrants attracted to natural amenities popular for outdoor recreation (e.g., mountains and bodies of water).[29] Some of these areas are also retirement destinations, but others attract relatively youthful streams of migrants. Rural amenity destinations saw substantial net migration gains during the COVID-19 pandemic as people sought to escape cities and remote work became more common.[30] A final example is the group of counties that are characterized by stable or growing populations because they are experiencing new flows of international migration (i.e., immigration), often from Mexico and Central America. The emergence of new rural *immigrant destinations* (which we discuss more in chapter 3) has offset the population decline occurring among the native-born population in such contexts.[31]

Rural Depopulation

Natural change and net migration combine to determine overall population gain or loss. Figure 3 shows population change by metro and nonmetro status from 2000 to 2020.[32] The data demonstrate that between 2000 and 2010, metro areas experienced greater natural increase and net migration than nonmetro areas, resulting in greater population growth overall. Nevertheless, the nonmetro population did grow over the period as well, driven by more births than deaths and more people moving in than out. The subsequent decade, however, was a different story. Between 2010 and 2020, natural increase and net migration again produced population growth in metro areas, albeit at a lower rate than in the previous decade, while nonmetro areas lost population. Rural depopulation over the decade resulted from a diminishing number of births only barely exceeding a rising number of deaths, as well as more people moving out than in. On balance, between 2010 and 2020, the total population of nonmetro America decreased by 0.6 percent, while the total population of metro areas increased by 8.8 percent.[33] This was unprecedented; never in history had rural America experienced an overall decadal population loss.[34]

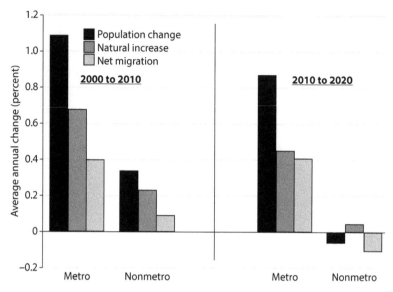

Figure 3. Population change by metro and nonmetro status, 2000–2020. *Note*: Counties are the unit of analysis. *Source*: Adapted from Johnson, 2022.

While rural depopulation was the dominant trend in the 2010s, figure 4 demonstrates that the experience was not monolithic.[35] Approximately two-thirds of nonmetro counties lost population between 2010 and 2020. Population loss was common in the agricultural heartland of the Great Plains and Farm Belt, much of the Deep South and Central Appalachia, and the mixed agricultural and industrial belt spanning from New York to Illinois. In contrast, suburban expansion and natural amenity attractions continued to drive growth in about one-third of nonmetro counties. These places were concentrated in the West, as well as in parts of the Southeast and New England.

That major macro trends mask a diversity of local experiences is, of course, nearly always true. Such is the nature of aggregation and averages. Even in the "rural rebound" of the 1990s, the trend was toward "selective deconcentration."[36] That is, while the general

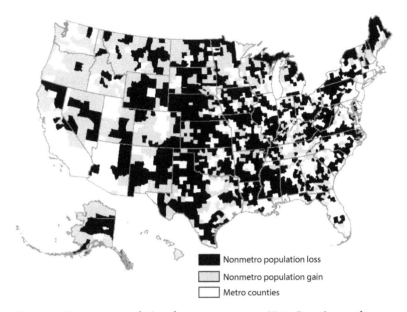

Figure 4. Nonmetro population change, 2010–2020. *Note*: Counties are the unit of analysis. *Source*: Author calculations based on data from 2010 and 2020 Decennial Censuses.

tendency was for population growth to favor rural over urban areas during that period, there were still many rural communities that continued to lose population. This was captured by Mark Baechtel in a story in the *Washington Post* in 2000. He had traveled to Lebanon, Kansas—a community positioned at the geographic center of the contiguous United States—to report on life in "middle" America at the millennium. Lebanon's population was 303 at the time. Despite the national trend toward rural population growth, he wrote:

> During the hours I walk up and down Main, the street stays so empty a dog could lie down in it for a long nap in no fear of being awakened, much less run over. The curbs are lined with crumbling Victorian gingerbread storefronts, mostly abandoned, dropping bricks and powdery mortar onto the sidewalk. No faces appear in their windows. Getting *whittled down* was the way one [local man] characterized the town.[37]

28   CHAPTER 1

Lebanon, Kansas, had clearly not participated in the 1990s rural rebound.

Depopulating rural areas face a unique set of challenges. These include the ability to maintain an adequate tax base to support critical infrastructure like roads, water systems, health care, and education. There are also challenges in terms of maintaining a vibrant economy, given fewer workers and less consumer demand for goods and services, as well as for social and civic life, given fewer people to serve on school boards and coach Little League. Growth also brings new demands, including the integration of newcomers, accommodation of increased calls for services and infrastructure (e.g., housing, health care, schools, traffic), and the need for planning processes that have not been used in the past (e.g., many rural communities have historically been resistant to land-use zoning). Ultimately, rural America faces a "demographic paradox."[38] That is, places are often viewed as demographic "winners"—those witnessing population growth and economic development but urbanizing in doing so—and demographic "losers"—those characterized by population loss and economic decline. This presents a critical challenge: Can communities strike a balance between social and economic vibrancy and rurality, or must growth underpin well-being?

Rural Natural Amenity Destinations

A notable set of rural places that have bucked the depopulation trend are those experiencing natural amenity–driven in-migration. Many people are drawn to the beauty of the rural outdoors, especially in areas with mountains, lakes, forests, and other attractive natural features. These factors, present in places like the mountain West, encourage people to move to areas boasting such features.

Figure 5 shows median percent population change among nonmetro counties from 1970 to 2015 by level of natural amenities.[39] The level of natural amenities is based on a scale constructed from

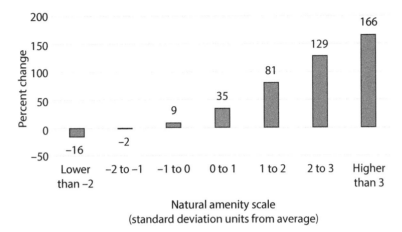

Figure 5. Median nonmetro population change by level of natural amenities, 1970–2015. *Note*: Counties are the unit of analysis, based on the 1974 metro-nonmetro delineation. *Source*: Adapted from U.S. Department of Agriculture, 2022a.

measures of climate, topographic variation, and water area. The data make clear that amenity levels in rural areas have been positively correlated with population change over the last four-plus decades. Nonmetro counties that are low in natural amenities have tended to experience population loss, while high-amenity nonmetro counties have seen population growth, sometimes at striking levels (over 100 percent). High-amenity settings are attractive for outdoor recreation enthusiasts and retirees for tourism, second-home ownership, and year-round residence. These types of communities have also become increasingly popular as technological innovations have untethered some people from their physical places of work. Indeed, during the COVID-19 pandemic, some rural high-amenity, high-growth communities came to be called "Zoom-towns," due to the influx of professional remote workers taking up residence (a play on the term "boomtown," applied to places experiencing rapid growth due to the discovery of a valuable extractive resource like oil or gold).

30   CHAPTER 1

Population growth in rural high-amenity areas can carry benefits in terms of economic development and community revitalization but can create new challenges as well. In addition to the general challenges of growth mentioned in the previous section, unchecked development and population pressure can degrade the very natural resources that people initially found attractive (e.g., via pollution, obstructed views, clearing land for building, the loss of peace and quiet). Research has documented not only community impacts from the increased volume of new people but also how the characteristics of newcomers tend to differ from longtime residents, giving rise to "culture clash" and new forms of inequality.[40] For example, Jessica Ulrich-Schad captured the following story from a longtime resident of a small town in the Rocky Mountains:

> One of my most negative things is the new people who move here and want to get us to be like where they came from. This is a great story, an older lady that I knew . . . was at the grocery store. This lady was behind a woman who was checking out. The woman was chewing out the checker, saying "I could not find any soft mozzarella! I just don't understand! When I was in California, I could always get. . . ." She was going on and on. The checker said 'I'm sorry. We don't get enough demand. We don't carry it." My friend said, "You know, ma'am, why don't you just move back to California?" There are people with that attitude who come in here. The first thing they want to do is change us.[41]

In-migrants to high-amenity rural areas often come from more urban places and have higher incomes and more education than longtime residents. Different cultural tastes and preferences and greater affluence among newcomers can create demands for new types of businesses and drive up real estate prices. While people often associate the term *gentrification*—the process by which the character of an area is changed by wealthier people moving in and displacing current residents—with urban settings, research provides ample evidence of gentrification in rural high-amenity communities as well.[42]

CHANGES IN POPULATION STRUCTURE AND COMPOSITION

As noted earlier, changes in population size tend to occur alongside shifts in population composition. Two noteworthy demographic changes in the rural United States over recent decades relate to its age structure and ethnoracial composition.

A change in age structure refers to an increase or decrease in the share of a population across different age groups. A population's age structure becomes younger if the share of residents in younger age groups (e.g., < 30 years) increases and becomes older if the share of residents in older age groups (e.g., 65+) increases. Research using the Census Bureau's definition of rural-urban shows that the share of and national trend toward older populations is more pronounced in rural America. Between 1980 and 2016, the percentage of the population aged 65 years and over in rural areas increased from 10.9 to 17.5 percent (6.6 percentage points). The corresponding trend in urban areas was a more modest increase, from 11.4 to 13.8 percent (2.4 percentage points).[43]

While population aging is common in rural areas, its causes are not uniform. In some places, population aging is driven by high rates of out-migration (and low rates of in-migration) among young adults described previously.[44] Importantly, the loss of these individuals not only reduces the population share in younger age groups, it also tends to reduce the origin community's birth rate (and thus the population share of children) since young adults take their reproductive potential with them when they leave.[45] In such situations, older residents age in place while the younger population declines, leading to relative increases in the population share at older ages. In another set of cases, rural communities have experienced increases in in-migration among older, retirement-age populations.[46] Even if the original population remained constant (i.e., there were no major changes in out-migration among young adults), these counties would experience aging given the influx of older in-migrants. Considering

32 CHAPTER 1

age differentials in employment, income, and the types of services people demand, population aging has implications for the size and composition of local economies (e.g., less demand for schools and business, professional, and hospitality services; more demand for health care; depressed labor force participation via retirement; and different housing needs).[47]

The second major compositional shift in the population of rural America is toward increasing ethnoracial diversity. The notion that rural areas are homogeneously White is a myth and misunderstanding. The rural United States has always been more ethnoracially diverse than commonly assumed, and this has become increasingly so in recent decades.[48] According to one study, 92.1 percent of all nonmetro counties experienced an increase in ethnoracial diversity between 1990 and 2010.[49] As of 2020, 76 percent of nonmetro residents were non-Hispanic (NH) White, 9 percent were Hispanic, 7.7 percent were Black, 3.4 percent were of other races (i.e., American Indian and Asian), and 3.9 percent were multiracial. Indeed, over the last decade, the largest population gain across these groups was among those who claimed a multiracial identity.[50] There are several factors contributing to increasing rural ethnoracial diversity, including the emergence of new immigrant destinations and White population decline.

New immigrant destinations represent a spatial diversification in the settlement patterns of immigrants away from traditional "gateway" cities and states.[51] In many cases, these changes have been driven by economic changes that increase demand for immigrant labor in new places and the quest to find affordable housing beyond high-priced gateway real estate markets.[52] This population movement, especially pronounced among Hispanic people, has provided a "lifeline" to many rural communities by offsetting population loss and aging.[53] Importantly, these contributions to population growth operate not only through migration but also through higher fertility among new immigrant populations (who tend to be younger than the native-born population) after they have settled.[54] Such dynamics

RURAL POPULATION CHANGE   33

represent a positively reinforcing demographic cycle, which contrasts with the cycle of out-migration and population decline that would occur in their absence. It also means that ethnoracial diversity among children in rural areas is more pronounced than among adults.

The other important driver of increasing ethnoracial diversity in rural America has been natural decrease in the rural White population. It is among White people that the demographic forces of declining fertility and increasing mortality in rural areas have been most profound. Between 2010 and 2020, the rural White population declined by approximately two million people.[55] The increasing ethnoracial diversity of rural America is a source of opportunity and challenge, most notably around the broad issues of equity and inclusion in social, economic, and civic life. We explore these issues further in chapter 3.

CONCLUSION

In this chapter we outlined major trends in rural population change in the United States. These include urbanization, depopulation (due to declining fertility, increasing mortality, and out-migration), natural amenity migration, aging, and increasing ethnoracial diversity. The patterns described have complex causes and consequences and are interrelated and dynamic.

An important consideration from a rural social change and challenges perspective is how the demographic processes covered in this chapter feed off one another. For example, youth out-migration is implicated in both reduced population growth (or population loss) and the aging of rural communities' populations. Both changes in turn can reduce the economic vitality of communities, increase deaths, and reduce births. This then sets the stage for more young people to leave the community in search of opportunity elsewhere. These "vicious" cycles are difficult to break and reverse. On the other

34   CHAPTER 1

hand, communities that can reverse such cycles and create "virtuous" cycles instead stand to benefit. The lifeline offered by population growth from both native-born and foreign-born Hispanics in rural America holds promise in this regard. But its success depends on the ability of newcomers and longer-term residents to accommodate one another and together weave a new community social fabric. Forging paths toward mutual accommodation between newcomers and old-timers is a challenge in growing rural high-amenity communities as well.

The idea that all rural communities are depopulating and fading away is a myth and misunderstanding. Many rural places are growing. The "demographic paradox" in rural America—the split between demographic "winners" (characterized by population growth and economic development, but urbanizing as a result) and demographic "losers" (characterized by population loss and economic decline)— begs a pivotal question: Is rural population decline a "social problem" (as it is commonly portrayed), or has it been improperly conflated with other conditions and processes causing difficulties in rural communities? Rural communities have small populations, and their populations must stay small to remain rural. Therefore, if the absence of sustained population growth is a social problem, it implicates rurality itself, promoting a decidedly urban-centric view of social and economic development. A more critical perspective suggests the need to develop ways to promote social and economic vitality within rural communities without necessarily undermining their rurality and prescribing for them an urban future.

2 Rural Economies and Livelihoods

When the mill went out, it was the other shoe dropping. I mean, it was devastating. . . . I seriously went home and was just like, "Oh my God." We all thought that within a few years our schools would be on the verge of closing. I thought my job may not be in existence. Everybody just sucked in, pulled back, and held on, and thought "What's gonna happen?"

You know, we had a lot of small fringe businesses that were making it, and when a hundred families moved out [after the mill closure], boom, that was it. You know, we had four grocery stores and we have two now. A lot of restaurants, a lot of gas stations . . . aren't here anymore.

—Jennifer Sherman, *Those Who Work, Those Who Don't*

These quotes from Jennifer Sherman's book *Those Who Work, Those Who Don't* highlight the challenges of economic change and disruptions to livelihoods experienced in many parts of rural America. In this chapter we explore trends in the transformation of rural economies and the implications those changes hold for how people make a living.

Popular stereotypes of rural areas often invoke bucolic images of farm life: red barns, rolling fields, and hearty salt-of-the-earth people making a living from the land. To be sure, agriculture has

36   CHAPTER 2

historically been central to life in much of rural America, and it remains a vital sector of the American economy. But like so many aspects of rural life, economies and livelihoods have undergone profound changes over time.[1] One goal of this chapter is to demonstrate that thinking of rural as synonymous with farming today is a myth and misunderstanding.

Relatedly, many people understand that vibrant and robust economies require diversity. Dependence on any single economic sector creates vulnerability to changes in the market as industries and economies restructure in response to innovation and changes in demand, a process that has been called "creative destruction."[2] However, owing in part to rural areas being defined by low population numbers and density, achieving appreciable economic diversity in such contexts presents a major challenge. Taking a deeper dive into the economic diversity dilemma for rural areas represents a second goal of this chapter.

Finally, it is common for people to think of poverty and economic hardship in geographic terms. For many, poverty suggests dense inner-city environments and concentrated neighborhood disadvantage. For others, poverty conjures images of rural contexts like the Oklahoma Dust Bowl or Appalachian coalfields, such as those so poignantly captured during the Great Depression by photographers like Dorothea Lange. However, the truth is that neither prosperity nor poverty is the exclusive domain of rural or urban areas. A third goal of this chapter is to describe key considerations in the geography of economic hardship and how people make ends meet in rural America.

ECONOMIC CHANGE IN RURAL AMERICA

The Agricultural Transition

As described in the introduction, for much of U.S. history most Americans lived in rural and small-town settings where people's livelihoods were centered on agriculture and natural resource extraction. But as the Industrial Revolution took hold in the late 19th and early 20th centuries, industrialization not only fueled urbanization, it also transformed the nature of the rural economy. Over time the locus of rural employment shifted away from agriculture and toward other sectors, leading to the abandonment of farming as a widespread rural livelihood strategy. The social significance of this shift in American life cannot be understated: "The exodus of Americans from farming is one of the most dramatic changes in the U.S. economy and society in the past century."[3]

In the early 20th century, agriculture was extremely labor intensive. As of 1900, more than 40 percent of the American workforce was employed in agriculture, a tremendous amount of human labor that was complemented by over 20 million work animals (e.g., horses and mules).[4] Farms in this period tended to be family-based operations, and while there were notable exceptions—such as the large-scale plantations devoted to commodities like cotton in the South—most were small in terms of acreage and diversified in terms of the goods they produced.

But over the course of the 20th century the United States witnessed a decline in the number of farms and the share of Americans working in agriculture (including owner-operators, tenant farmers, and laborers). This coincided with increases in farm size and capital intensity (i.e., assets required for production, like property and equipment), as well as specialization in the production of a limited variety of commodities.[5] These changes were facilitated by federal policy interventions born of the New Deal and the adoption and diffusion of new technologies, the latter of which took place at an especially rapid pace after World War II. While agriculture was overwhelmingly reliant on animal power in 1900, in the postwar period tractors replaced animal power, and mechanical crop harvesting became widespread. Mechanization, combined with advancements in plant and animal breeding and the extensive use of chemical inputs (i.e., fertilizers and pesticides), meant both increases in

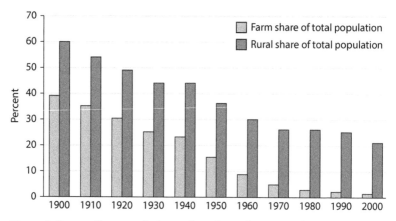

Figure 6. Percent farm population and rural population as a share of overall U.S. population, 1900–2000. *Note*: USDA defines a farm as any operation with the ability to produce at least $1,000 in agricultural goods each year. This definition has changed over time, though the current definition has stood since 1975. *Source*: Dimitri et al., 2005.

productivity and decreases in labor demand in the agricultural sector. By 1970 only 4 percent of Americans were employed in agriculture. And by 2000 that number had fallen to less than 2 percent.[6] Periodic crises put additional pressure on farmers amid these long-term trends. For example, the Dust Bowl of the 1930s forced at least 2.5 million people (many of whom had been farmers) out of the Plains states.[7] And in the 1980s a devastating agricultural recession led many family farms into heavy debt and caused mass farm foreclosures, especially in the Midwest.[8]

Figure 6 shows that over the last 100 years the share of Americans engaged in farming has undergone a marked decline relative to both the total population and the rural population specifically. Today agriculture accounts for less than 10 percent of employment even in counties that are completely rural.[9] Moreover, by the beginning of the 21st century, more than 90 percent of farm households claimed off-farm income, a livelihood strategy often undertaken by families to supplement their finances and gain access to employer-based health insurance offered to workers in other sectors.[10]

Manufacturing and Deindustrialization

In early industrialization, rural areas played a vital role by supplying the raw materials and much of the labor (through rural-to-urban migration) that fueled the process. The historical heyday for manufacturing in the United States was the period spanning from the end of World War II to the 1970s. Due in part to the devastation the war had brought to much of the rest of the industrialized world at the time, this stage of development saw U.S. manufacturing rise to global dominance. Nationally, employment in manufacturing reached its peak in the 1950s, when nearly one in three American workers were employed in the sector, though it remained the largest single sector of U.S. employment through the 1970s.[11]

Starting in the 1970s, however, the U.S. manufacturing sector began to face more intense international competition as the process of globalization—the increasing interconnectedness and interdependence of people, businesses, and governments worldwide—reshaped the economic landscape. Increased import competition drove U.S. manufacturers to cut costs. For some this meant moving production to less developed countries. But for manufacturers who kept their production domestic, many met the goal of lowering expenses by moving to rural areas where wages, land, and local tax costs were generally lower than in urban locales, and where workers had less bargaining power (e.g., a more limited opportunity structure and lower union density). By the 1980s, the manufacturing sector's share of employment and earnings in rural areas exceeded that of urban areas.

As illustrated in figure 7, this pattern holds to the present. While rural and urban America alike have witnessed deindustrialization over recent decades (i.e., declining employment in manufacturing), manufacturing continues to provide a greater share of jobs and

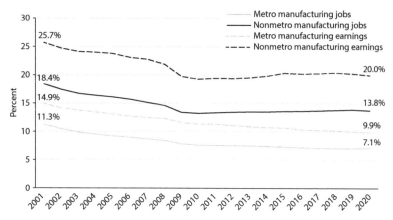

Figure 7. Percent manufacturing sector share of private nonfarm jobs and earnings in metro and nonmetro areas, 2001–2020. *Note*: Start- and end-point values included on trend lines. *Source*: Author calculations using data from U.S. Bureau of Economic Analysis, 2022.

earnings in rural areas than other sectors people often assume predominate, like timber and agriculture, though important sectoral linkages certainly exist (e.g., lumber mills, vegetable and fruit processing, and meatpacking). Over the last two decades, manufacturing has averaged 14.7 percent of jobs and 21.5 percent of earnings in nonmetro areas, compared to 8.2 percent and 11.8 percent in metro areas. The relative importance of rural manufacturing amid deindustrialization represents an ongoing challenge in many small towns across the country. As illustrated by the quote at the beginning of the chapter, when a plant has come to define the identity and economy of a community for generations, its closure is especially painful.

The Rise of the Service Sector

As the process of globalization progressed, the economic landscape for American workers continued to change in rural and urban areas alike.[12] The trend toward deindustrialization was accompanied by a rise in service sector employment (i.e., the portion of the economy that produces intangible goods, as opposed to raw materials in the extractive sector or tangible goods in the manufacturing sector). Nationally, the service sector surpassed manufacturing as the largest sector of employment in the 1980s, and during the 1990s services accounted for nearly all U.S. job growth.[13] By 2020, 80 percent of national employment was in service-producing industries.[14] Today services comprise the largest share of employment in both rural and urban settings.

Common jobs in the rural service sector include those in educational and health-care services as well as entertainment, recreation, accommodation, and food services. Given the size of the service sector, it encompasses many types of jobs that vary in quality. A source of concern with service industries is that they are characterized by a "good jobs" versus "bad jobs" divide. That is, jobs are split between some providing workers a desirable standard of living, job security, and fringe benefits (e.g., health care and retirement plans) and others providing low wages, insufficient and unstable hours, high turnover, and meager (or absent) benefits.[15] A related trend in the American labor market has been the rise in nonstandard employment (i.e., temporary and contingent work). These jobs stand in contrast to standard employment, where there is an assumption of a long-term relationship between employer and employee if demand and performance are maintained. Nonstandard jobs are typically of poorer quality in terms of pay and benefits, and rural workers are more likely to be employed in nonstandard work than their urban counterparts.[16]

Taken together, the trends described here culminate in several important considerations. The first is that it is a myth and misunderstanding to think of rural as synonymous with farming. While most farming does occur in rural areas, very few people in contemporary rural America are employed in farming directly. In addition, while manufacturing is often associated with an urban landscape, in comparative perspective manufacturing plays a more prominent role in

42   CHAPTER 2

rural employment today. This means that the well-documented hardship and dislocation from deindustrialization has been and continues to be felt acutely in small-town America. Finally, the service sector has grown to claim the dominant share of jobs in both rural and urban areas of the United States. This suggests that research and policy attention to the prospects and problems associated with this vast sector has the potential to serve rural and urban communities alike.

ECONOMIC DIVERSITY AND DEPENDENCE

Economic diversity—having a balanced mix of jobs and industries in a local area—helps communities weather economic shocks and changes. If any one part of the economy takes a hit, there are other industries and job opportunities available to help soften the blow. In contrast, economic dependency refers to being highly leveraged on a particular industry or employer. This is a precarious economic position because all businesses are subject to "creative destruction." The risk in such a situation is captured by the adage that it is unwise to "put all your eggs in one basket."

Although most people recognize that economic diversity is desirable, rural areas face several obstacles to its achievement. Small populations, physical isolation and distance, less developed infrastructure, and inherent disadvantages in agglomeration economies (i.e., the market benefits to firms from clustering near one another) all deter rural economic diversification. On the other hand, as noted in the previous chapter, rural areas that are successful in growing and attracting substantial investment can in turn transition from being rural altogether (and become urban). This trade-off represents a major dilemma in rural development.

The USDA Economic Research Service issues an economic typology that helps put the challenge of rural economic dependency in stark perspective.[17] It divides all counties in the United States into one of six mutually exclusive categories: farming dependent, mining dependent, manufacturing dependent, federal/state government dependent, recreation dependent, and nonspecialized. The first five categories refer to counties that rely heavily on a particular sector of the economy. Figure 8 presents maps of counties defined as dependent on farming, mining, and manufacturing, respectively. A total of 444 counties are defined as farming dependent; this includes 19.8 percent of nonmetro counties (compared to 4.5 percent of metro counties). Most farming-dependent counties are clustered in the Great Plains, spanning from North Dakota to Texas. When contrasted against overall trends in rural agricultural employment described previously, it is important to note that these are some of the most sparsely populated areas of the country. Further, 221 counties are defined as mining dependent; this includes 9.3 percent of nonmetro counties (compared to 3.2 percent of metro counties). Regional clusters can be observed in Appalachia (coal), Oklahoma and Texas (oil and gas), and the mountain West (metals and non-metallic minerals). Finally, 501 counties are defined as manufacturing dependent; this includes 17.6 percent of nonmetro counties (compared to 13.1 percent of metro counties). These places are primarily clustered in the eastern half of the United States.

In addition to the county economic types displayed in figure 8, 11.6 percent of nonmetro counties are defined as recreation dependent (compared to 8.9 percent of metro counties). In fact, according to the USDA typology, 70.4 percent of all nonmetro counties are defined as being dependent on a particular economic sector (compared to 44.1 percent of metro counties). Viewed against this backdrop, uneven development and the "creative destruction" of industrial change clearly generate unique economic risks for many rural areas. As summarized by Katherine Curtis and colleagues, "places dependent on distressed sectors become distressed places."[18]

Of special note here is the substantial body of scholarship that has emphasized the implications of dependence on natural resource extraction (e.g., oil, gas, mining, and timber) for rural communities. Despite relatively high wages paid to those directly employed in these

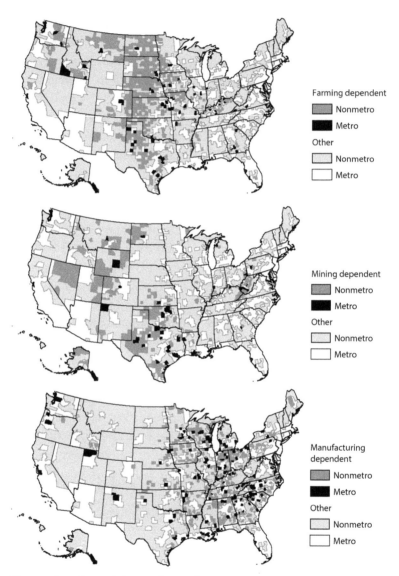

Figure 8. Farming-, mining-, and manufacturing-dependent counties. *Note*: Data based on the 2015 edition of the County Typology Codes. *Source*: U.S. Department of Agriculture, 2019b.

industries in the short term, studies have generally shown elevated social disruption associated with their boom-and-bust cycles, as well as high levels of underemployment, poverty, and inequality over the longer term in places dependent upon these sectors.[19] While not extractive in nature, economies reliant on natural amenity recreation and tourism have also been shown to provide limited opportunities for local workers (i.e., mainly low-wage service sector employment).[20]

UNDEREMPLOYMENT AND POVERTY

For most American households, employment is their principal source of income. However, a persistent problem in rural America is that work tends to provide less protection from economic hardship than it does in urban areas.[21] Many factors contribute to this rural disadvantage, including the structural features of rural labor markets described earlier. It is also the case that lower educational levels prevail in rural areas, an issue exacerbated by the out-migration of educated youth.[22] Relatedly, research has shown that rural workers receive lower returns for the educational credentials they do possess than their urban counterparts.[23] This reality creates a dilemma for leaders in many small communities who know that the modern economy demands educated workers and often place high value on education in its own right, but also know that educated young people are either going to leave town in search of opportunities elsewhere or have their education be undervalued in the local labor market.[24]

Underemployment

High underemployment is a long-standing feature of rural and small-town America.[25] A prominent method for measuring underemployment is the Labor Utilization Framework.[26] This approach defines four states of underemployment:

46   CHAPTER 2

Discouraged workers: individuals who would like to be employed but are currently not in the labor force (i.e., not working and not looking for work in the previous four weeks) due to discouragement with their job prospects.[27]

Unemployed workers: individuals who are not employed but (a) have looked for work during the previous four weeks or (b) are currently laid off but expect to be called back to work (this category is consistent with the official definition of unemployment).

Low-hour workers (or involuntary part time): individuals who were employed less than 35 hours in the previous week only because of slack work or being unable to find full-time employment.

Low-income workers: individuals who are otherwise not underemployed as defined here and whose annualized weekly earnings are less than 125 percent of the poverty threshold for a single person.

Workers who do not fall into one of the four states of underemployment are defined as *adequately employed*, while individuals who are not employed and do not indicate a desire to be employed are defined as *not in the labor force*.

Figure 9 shows the percentage of those aged 18 to 64 underemployed by residence from 1968 to 2017 (restricted to those in the labor force as defined earlier).[28] The data demonstrate two important points. The first is that underemployment among nonmetro workers has exceeded that of metro workers at every point over the last 50 years. During this period, nonmetro underemployment averaged 20.4 percent (one in five workers), compared to 16.6 percent in metro areas. However, the second point is that the nonmetro-metro underemployment gap has been narrowing in more recent decades. The gap was largest in the mid-1980s at over six percentage points but closed to about two percentage points since the Great Recession circa 2008. Notably, the more recent trend toward metro-nonmetro convergence in underemployment was driven by underemployment growing more prevalent in metro settings, rather than by improvements in nonmetro labor markets.

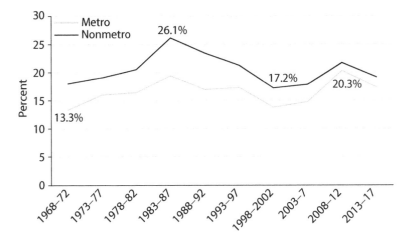

Figure 9. Percent underemployed in metro and nonmetro areas, 1968–2017. *Note:* Analysis restricted to those aged 18–64. High- and low-point values included on trend lines. *Source:* Slack et al., 2020.

The employment difficulties described here are more layered than people's ability to make ends meet, as important a consideration as that is on its own. For example, qualitative research has demonstrated the importance of a moral discourse that emphasizes individualism and self-sufficiency in rural America, with strong distinctions between the *deserving* and *undeserving* poor.[29] This conceptualization casts poor able-bodied adults as undeserving of aid based on the expectation that they should support themselves and their families through work. Paradoxically, the power of this type of moral discourse may grow even stronger in rural contexts where stable and well-paying jobs are in short supply.

Poverty

Poverty also represents a persistent challenge in rural America.[30] The idea that high and concentrated poverty is an exclusive condition

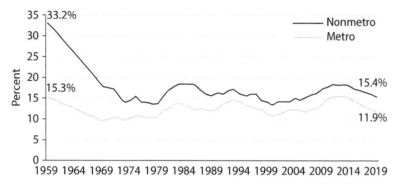

Figure 10. Percent poor in metro and nonmetro areas, 1959–2019. *Note*: Start- and end-point values included on trend lines. *Source*: U.S. Department of Agriculture, 2022b.

of the inner city is a myth reinforced by media portrayals. In fact, for the entire history that the U.S. government has officially measured poverty, it has been higher in rural America.[31] This reality was noted during the War on Poverty of the 1960s in the pioneering federal report on rural poverty, aptly titled *The People Left Behind*.[32]

Figure 10 shows the percentage poor by residence from 1959 to 2019 according to the official poverty measure (OPM).[33] The long-term trends in poverty as officially measured by the federal government illustrate three key facts. The first is that the poverty rate among nonmetro families has been greater than among their metro counterparts at every point over the last 60 years. During this period, poverty averaged 17.8 percent in nonmetro areas compared to 12.5 percent in metro settings. Second is that similar to underemployment, there is evidence this gap has been closing over time. At the beginning of the period, poverty stood at a staggering 33.2 percent (one in three people) in nonmetro areas, while the comparable number was less than half that level (15.3 percent) in metro contexts. However, by the 2010s that gap had narrowed to just 1.8 percentage points on average. A final observation is that after falling precipitously in the 1960s, since the 1970s poverty rates have

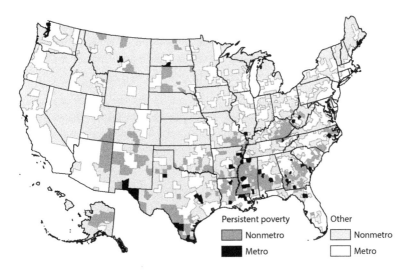

Figure 11. Persistent poverty counties. *Note*: Data based on the 2015 edition of the County Typology Codes. *Source*: U.S. Department of Agriculture, 2019b.

been largely stagnant in rural and urban America alike, fluctuating within about five percentage points countercyclical to the performance of the economy (i.e., when the economy contracts, poverty rises; when the economy grows, poverty declines).

It is also the case that areas of the country where poverty is chronically highest are largely rural. The USDA Economic Research Service defines persistent poverty counties as those where 20 percent or more of county residents have been poor for the last 40 years. That is, these are places where not only is poverty high, but it has been so for decade upon decade. Figure 11 is a map of these counties that illustrates two key points. First, of the 353 persistent poverty counties nationally, most are nonmetro. Persistent poverty afflicts 15.2 percent of nonmetro counties versus 4.5 percent of metro counties. Second, the distribution of these counties is not random. Instead, they show clear regional patterns. Namely, these places are: Central Appalachia, the Black Belt, the Delta, the Rio Grande Valley (or Texas Borderland), and American Indian country. In all cases,

50   CHAPTER 2

besides Appalachia, persistently poor regions of the United States are characterized by significant populations of rural minoritized ethnoracial groups (an issue to which we devote further attention in chapter 3). Moreover, each of these areas can trace its history to particular political economies and systems of stratification.[34]

Conditions in Appalachia, represented by the clustering of counties in eastern Kentucky and southern West Virginia, are linked to vast inequities in ownership of the region's rich natural resource base, its coalfields especially, and the methods used by elites to exploit labor and land in the process of resource extraction. Economic hardship in the Black Belt (spanning from the Carolinas down to eastern Mississippi) and the Delta (straddling the Mississippi River in Arkansas, Mississippi, and Louisiana) has its roots in the history of Black enslavement in plantation agriculture and the institutional mechanisms used to continue labor exploitation and racial subjugation after slavery was abolished (e.g., Jim Crow, sharecropping, and tenant farming). In the Rio Grande Valley of south Texas, high poverty is tied to the geopolitics of the U.S.-Mexico border and comparatively lower standards of living to the south of that divide. In fact, it is for this reason that the valley is the only persistently poor region of the country characterized by significant in-migration (people typically out-migrate from high poverty areas in search of better opportunity).[35] The valley has historically been a major source of the low-wage migrant farm labor upon which U.S. agribusiness depends, the lion's share of which is performed by workers of Mexican descent. Last, poverty in Native American country—observed in places like the Dakotas, the Four Corners, and Oklahoma—is the product of an express policy of oppression and violence by the U.S. federal government, including brutal military conquest, forced migration, and an array of efforts to extinguish tribal cultures (e.g., youth boarding schools and urban relocation programs).[36] In short, historical and contemporary political economies and related inequality have produced the regional geography of rural persistent poverty.

With these facts in mind, the OPM also has well-known shortcomings that complicate rural-urban comparisons.[37] The measure was developed in the 1960s during the federal government's War on Poverty. After all, if the government was going to declare a war on poverty, it needed a metric to determine its progress. In the OPM framework, a family is poor if their pretax income is less than the poverty threshold for a family of their size and age composition (i.e., number of adults and number of children). The assumption is that the poverty thresholds represent the income needed for a family to support its basic needs. Criticisms of the OPM have been made on many grounds, but a chief limitation given the focus of this book is that the OPM makes no adjustments for geographic differences in the cost of living. Thus, the OPM thresholds are the same, for instance, whether one lives in New York City or rural Alabama. In recognition of this and other limitations of the OPM, since 2009 the federal government has also calculated a supplemental poverty measure (SPM), which includes an adjustment for geographic variation in housing costs.

Comparing estimates from the two measures for metro and nonmetro areas, the relationship for the SPM is the opposite of that for the OPM: the nonmetro SPM is consistently lower than the metro SPM. So, is poverty higher in rural or urban areas? The answer depends on how we measure poverty.[38] Importantly, the SPM is used by the federal government to provide additional information, not to replace the OPM or the prominent role it plays in public policy. In addition, while the SPM incorporates geographic variation in housing costs, it does not account for other costs of living that are known to vary spatially. Analysts continue to work through the best technical approaches to the measurement issue.[39] But the critical point here is that there are undoubtedly meaningful differences across rural and urban places in what it costs to get by. Urban residents tend to face higher costs for housing and food, while rural residents face higher costs for transportation and health care.[40] Sometimes, however, thinking through what it "costs" to live in rural

52   CHAPTER 2

and urban areas can be difficult to decipher. For example, the direct cost of childcare, a significant expenditure for working parents, is typically higher in urban areas. Yet access to licensed childcare centers is much lower in rural areas, in part because lower population numbers and density present challenges to the economic viability of such businesses.[41] The direct costs of childcare and the absence of childcare centers both impose costs on working parents. As another example, while a greater share of urban residents have been shown to be housing-cost burdened than their rural counterparts (i.e., 30 percent or more of their monthly income is spent on housing), it is still the case that more than one in five rural residents (21 percent) face this form of economic hardship, with its prevalence running as high as one in three among rural Black households.[42] Housing cost burdens are especially acute in rural high-amenity communities, where in-migration among wealthy newcomers serves to drive up housing costs and price out longtime locals (i.e., rural gentrification).[43] Taken together, these considerations mean many families in both rural and urban settings routinely face difficult choices about how to make ends meet.

INFORMAL WORK

> There's lots of people that work under the table around here. You know, odd jobs for cash. Like when I used to work out at the bar, that was just straight up cash there. And just the other day, this guy down the road here needed help unloading a truck and I did that. You know, things just come up, somebody needs something done, and they offer to pay you for it.
>
> . . .
>
> We get paid in different ways: 20 bucks, a bag of tomatoes, it just depends. Like the guy I clean house for, he takes me to work in the winter. He's got a four-

wheel drive truck. So that's how I get paid there. We
often get paid by *things*. And a lot of the time when we
do things for people around here it's in exchange for
another job. Like [my husband], he just finished
painting a house. Well, he's getting paid in two
truckloads of stone for our road out there. That's a hell
of a lot of money we saved [on that gravel].
. . .
[My husband sells] car parts and stuff. In fact, he has a
motor out here right now. The guy that wants it, he
grinds tree stumps, and we have a whole bunch [of
stumps] in our backyard, so he's gonna grind those up
in exchange for that motor.[44]

These quotes from Tim Slack and Leif Jensen's study "Informal
Work in Rural America" illustrate that people support themselves
not only via formal employment but by other types of work as well.
Economic activities can be broadly defined as occurring in the formal economy, informal economy, and criminal economy.[45] The *formal economy* includes activities undertaken within the legal and
regulatory framework of the state (e.g., tax, labor, and environmental laws), while the *criminal economy* refers to the production of
goods and services that are expressly illegal as defined by the state.
The *informal economy*, in contrast, refers to economic activities that
are pursued outside the scope of state regulation but are mostly legal
(albeit sometimes bypassing government rules). Examples include
working under the table in a formal business for cash, doing jobs or
providing services for cash or in-kind payment (e.g., repair work,
landscaping, childcare, hairstyling), and barter.

In less developed nations where state regulation is not robust
and much trade is unregistered, such activities are commonplace.
Scholars have traditionally maintained that as capitalist economies
develop and the formal sector grows, informal work activities will
undergo an accompanying decline. More recently, though, there

54   CHAPTER 2

has been growing recognition that the informal economy remains a persistent structural feature of modern and highly developed societies.[46] In fact, not only has informal work not faded away in such contexts, there is reason to believe it has actually "grown in significance with the development of the modern world."[47] Reasons for this include rapid rates of "creative destruction" brought about by globalization and related industrial restructuring, political retrenchment of the welfare state (i.e., scaling back government social programs), and other social forces creating economic precarity and uneven development.

Research shows that it is neither people with the lowest incomes nor those with higher incomes who most often pursue informal work, but those who occupy a class position in between.[48] Studies have demonstrated that attachment to the formal economy and greater social capital (i.e., social ties, group memberships, and mutual trust) are significant positive predictors of participation in informal work.[49] These findings point to a seminal idea in economic sociology: *embeddedness*. Pioneered by Mark Granovetter, the concept of embeddedness emphasizes how people's social ties variously facilitate and constrain economic action, and how people's networks serve to generate norms of trust and reciprocity that are critical in undergirding economic transactions.[50] While embeddedness shapes all kinds of economic activity, it is perhaps most crucial in the informal economy.[51] This is because in the absence of the state regulation and enforcement (i.e., laws and government agents) that exists in the formal economy, social capital becomes even more important in ordering economic behavior. Embeddedness allows for access to informal transactional networks, and malfeasance is sanctioned with exclusion. For instance, if two people agree to an informal exchange and one party violates the terms, the person who was wronged is not only unlikely to trade with the wrongdoer again in the future but is also likely to let others in their network know the wrongdoer is not to be trusted. The offending party will then find limited options for informal economic activities going forward once this news is shared.

Given this risk, most people take the long view and choose to maintain relationships over cheating for short-term gain.

There are a host of reasons to believe that informal work might be more common in rural America.[52] For example, social networks in rural areas have been shown to contain ties of greater intensity and role multiplexity.[53] Relatedly, gemeinschaft relations, described in the introduction, often thought to be more typical of rural areas, stand to facilitate informal work. And patterns of uneven development, documented in this chapter, may also make informal work a more attractive complement to or substitute for formal sector employment in rural areas. Moreover, many types of informal work require access to land or other natural resources that are more accessible in the countryside (e.g., hunting, fishing, and gathering).

Table 2 shows data on the prevalence of informal work by type of activity in metro and nonmetro areas from a national sample of U.S. households.[54] The data demonstrate several important points. The first is that, overall, informal work is quite common, with more than two-thirds (67.0 percent) of U.S. households reporting participation. Second, engagement in informal work is higher among nonmetro (72.1 percent) than metro (66.0 percent) households, and nonmetro households undertake more informal activities on average. Third, in every case where there is a significant metro-nonmetro difference in specific types of informal work activities, nonmetro households report greater participation. Additional findings from this research (not shown) confirm that informal work is more prevalent among nonmetro than metro households, even after controlling for a range of other factors (e.g., demographics, income, and social capital).

The informal economy holds promise in terms of rural economic development. Micro-credit and micro-enterprise programs that make capital and business planning services available to informal entrepreneurs have the potential to develop locally owned businesses deeply rooted in their communities. However, while programs can help people overcome barriers to formality when that outcome is desired, a caution for policymakers is to not neglect the

Table 2 Percent of Households Engaging in Informal Work by Type and Residence

	Total Sample	Metro	Nonmetro
Any informal work	67.0	66.0**	72.1
Grow or produce food products	26.4	25.1**	32.5
Home repair or improvement	24.0	23.2	27.9
Repair vehicles, appliances, or other mechanical work	18.6	17.9	22.0
Personal service	17.3	17.4	17.1
Hold or contribute to garage sale/flea market	17.2	16.3*	21.4
Reuse/fix things others discarded	17.3	17.0	18.5
Sell or trade clothes, makeup, scrap metal, etc.	15.5	14.5**	20.4
Hunt, fish, or gather from land	15.0	12.5**	26.8
Landscaping, snow removal, etc.	12.7	11.9*	16.9
Provide blood or blood products (e.g., plasma)	12.6	12.7	12.3
Crafts, collectibles, or sew/do alterations	8.9	8.8	9.2
Other informal work not mentioned	8.3	8.4	7.4
Accounting or computer work	7.4	7.5	6.7
Give lessons (e.g., music, language, sports)	7.0	7.0	7.0
Breed, board, or tend nonfarm animals	4.6	4.6	4.4
Clerical work (e.g., typing)	4.4	4.2	5.4
Take in boarders	2.1	2.1	2.5
Bartending or catering	1.5	1.5	1.9
Street vending/roadside sales	1.4	1.3	1.6
Number of activities reported			
Mean overall	2.2	2.1**	2.6
Mean among those engaged in 1 or more	3.3	3.2*	3.6
Maximum	16.0	16.0	15.0

SOURCE: Jensen et al., 2019.
*Metro/nonmetro difference significant at $p < .05$.
**Metro/nonmetro difference significant at $p < .01$.

value of informal work in and of itself.[55] Informal work not only carries economic benefits; it can also be important culturally in terms of reinforcing group values, norms, and identity.

SAFETY NET PROGRAMS

The social safety net refers broadly to the range of government programs aimed at relieving economic hardship and poverty. Many safety net programs target demographic subpopulations, like children or those age 65 and older. Nonetheless, general poverty-reducing effects across rural and urban areas can be compared. Using the SPM, research shows that Social Security has (by far) the greatest overall anti-poverty effect in both rural and urban areas, and that the reduction in poverty associated with the program is more pronounced in rural than urban contexts.[56] This makes sense given that Social Security is primarily aimed at older populations, and rural America is home to a greater relative share of older adults. Among children, refundable tax credits (e.g., the Child Tax Credit and the Earned Income Tax Credit) have the greatest poverty-reducing effect, and this holds in both rural and urban areas. The direct economic benefit of the Child Tax Credit to working families, for example, is why its expansion and advanced payments to families were a centerpiece of federal relief efforts during the COVID-19 pandemic. The anti-poverty impacts of other safety net programs are also similar across rural and urban areas, apart from housing subsidies, which have a bigger impact in cities, and unemployment insurance, which has a bigger impact in rural settings.

Studies have also shown the prevalence of disability is substantially higher in rural America,[57] with the relatively rural states of West Virginia, Alabama, Arkansas, and Mississippi leading the nation in disability benefits receipt (more than one in ten residents in each state are on disability).[58] This is not just important from a programmatic perspective but also has implications for other

58   CHAPTER 2

dimensions of well-being. For example, nearly 30 percent of rural adults with disabilities are housing-cost burdened.[59] In addition, the prevalence of Supplemental Nutrition Assistance Program (SNAP, formerly Food Stamps) receipt has also been shown to be significantly higher in rural regions like Appalachia, the Rio Grande Valley, and the Delta, even after accounting for local variation in poverty, labor markets, and population structure.[60]

One current program that plays little role in poverty reduction in either rural or urban areas is Temporary Assistance for Needy Families (TANF).[61] This may be surprising to some, as TANF is the nation's primary cash assistance program for the poor (i.e., it is the program people commonly think of when they refer to a "welfare check"). At one time, receipt of cash assistance aimed at poor women and their children was much more common. But in 1996 the Personal Responsibility and Work Opportunity Reconciliation Act (PRWORA), more widely known as "welfare reform," became federal law. President Bill Clinton vowed at the time that this represented the "end of welfare as we know it," and he was right. Welfare reform replaced Aid to Families with Dependent Children (AFDC) with TANF, which imposed time limits on receipt (i.e., people are eligible for only 60 months over their lifetime) and required adult recipients to engage in work activities as a condition of receipt or face sanctions (e.g., termination of benefits). The latter posed a dilemma in contexts where job options were few to begin with. Combined with low cash benefit levels in most states (e.g., in 2021, the average grant in Louisiana was $240 per month for a three-person household), the net result has been a precipitous decline in TANF caseloads in the decades since 1996, a trend that continued through periods of high economic distress like the Great Recession.[62] What this means is that cash welfare grants based on low income alone are largely a thing of the past for the American social safety net, even in rural and urban areas where poverty is high. Was welfare reform a success? The answer depends on how success is measured.[63] Caseloads have dropped from being a prominent part of the U.S. social safety net to being an extremely marginal one, while poverty has remained a stubborn structural reality.

Beyond Social Security, other safety net programs for older adults are also critical but often underresourced in rural areas. The Older Americans Act (OAA) is a federal program that funds services through grants to help older adults access home- and community-based services. Area Agencies on Aging (AAA) are responsible for administering these services, and 80 percent of AAA service areas are at least partially rural.[64] However, widely dispersed populations, a small and shrinking supply of social service professionals, and poor infrastructure (e.g., limited transportation, low-quality housing, and insufficient broadband) in rural areas mean that AAA services for older adults are often more difficult to administer in these places. As a result, rural AAAs are less likely than their urban counterparts to provide critical services to older adults, including adult day care, care transition, money management counseling, and integrated care. Even when such services are available, rural older adults often face long waitlists due to high demand.[65]

CONCLUSION

The overarching theme of this chapter is that profound change has characterized rural economies and livelihoods over the course of American history. Contrary to popular stereotypes of rural areas being reminiscent of a time gone by when most people made a living from the land, rural America has been fundamentally enmeshed in processes such as the agrarian-industrial-postindustrial transition and globalization. Further, thinking about prosperity or poverty in exclusive rural or urban terms is misguided; neither is confined to either context.

More specifically, the assumption that contemporary rural economies are synonymous with farming is a myth and misunderstanding. While agriculture remains a critical industry, over the last century

60   CHAPTER 2

the sector has witnessed a marked decline in its employment share and today constitutes only a small segment of rural employment. Further, despite industrialization often being conflated with urban contexts, today manufacturing represents a larger share of employment in rural than in urban America. When contextualized within the broader trend of deindustrialization, the magnitude of the challenge this poses for many small communities becomes apparent. It is one thing to lose a plant in a large and economically diversified metropolis; it is quite another when it is the main employer in town.

Relatedly, industry and job diversity are critical for vibrant and robust local economies. However, achieving appreciable economic diversity presents a major challenge in many rural contexts. Low population numbers and density place limits on the ability to build and maintain a diverse mix of employers and jobs. The dominant economic paradigm in American society is to achieve this end through growth. But rural communities that are successful in engaging this strategy often transition from rural to urban. A puzzle in rural development is how to avoid the pitfalls of economic dependence while also preserving rurality.

Last, conceptualizing economic hardship as being exclusive to rural or urban settings is a misunderstanding. Underemployment represents a particular challenge in rural America. And according to the OPM, poverty is consistently higher in rural than urban areas (though the SPM tells a different story). On balance, we must be clear that neither prosperity nor hardship is the exclusive domain of rural or urban America, and that the struggles of the poor are very real in both contexts.

3 Rural Ethnoracial Diversity and Inequities

Perry, Iowa (population 7,929) was like many other small towns until the 1990s. Nearly all residents were White, with roots going back generations. Perry's first meatpacking plant opened in 1920. By the 1960s, the local Oscar Mayer plant was home to some of the most desirable jobs in town that came with good wages and benefits. Everything changed when Oscar Mayer sold the plant to Beef Packers in 1988. Taking advantage of loosening labor laws and new technology that reduced the need for skilled butchers, Beef Packers slashed wages and benefits and increased production speeds. Contending with inevitable worker shortages, Beef Packers began recruiting Hispanics, first from U.S. cities, and then directly from Mexico and parts of Central America. As of 2021, nearly one in three residents of Perry were Hispanic.

—Lay, *Rural Poverty in the United States*

When you think of the racial and ethnic composition of rural America, do you think of Whites with European ancestry? If you said yes, you are not alone. The conventional view of rural America—one often reinforced by the media—is that it is composed almost entirely of White people. This is among the most common myths and misunderstandings about the rural United States. In fact, rural

62   CHAPTER 3

America has always been more ethnoracially diverse than is commonly assumed, and it is becoming increasingly more so. However, rural America's minoritized ethnoracial populations are often geographically and socially isolated from White people, concentrated in small towns in the southern Black Belt,[1] on remote American Indian reservations,[2] and in U.S.-Mexico Borderland colonias—all places with long histories of exploitation, chronic poverty, and deprivation.[3] Rural minoritized populations are also often forgotten or ignored by politicians and the media.[4] This is a mistake given the important implications of ethnoracial diversity and change in rural America.

This chapter describes the ethnoracial composition of the rural United States, as well as contemporary changes in ethnoracial composition and diversity. We also discuss historical settlement patterns, integration, and inequality, with special attention to the experiences of rural American Indian, Black, Hispanic, and Asian people. Woven throughout are considerations of America's long history of structural racism—violence, conquest, genocide, forced migration, slavery, theft, and subjugation—which along with its more contemporary manifestations is the foundation for the current spatial settlement patterns we observe and the ethnoracial inequities therein. We also give attention to the long history of rural minoritized groups' resistance to structural racism. Before we begin, however, it is important to discuss the terminology we use to describe ethnoracial groups.

THE SOCIAL CONSTRUCTION OF RACE: ETHNORACIAL TERMINOLOGY

In the past, race was commonly conceived and promoted by White scientists as a biological concept based on groups' physical and genetic traits. However, most scholars now view race as a *social construction*, in which the categories, terminologies, and meanings

RURAL ETHNORACIAL DIVERSITY AND INEQUITIES   63

change over time and place. This does not mean that race is not real. "Racial distinctions are real and meaningful . . . to the extent that people are treated differently and have different kinds of life experiences and outcomes."[5] Not all societies categorize people based on race. The existence of "racial minorities" is a "feature of a *racialized social system*—a society in which one social group secures economic, political, and cultural domination over others in part through the construction of an ideology of racial difference."[6]

A prime illustration of the social construction of race in the United States is in how the U.S. Census Bureau has changed its collection and categorization of racial and ethnic identity over time. The first U.S. Census, collected in 1790, captured only three "racial" groups: Slaves, Free Whites, and All Other Free Persons. A century later (1890), the Census included Indian; Chinese/Japanese; Black, Mulatto, Quadroon, Octoroon; and White. By 1990 the Census captured Aleut, Eskimo, American Indian; Asian or Pacific Islander, Chinese, Filipino, Hawaiian, Korean, Vietnamese, Japanese, Asian Indian, Samoan, Guamanian, Other Asian or Pacific Islander; Black or Negro; White; and Other Race. In 2000, for the first time respondents were allowed to select more than one race. Before this, respondents were forced to select the single category they thought best represented them. Moreover, it was only in 1960 that people were first able to self-identify their race. Until then, Census enumerators assigned race to respondents. In sum, the Census Bureau has not only changed how race is defined over the years, but it has also long failed to accurately capture many individuals' full racial identities.

You may have noticed that Hispanic and Latino are not listed in these categorizations. This is because the Census Bureau considers Hispanic/Latino to be an ethnicity rather than a race.[7] Census respondents are instructed to select both their race and whether they consider themselves to be of Hispanic, Latino, or Spanish origin. Whereas *race* typically refers to a group of people who are perceived by themselves and others as possessing distinct phenotypic

64   CHAPTER 3

characteristics (e.g., skin color), *ethnicity* differentiates groups by their origin culture.[8] Nevertheless, the terms *race* and *ethnicity* are often used interchangeably, and Hispanic ethnicity is often racialized, in contemporary U.S. society.

Throughout this chapter, we typically use the official U.S. Census terminology for different groups. Broadly, "White" is used for non-Hispanic (NH) White, "Black" for NH Black, "Indigenous" or "American Indian" for NH American Indian or Alaska Native (AIAN), "Asian" for NH Asian and Pacific Islander, and "Hispanic" for Hispanic of any race. We understand that these terms are fraught, and people disagree about the most appropriate terminology. For example, there is no consistently agreed upon term for Indigenous populations, for whom the terms American Indian, Native American, Native People, tribal communities, Indigenous, and First Nations are commonly used both by members of these groups and by outsiders. It is also worth noting that academic elites and activist groups sometimes revise terms and advocate for new terminology with which the people being categorized do not even agree (e.g., in 2020, less than one-quarter of those who self-identified as Hispanic or Latino had ever even heard of the term Latinx, and only 3 percent used it to self-identify).[9] In sum, there are no universally agreed upon terms for the groups we describe in this chapter and throughout the rest of the book. Moreover, all methods of categorization mask diversity within groups. Indigenous populations include a substantial number of different tribes (574 are federally recognized). Other ethnoracial groups, particularly Hispanic and Asian populations, encompass people from a variety of origins. As noted at the outset of this book, we typically invoke the term *minoritized* in our discussion to center how individuals and groups have been systematically marginalized based on race and/or ethnicity. But sometimes we use *non-White* for clarity and brevity, particularly when summarizing U.S. Census data. It is important that we all grapple with the reasons these terms are contested and evolve over time.

RURAL ETHNORACIAL POPULATION TRENDS

Rural America is currently, and has been throughout its history, home to large numbers of minoritized people.[10] As a case in point, prior to European settlement, Indigenous populations were the majority ethnoracial group in what is the present-day rural United States.

Over the past several decades, U.S. society has become increasingly racially and ethnically diverse overall, and the same is true for rural America. The proportion of the overall U.S. population that is non-White increased from 24.4 percent in 1990 to 42.4 percent in 2020. Likewise, although non-White people continue to comprise a smaller share of the overall nonmetro than metro population, their share of the nonmetro population increased from 14.3 percent in 1990 to 24 percent in 2020 (see figure 12).[11]

The increase in the rural non-White population share is due both to increases in the absolute number of non-White people living in rural areas and declines in the absolute number of White people (insufficient births and in-migration to offset deaths) over the past couple of decades. The number of non-White people living in nonmetro counties increased by over five million during this period.[12] That number is slightly larger than the entire population of Ireland.

Minoritized ethnoracial people now comprise nearly one in four rural residents, with Hispanic people representing 9 percent (4.1 million people), Black people 7.7 percent (3.5 million people), American Indian/Alaska Native people 2 percent (nearly 1 million people), Asian people 1 percent (half a million people), and mixed-race and other race people just over 4 percent (nearly 2 million people) in 2020. Although American Indians comprise a relatively small share of the overall nonmetro population, 40 percent live in a nonmetro county (the largest nonmetro percentage of any ethnoracial group),[13] and it is estimated that 54 percent live in rural and small-town areas more broadly defined.[14]

The largest percentage gain between 1990 and 2020 was among mixed-race people. This increase reflects changes in how the Census allows respondents to identify (i.e., the option to select more than one race was added in 2000), growing cultural acceptance and individual embrace of multiracial identities, and more births among interracial

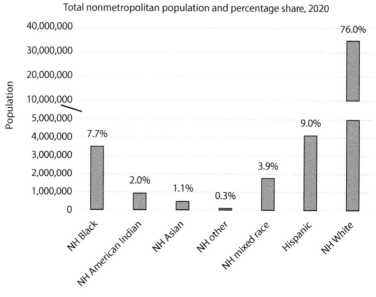

Total nonmetropolitan population and percentage share, 2020

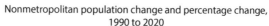

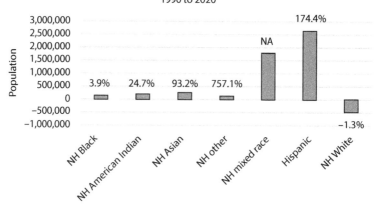

Nonmetropolitan population change and percentage change, 1990 to 2020

couples.[15] Another change is that while the Black population long comprised rural America's largest minority group, the rural Hispanic population surpassed that of the Black population in 2010. Whites were the only ethnoracial group in rural America to lose population between 1990 and 2020. There were nearly half a million fewer White people living in nonmetro counties in 2020 than there were in 1990.

The increase in the rural non-White population, while occurring across all age groups, has been especially striking among children. As of 2020, nearly one in three rural residents under age 18 was non-White (see figure 13). Hispanic and mixed-race children are driving this trend. Whereas Hispanic people comprise 7.6 percent of all rural adults, they comprise 14 percent of rural children. Likewise, whereas mixed-race individuals comprise 3.2 percent of rural adults, they comprise 6.2 percent of rural children. Conversely, White people comprise 78.4 percent of the rural adult population but a smaller share (67.5 percent) of rural children.

Several demographic phenomena intersect to explain the growth in the rural non-White child population.[16] First, the share of White women who are in their childbearing years has declined. Relatedly,

Figure 12. (*Opposite*) Nonmetro population, 2020 (top), and population change by race and Hispanic origin, 1990–2020 (bottom). *Note*: NH = non-Hispanic. The Hispanic category includes Hispanics of any race. All other categories include only non-Hispanics. In the top graph, the slashed line on the y axis and the break in the bar for NH White is to notify the reader of the change in the y axis value intervals to accommodate the large difference in population sizes between NH Whites and other groups. The American Indian category includes Alaska Natives. The Asian category includes Pacific Islanders. The Census did not add the option to select more than one race until 2000. Therefore, individuals who might have identified with more than one race are included in one of the single-race groups in the 1990 Census. The growth observed in the NH mixed race population between 1990 and 2020 is due to the addition of the more-than-one-race option. *Source*: Author calculations using data from U.S. Census 1990 and Census 2020 Preliminary file. Based on 1,976 nonmetro counties defined using the 2013 USDA Economic Research Service RUCC.

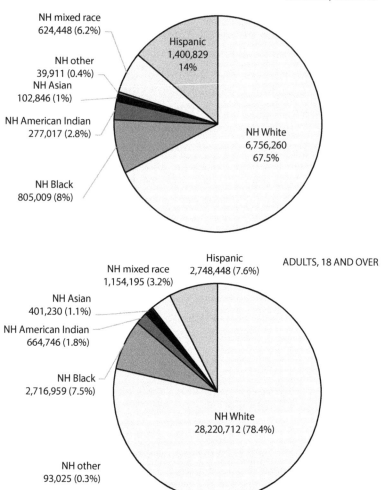

Figure 13. Nonmetro population under age 18 (top) and age 18+ (bottom) by race and Hispanic origin, 2020. *Note*: NH = non-Hispanic. The Hispanic category includes Hispanics of any race. All other categories include only non-Hispanics. The American Indian category includes Alaska Natives. The Asian category includes Pacific Islanders. *Source*: Author calculations using data from U.S. Census 2020 Preliminary file. Based on 1,976 nonmetro counties defined using the 2013 USDA Economic Research Service RUCC.

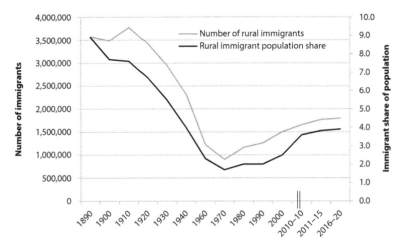

Figure 14. Foreign-born population totals and population share in nonmetro counties, 1890–2020. *Note*: Numbers for 1890–2000 represent "rural areas" as defined by the U.S. Census Bureau. The final three time points represent nonmetro counties. Therefore, there is a break in the trend; data are not perfectly comparable before and after the break. The difference in definitions is due to changes in how the Census made data available over time. *Source*: For 1890–2000, data are from Gibson and Jung, 2006; for 2006–2020, data are from the American Community Surveys, 2006–2010, 2011–2015, and 2016–2020.

many non-White groups, particularly Hispanics, are younger on average than Whites, meaning that larger shares of non-White people are in their childbearing years. Finally, some minoritized ethnoracial groups, especially Hispanics, have higher fertility rates (number of births per woman in her lifetime) than Whites. Taken together, "working in demographic concert, White population decline coupled with widespread ethnoracial minority population growth is gradually transforming the racial and ethnic composition of rural and small-town America."[17]

Immigration is also an important part of the story. The U.S. rural immigrant population has fluctuated substantially since data were first reported (see figure 14). Immigrants comprised 8.9 percent of

70   CHAPTER 3

the rural population in 1890 (almost entirely those of European origin), thereafter steadily declining to a low of 1.7 percent in 1970. The share of immigrants living in rural areas then increased steadily from 1970 onward. Immigrants now comprise 3.9 percent of the U.S. rural population, with most recent rural immigrants originating from Mexico and Central America.[18] We discuss the political, legal, and economic reasons for these trends later in the chapter.

GEOGRAPHIC VARIATION IN RURAL ETHNORACIAL POPULATION COMPOSITION AND DIVERSITY

The preceding section demonstrates that rural America is trending toward greater absolute numbers and shares of minoritized ethnoracial populations and thus increasing ethnoracial diversity. However, *where* this is happening is highly unequal and regionalized. Whereas some parts of rural America have long been home to large shares of minoritized groups, and some have experienced major increases in their minoritized populations over the past few decades, others have remained largely White.

Although the term *diversity* is often used to refer to the presence of minoritized groups, a more accurate definition captures both the absolute and relative sizes of ethnoracial populations. A place that comprises equal shares of multiple groups is considered diverse, whereas a place that comprises an exceptionally large share of any one group is not diverse. This means that a place can have a large minoritized population and still not be diverse if there are few members of other groups.

As shown in the maps in figure 15, most rural counties are majority White (and therefore not diverse). About 88 percent of nonmetro counties have a population that is over half White. But this is not that different from metro counties, among which 86 percent are majority White. Of the 229 nonmetro counties that are majority-minority, 67 are majority Black (29 percent), 72 are majority

Hispanic (31 percent), and 27 are majority American Indian (12 percent). The current majority-minority share of nonmetro counties (11.6 percent) represents an increase since 1990, when only 7 percent were majority non-White. This rate of growth is comparable to the growth in majority-minority central cities and suburbs over the same period.[19]

Among the most striking features of the ethnoracial geography of the rural United States is the regional concentration of minoritized ethnoracial groups. Black people are by far the most regionally concentrated, with close to 90 percent of all rural Black people residing in the South (mostly in Louisiana, Mississippi, Alabama, and Georgia, including the Black Belt and Delta). American Indian people are somewhat less regionally concentrated, though just over half live in five states (Oklahoma, Arizona, New Mexico, Alaska, and North Carolina), with one in three rural American Indian people living on reservations or tribal lands. In Montana, Wyoming, and South Dakota, more than four in five American Indian people live in a small town or rural area.[20] Majority Hispanic counties are clustered along the U.S.-Mexico border region of Texas, New Mexico, Arizona, and California, with one in four rural Hispanic people living in Texas alone.[21] These spatial patterns are not accidental or random; they are the product of historical racialized economic, political, and social processes that systematically concentrated these groups in particular regions—a topic to which we return later.

There are also newly emerging majority-minority rural places—counties that achieved over 50 percent non-White populations after 2000.[22] They are found along the West Coast and eastern seaboard. They are also scattered throughout the Midwest, a pattern consistent with the emergence of new Hispanic destinations, which we prefaced in the anecdote that began this chapter.

As shown in figure 15, there are many additional counties where minoritized groups comprise a larger share of the population than their share in the United States overall, but where there are also large shares of White people. We might think of these as

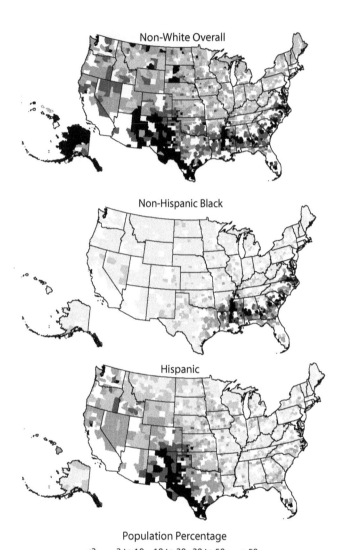

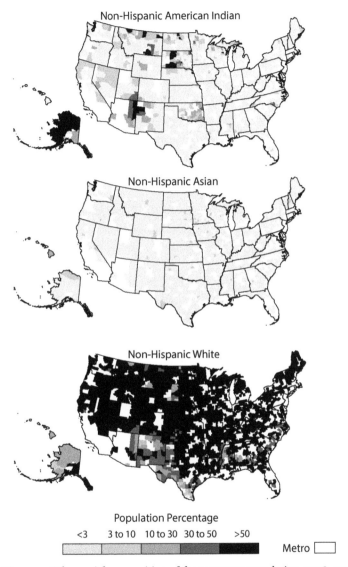

Figure 15. Ethnoracial composition of the nonmetro population, 2016–2020. *Note*: The Hispanic category includes Hispanics of any race. All other categories include only non-Hispanics. The American Indian category includes Alaska Natives. The Asian category includes Pacific Islanders. *Source*: American Community Survey, 2016–2020.

74 CHAPTER 3

truly diverse counties. For example, in addition to the Southeast, there are rural counties with larger than average Black population shares throughout the Northeast, Midwest, and Texas. The Hispanic population, once highly concentrated in large urban hubs and rural border towns, now comprises notable population shares in nearly all parts of the rural United States. Although there are no majority Asian counties—regardless of metro status—15 nonmetro counties had larger Asian population shares than the United States overall, with most of these located in Alaska.

Overall, the greatest ethnoracial diversity is found throughout the Southeast and Southwest and in some nonmetro counties that are adjacent to metro areas. In contrast, New England, the northern Great Lakes, northern Appalachia, and the northern Great Plains are the least diverse.[23] As discussed in the previous section, the growth in the minoritized child population (particularly Hispanic and mixed race) means that there is greater diversity across the rural United States among children than among adults, a trend that will mean continued growth in rural diversity in the coming decades.

HISTORY OF ETHNORACIAL GROUP SETTLEMENT IN RURAL AMERICA

Today's ethnoracial population patterns reflect both historical processes and contemporary economic, political, and social shifts. This is a story that must be understood within the context of institutionalized systems of racial domination. Accordingly, we infuse our discussion of ethnoracial group settlement with a discussion of racialization processes and racialized social structures. As articulated by Mark Harvey:

> [R]acialization, or the invention of the social category of race, was crucial to the development of the modern global capitalist economy and nation-state system. The idea of race provided the moral justification and legal basis for the conquest, extermination, and enslavement of

non-European people by Europeans. By defining non-Europeans as something less than men, race made the crimes committed against them morally acceptable. For example, although slavery had existed in various forms since the dawn of history, the uniquely dehumanizing and commoditized form of *chattel* slavery practiced in the U.S. South only emerged in the 17th century through the combination of a rise in demand for field labor with the emerging practice of ascribing essential meaning to human bodies based on color and geographic origin. The ascription of racial meaning did not reflect any real differences between people assigned to what eventually came to be seen as the "black" and "white" races. Rather, the practice of ascription itself, *combined* with the practice of chattel slavery, functioned to *racialize* the social relation between people of European origin and those of African origin, transforming them into permanently different and unequal "races."[24]

In the following subsections we discuss how racialization has manifested through different forms of racial domination—conquest, violence, slavery, legal apparatuses, and institutional arrangements —throughout American history. We end this section by drawing attention to the ways rural America's historically marginalized ethnoracial groups have resisted and persisted against these oppressive systems and structures.

Indigenous Populations

There is substantial diversity in the historical experiences and settlement patterns of Indigenous populations, though most share a common history of violence, trauma, theft, and exploitation. The history of American Indians in what is now the United States predates the birth of the nation by centuries. Estimates of the number of Indigenous inhabitants at the time of Jamestown's establishment in 1607 vary from 1 to 10 million. After declining dramatically from the 1600s to 1800s, the American Indian population reached a low of half a million in 1890. This massive population decline was directly attributable to the arrival of European colonists, who brought disease and wrought warfare and displacement.

76   CHAPTER 3

U.S. military conquest resulted in mass death and land loss among Indigenous people and led to their forced removal from native lands to geographically isolated and resource-deprived rural reservations. Indigenous populations living on and around reservations were denied formal citizenship until 1924 and were prohibited from voting in some states until 1957. For 150 years (from 1819 to 1969), the U.S. government forcibly separated American Indian children from their families and sent them to over 400 residential boarding schools throughout the United States. Often run by religious organizations, in these institutions children were forced to learn English and assimilate to White European culture; exploited as free labor; subjected to abuse, disease, and malnourishment; and even killed.[25] The express purpose of these schools was to "civilize" American Indian children by stripping them of their Indigenous identity. In addition, federal policies, such as the Dawes Act of 1887, transferred tribal land to White settlers, leading to the spatial and social fragmentation of tribal communities.[26] All of these factors contributed to myriad forms of oppression, subjugation, and disadvantage for Indigenous people, but this history is also marked by considerable resistance and persistence.[27]

The American Indian population has experienced remarkable growth since the 1970s, owing to natural increase, a resurgence in self-reports of Indigenous heritage, and improvements in Census enumeration.[28] Today, the United States is home to around 3.1 million people who identify as solely American Indian or Alaska Native (AIAN) and another 5.7 million who partially identify as such, comprising about 2.6 percent of the total U.S. population.[29] The actual population is likely higher given that American Indian people have historically been severely undercounted in decennial censuses.[30] As of 2023, there were 574 federally recognized AIAN tribes spanning 37 states, several additional state-recognized tribes, and many tribal groups that are not state or federally recognized.

The U.S. Constitution ensures tribal sovereignty; with few exceptions, recognized tribes have the same powers as federal and state governments to regulate their internal affairs. Even so, tribal nations face various challenges to economic development due to decades of federal policies that prohibited tribal governments from owning and operating reservation businesses, and today by severely underdeveloped financial, physical, and political/legal infrastructures and ongoing U.S. colonial relationships with tribal governments. For example, banks and other forms of credit are sparse on tribal lands, limiting entrepreneurship. Tribal communities are also disadvantaged by insufficient physical infrastructure (e.g., roads, utilities, and high-speed internet).[31] Nonetheless, tribes have proactively attempted various economic development strategies over the past several decades. Nations that are proximate to urban markets can benefit from legalized gaming, but it is a myth that casinos have been an economic salvation for all tribal peoples. On the one hand, in some cases the income derived from casinos has indeed led to better infrastructure and improved services for the small share of tribes who control them. On the other hand, most gaming operations are small, few are lucrative (e.g., only 5 percent of all tribal gaming operations generate 40 percent or more of total tribal revenue), and only a small share pay dividends to tribal members.[32] Tribal governments cannot act unilaterally on casinos; they must negotiate with state governments to receive permission to open them and determine how revenues can be spent. And legalized gaming contributes to gambling addiction and other social problems that harm American Indian communities. Beyond casinos, some tribes that possess natural resources have been able to generate revenue from the land. Still other tribes are isolated from urban markets, do not possess or do not wish to exploit resource-rich land, and/or have struggled to kickstart private entrepreneurship.

Tribal and federal governments tend to be the largest employers on reservations. Jobs and economic opportunity are often scarce; many households are overcrowded and substandard; homelessness is high; and social security, disability, or veterans' income are the main income sources for many households. The nearly 2.6 million

78   CHAPTER 3

American Indian members of federally recognized tribes are provided education and health assistance through the Indian Health Service (IHS), which operates within the U.S. Department of Health and Human Services.[33] But these services are chronically underfunded, making the quality subpar.[34]

Finally, efforts to understand and improve conditions among rural Indigenous populations are hampered by inaccurate data collection and media representations. Rural American Indian communities are made "twice invisible" by policymakers and philanthropists because of both the lack of understanding and the isolation of remote rural communities and reservations where many Indigenous people live.[35]

White Populations

In 1606, King James I sent the Virginia Company (a group of 105 soldiers, laborers, and elites from London) to establish an English settlement in the Chesapeake region of North America. Arriving in 1607, the population soon dwindled due to disease, starvation, and attacks by the neighboring Powhatan tribe. England continued to send ships to replenish people and resources. However, the settlers faced the problems of insufficient labor and inability to feed themselves. In 1619, the first ship carrying captive African people arrived in Jamestown, and enslaved people from Africa soon became the new colonies' economic foundation. The American Revolution, founding of the new United States, and its subsequent national expansion unfolded over the next two centuries, sending White Europeans westward. Black enslavement and Indigenous land theft were foundational dimensions of this national expansion.[36]

Immigrants to the United States in the late 19th and early 20th centuries remained nearly entirely of European origin. For example, the roots of today's rural White population in the agricultural Midwest are immigrants from Northern Europe—mainly Germany and Scandinavia—who settled in the region to develop family farms. In Appalachia, other White immigrant groups, such as the Scots Irish,

RURAL ETHNORACIAL DIVERSITY AND INEQUITIES   79

settled in small towns to work in coal mines, on railroads, and in the timber industry.[37] Certain White ethnic groups (especially Jews, Irish, Poles, and Italians) were not initially considered "White" by prior groups from Northern Europe. As such, they often faced xenophobic exclusion, violence, discrimination, and stigma.[38] However, the oppression of these groups was far less systematic and enduring than of other ethnoracial populations—American Indian and Black people in particular—and over time European ethnic groups generally assimilated into "whiteness."

Black Populations

Black population settlement in what is now the United States has its history in forced migration and enslavement, first when millions of West and Central African people were violently transported to American colonies and later when they were enslaved in plantation agriculture and other industries concentrated largely in the rural U.S. South. Indeed, enslavement was integral to the development trajectories of the North and South alike (e.g., southern cotton plantations were linked to northern textile mills, and New York's Wall Street was home to a major slave market for the South).

After the Civil War and constitutional amendments ended slavery and conferred citizenship on Black people, Reconstruction (1865–1877) brought temporary hope for equality. Black people gained the right to vote, and some were elected to state legislatures and the U.S. Congress. However, that hope was short lived, as most of the promises the U.S. government made to "freedmen" were never fulfilled, leaving Black people socially and economically marginalized, especially in the rural South. By the late 1870s, Black people were once again relegated to second-class citizens who were denied the right to vote; were subjected to intimidation, violence, and lynchings; and faced severe restrictions on employment and education. As a result, Black people in the rural South often worked as sharecroppers and tenant farmers, with limited power and heavy

80   CHAPTER 3

debt burdens that kept them tethered to the land and unable to achieve upward mobility.[39]

The Jim Crow era, which lasted from the late 1870s until the passage of landmark civil rights laws in the mid-1960s, enforced Black-White segregation in the U.S. South. Sanctioned by state and local laws and the U.S. Supreme Court's decision in *Plessy v. Ferguson* (1896), which upheld the constitutionality of segregation, rural southern Blacks were trapped in conditions of quasi-slavery for another hundred years after emancipation.[40] "Separate but equal" was always separate and fundamentally unequal by design. Moreover, "sundown towns," established throughout the country during the first half of the 20th century, were especially concentrated in the Midwest, Northeast, and Northwest. These were communities where Black people and other minoritized groups were targeted for exclusion by requiring that they leave town by dusk or risk arrest by the police or worse. Most sundown towns were places with relatively small populations because the enforcement mechanisms were often impractical in larger cities (e.g., forcing minoritized people to leave the community by nightfall).[41] As late as the 1960s, there were at least 100,000 such towns in the United States, and many remain places with few Black or other non-White residents to this day.[42]

Facing violence, discrimination, and systematic exclusion from social, economic, and political institutions, in a "striking regional redistribution" of the U.S. population, Black people left the rural U.S. South en masse between 1910 and 1970 to relocate to cities in the Northeast and Midwest in what was termed the "Great Migration."[43] Whereas about 75 percent of Black people lived in the rural South in 1900, that share had dropped to 12 percent by 2000. Although Black people faced less oppression and violence in the urban North than they had in the rural South, they were still subjected to systematic discrimination in labor, finance, insurance, and real estate markets and were severely residentially segregated in northern cities.[44]

The civil rights movement of the 1950s and 1960s led to federal legislation that overturned the legal framework that supported discrimination against Black people (e.g., the *Brown v. the Board of Education* Supreme Court decision of 1954 struck down "separate but equal"; the Civil Rights Act of 1964 prohibited racial discrimination in employment, public accommodations, and housing market transactions; and the Voting Rights Act of 1965 prohibited racial discrimination in voting) and led to improvements in the economic situation and political power of Black people. In this legal context, and amid worsening economic conditions in the urban North and improving conditions in the rural South, a large share of southern-born Black people who had moved northward during the Great Migration began returning to the South in the 1970s.[45]

Hispanic Populations

As with American Indians, the history of Hispanics in the rural United States far predates the birth of the country. Spanish colonial settlements were subsumed into the United States by the annexation of territory in Florida in the early 1800s.[46] In the mid-1880s, over 100,000 Mexicans became "American" during the U.S. conquest of the Southwest, when roughly half of Mexico's territory was lost to the expanding nation (comprising the states now known as Texas, California, New Mexico, Nevada, Arizona, Utah, and Colorado). Other Hispanic people from Mexico and elsewhere arrived later through immigration. Accordingly, the U.S. Hispanic population represents Indigenous, native-born, and immigrant populations.[47]

U.S.-born Mexican people were not eligible for citizenship until 1898, depriving them of political and economic power. In much of the rural Southwest, "a thoroughly racialized social structure akin in many ways to that of the Black Belt placed most land and political power into the hands of Whites and reduced Mexican Americans to politically disenfranchised laborers."[48] Mexican immigrants were often highly recruited during U.S. labor shortages, but at other times they were encouraged or forced to return to Mexico. The Bracero Program, which operated from 1942 to 1964, serves as a prime

82   CHAPTER 3

example. Under this policy, Mexican nationals were recruited to work in the United States in agriculture during World War II labor shortages. Although the program called for wage guarantees, housing, and food, those terms were not well enforced and were often disregarded by farm owners. In the 1950s, amid public pressure to stem the growth of undocumented workers encouraged by lax administration of the Bracero Program, the U.S. government enacted the pejoratively termed "Operation Wetback," a military-style round-up and mass deportation of roughly a million Mexican people, including many U.S. citizens of Mexican descent.[49] Following these events, the United States enacted several programs through the Immigration and Nationalization Act (1965) and Immigration Reform and Control Act (1986) that legalized certain forms of new immigration and legalized the status of approximately 2.8 million undocumented immigrants already in the United States.[50] The IRCA also included provisions and additional resources for border enforcement that made it more difficult for migrants to travel back and forth across the U.S.-Mexico border. Complex relationships between U.S. immigration policies (e.g., the IRCA and the H-2A visa program for temporary agricultural workers) and demand for workers in agriculture, food processing, and other low-wage industries continue to drive contemporary patterns of rural Hispanic settlement, population growth, and labor exploitation today.[51]

Although the contemporary U.S. Hispanic population is mainly concentrated in large cities (e.g., Los Angeles, Miami, New York, Houston, and Chicago), one of the most profound demographic trends of the late 20th century was the large-scale movement of Hispanic people away from these cities into many parts of rural America.[52] For example, whereas only 9 percent of Mexican immigrants settled outside of traditional gateway states in the 1970s, one-third of Mexican immigrants to the United States in the 1990s settled outside them.[53] In 1990, rural America was home to just over 1.5 million Hispanic people, with most living in Texas and California alone. Today, over 4 million Hispanic people live in rural counties spread

RURAL ETHNORACIAL DIVERSITY AND INEQUITIES   83

throughout the United States, from upstate New York (attracted by work on dairy farms and as migrant crop harvesters) to Iowa, Arkansas, and North Carolina (where they serve as the main labor force in meat processing).

The rise of these new Hispanic destinations in rural and small-town America during the 1990s and 2000s was driven by numerous economic, political, and social forces, including anti-immigrant legislation in traditional gateways, increased danger of traveling back and forth across the U.S.-Mexico border, a desire for affordable housing, and economic restructuring that began decades earlier (including factory relocations from the heavily unionized Northeast and North Central regions to the less-unionized rural Southeast and Midwest) in search of lower-paid labor with less bargaining power.[54] In addition, Hispanic people have been drawn to service and construction jobs in rural retirement and amenity destinations, illustrating the intersection of two major demographic trends of the late 20th and early 21st centuries: White population aging and Hispanic population growth.[55] Although immigration to the United States has been in decline since the mid-2000s, the rural Hispanic population continues to grow through natural increase.

Hispanic population growth has provided a demographic and economic lifeline for many dying small towns, offsetting out-migration and natural decrease among the White population. For example, if not for Hispanic population growth, over 200 rural counties would have experienced overall population decline during the early 2000s.[56] This rapid population change has also created new challenges for these communities.[57] While Hispanic people living in established destinations benefit from prior generations of coethnics who can provide support, advocacy organizations that can provide information and assistance, and infrastructure and staff with experience working with these populations (such as in schools and hospitals), these supports and services are largely absent in new destinations.

Moreover, while numerous studies show that immigrants' contributions to U.S. society generally, and rural areas specifically, far

84   CHAPTER 3

exceed their costs,[58] Hispanic immigrants continue to face hostility and stigma. These hostilities metastasized during Donald Trump's first presidential campaign and his ensuing presidency. The heavy rural vote for Donald Trump in 2016 and 2020 (discussed more in chapter 5) may have partly reflected long-simmering White feelings of racial threat in small towns with a growing Hispanic presence.

Asian Populations

Asians are the fastest growing ethnoracial group in the United States. Though Asian settlement and population growth has historically been and continues to be concentrated in metropolitan areas, it would be a misunderstanding to think that Asian people do not live in rural America. Asians' history of settlement in rural America spans over three centuries and involves multiple pan-ethnic groups. Settlement patterns have been diverse and driven by multiple causes, including U.S. demand for labor, forced migration, and refugee migration.

The Chinese were the first large group of Asian people to have a presence in the United States. In the mid-1800s, Chinese immigrants arrived in substantial numbers in the West (particularly California) to work in low-paying, labor-intensive jobs, first in the Gold Rush and on the transcontinental railroad and then on large farms.[59] While the contributions of Hispanic migrants to agriculture are generally well known, as of the 1880s, 75 percent of seasonal farmworkers in California were of Chinese descent.[60] However, as Chinese immigrants became more prominent in better-paying industries and built their own businesses, anti-Chinese sentiment rose. In 1882 the U.S. government passed the Chinese Exclusion Act, the first federal law that targeted a specific ethnic group. The act prohibited the immigration of Chinese laborers to the United States for 10 years and denied naturalization to Chinese people, with few exceptions. Subsequent laws (e.g., the Geary Act of 1892 and the Extension Act of 1902) renewed these provisions until the Chinese Exclusion Act's repeal in 1943.[61] The Chinese Exclusion Act institutionalized racial discrimination against Chinese people, contributed to a climate of hostility, resulted in the separation of families, and undermined economic opportunity and upward mobility for this group.

With the flow of Chinese laborers cut off by the Chinese Exclusion Act, Japanese immigrants began arriving in the United States in the late 1800s, primarily to work in agriculture.[62] In the early 1900s, Japanese migrants and their U.S.-born descendants established farming communities in rural areas along the West Coast, playing a crucial role in developing the agricultural industry in that region. However, after the Japanese government's attack on Pearl Harbor in 1941, the U.S. government forcibly interned approximately 120,000 Japanese Americans (no similar action was taken against people of German or Italian ancestry). Following World War II and their release, some interned Japanese Americans returned to the rural West, but they often faced difficulty reclaiming their former property. Others moved on to different parts of the country but faced substantial discrimination and continued hostility.[63]

The IRCA resulted in the rapid growth and diversification of the Asian population in the rural United States throughout the late 20th century, including people hailing from the Philippines, Korea, China, India, and Pakistan. In addition, during and following the Vietnam War in the 1970s and 1980s, the U.S. government admitted large numbers of refugees from Southeast Asia, including Vietnam, Cambodia, and Laos, and the Hmong. Many of these refugees settled in rural parts of Minnesota, California, and Washington, where they too were recruited to work in agriculture and the food processing industry. Today, the largest concentrations of Asian people living in the rural United States can be found in California's Central Valley, the Hawaiian Islands, the Pacific Northwest, the upper Midwest, and on the Gulf Coast.

The settlement histories of the minoritized ethnoracial groups discussed here have several commonalities. As articulated by C. Matthew Snipp:

86   CHAPTER 3

Perhaps most profound is that reservations, colonias, and rural African American communities, unlike other communities, share the experience of living in close proximity to the historical remnants of institutions explicitly created to conquer, oppress, and maintain their subordinate position in society. A list of these institutions is easy to construct: labor contractors, immigration authorities, slavery, Jim Crow, sharecropping, plantation agriculture, the Bureau of Indian Affairs, and tribal police, to name only a few. These institutions were first established in rural areas, and they have survived longer in rural areas than anywhere else.[64]

Another commonality has been resistance and persistence in the face of these oppressions. Rural minoritized ethnoracial groups have led national and local social and political movements and engaged in protracted efforts to change laws, policies, and institutions, securing victories in several arenas, including desegregation, voting rights, Black agrarianism, stolen land reclamation, economic development, education, collective bargaining, political representation, environmental justice, and the reclamation and promotion of authentic cultures.[65]

Resistance efforts have also involved the institution of higher education. The prominent Black academics Booker T. Washington and W. E. B. Du Bois established rural sociology programs at historically Black colleges and universities (HBCUs) and 1890 Land Grant Universities to promote research on the social and economic conditions facing rural Black populations.[66] Du Bois—America's first rural sociologist—pioneered "emancipatory empiricism" by using rigorous research methods to challenge myths and misconceptions about rural Black people and to document the influence of social structure and agency on rural Black well-being.[67]

Such efforts have led to meaningful progress, though substantial ethnoracial inequities persist, and recent democratic backsliding in the United States (e.g., gerrymandering, increased restrictions on voting rights, vilification of mainstream media, restrictions on educational curricula about race) threaten to reverse this hard-won progress. While today's systems of racial oppression look quite different from those of the past, rural America's history of structural racism continues to reinforce marginalization and inequity. It is to this issue we now turn.

RURAL ETHNORACIAL INEQUITY

Three decades ago, a working group of the Rural Sociological Society concluded that rural minoritized populations face the "double jeopardy" of being both rural and non-White.[68] American Indian, Black, Hispanic, and Asian people have long been excluded from full incorporation into the U.S. institutions and residential environments that facilitate economic well-being and upward mobility. These challenges are magnified in rural communities that are geographically isolated, economically disadvantaged, and underresourced.

The legacies outlined in the previous section have created a complex mix of progress and persistence in rural ethnoracial inequity. On the one hand, there have been substantial improvements in economic well-being and living conditions of rural minoritized populations over time. This progress was hard won and should not be ignored. On the other hand, due both to the legacy of historical racism and contemporary political-economic regimes, rural minoritized populations continue to experience worse economic, housing, and health outcomes than both their rural White and urban minoritized counterparts.

Rural minoritized populations have lower educational attainment and higher rates of unemployment and poverty than both rural Whites and urban minoritized populations (see table 3). The only exception is rural Asians, who have lower unemployment than rural White or urban Asian people. Based on Census data from 2016–2020, the shares of rural Black, American Indian, and Hispanic people who have a four-year college degree are half that of rural White people, with even lower educational attainment

Table 3 Economic Well-Being by Ethnoracial Group in Nonmetro and Metro Counties, 2016–2020

	Nonmetropolitan					Metropolitan				
	Black	American Indian/ Alaska Native	Hispanic	Asian	NH White	Black	American Indian/ Alaska Native	Hispanic	Asian	NH White
Educational attainment for population ages 25 and older (%)										
Less than high school	21.0	19.2	34.5	14.7	10.3	12.6	19.5	29.4	12.7	6.0
4-year college degree or more	11.2	11.3	11.1	39.7	22.3	23.7	17.6	18.0	55.4	39.7
Poverty rate	31.0	30.3	23.0	14.1	12.9	21.2	20.6	18.0	10.5	8.5
Unemployment rate for population ages 16 years and older	10.1	12.0	6.4	3.8	4.6	9.1	8.6	6.2	4.3	4.3
Homeownership (% of housing units)	50.5	61.8	58.3	58.3	75.1	41.7	51.7	47.9	60.1	71.6

SOURCE: U.S. Census Bureau, 2021d.

NOTE: NH = non-Hispanic. The ACS tables for these well-being estimates do not enable disaggregation by Hispanic ethnicity for Black and American Indian/Alaska Native populations. Therefore, the values presented for the Black and AIAN categories include Hispanic people who selected those respective racial groups, and the Hispanic category is not exclusive.

among American Indians living on reservations.[69] Conversely, a much larger share of rural Asian people have a four-year college degree than do rural White people. Rural Black people face the highest poverty rate (31 percent), followed by American Indians (30.3 percent) and Hispanics (23 percent). Rural White and Asian people, in contrast, have much lower poverty rates (13 and 14.1 percent, respectively). Moreover, poverty rates are nearly 10 percentage points higher among rural Black and American Indian people than among their urban counterparts. Perhaps especially concerning is the extremely high poverty experienced by rural minoritized children. Whereas the poverty rate among rural White infants is shameful enough (24 percent), rates among rural Black (55.3 percent), American Indian (46.6 percent), and Hispanic (40 percent) babies are downright staggering.[70]

Poverty among rural minoritized populations is also decidedly regionalized. Chapter 2 identified three rural regions where poor minoritized populations are concentrated—the Delta and Black Belt in the South, the Borderlands in the Southwest, and American Indian reservations in the Southwest and northern Plains. (It also highlighted Appalachia, where rural White poverty is highly concentrated.) Rural minoritized populations who are poor tend to be geographically concentrated in "high poverty" places—counties with poverty rates of 20 percent or higher. Two-thirds of poor rural Black people and 40 percent of poor rural Hispanic people live in high poverty counties—a much greater share than the 20 percent of poor rural White people who do so.[71] American Indian people living on reservations also often experience extreme poverty.

One proximate reason for high poverty rates is that rural minoritized people experience pronounced labor market disadvantages. Whereas the unemployment rate among rural Whites was 4.6 percent in the late 2010s (a strong macroeconomic period), 10.1 percent of rural Blacks, 12 percent of rural American Indians, and 6.4 percent of rural Hispanics were unemployed (see table 3). In fact, seasonal unemployment runs as high as 60 percent on some reservations.[72]

90   CHAPTER 3

Tim Slack and colleagues show that rural minoritized populations also have much higher underemployment rates (defined in chapter 2) than both rural Whites and their urban minoritized counterparts.[73] Rural Black people are particularly disadvantaged in this regard.

While rural Hispanic people have somewhat better labor market outcomes than rural Black and American Indian people, work in new Hispanic immigrant destinations tends to be difficult, is sometimes dangerous, and comes with low wages and few to no benefits. Indeed, these are the jobs that many people consider undesirable and thus have difficulty attracting U.S.-born workers. Hispanic immigrants in new destinations also tend to have lower educational attainment, are more likely to be unauthorized, and face substantial language and cultural barriers, making full economic and social integration difficult. Children of immigrants in these places often "start life behind the starting line," facing major impediments to upward mobility due to having lower-income parents who may not speak English well and have limited power in their workplaces and communities.[74]

In the United States, homeownership has historically been seen as evidence of economic security, a buffer against economic hardship, and a foundation for building wealth. Indeed, homeownership is the single greatest source of wealth among American families overall. Wealth is accumulated through appreciation in housing values, against which families can borrow in times of economic hardship. Rural minoritized populations have higher rates of homeownership than their urban counterparts, except for Asians, whose homeownership rates are comparable in rural and urban areas. However, rural minoritized populations have homeownership rates well below those of rural Whites. Compared to the rural White homeownership rate of 75.1 percent, rates are 50.5 percent, 61.8 percent, 58.3 percent, and 58.3 percent for rural Black, American Indian, Hispanic, and Asian households, respectively (see table 3). Moreover, home values are much lower among minoritized groups than among Whites.[75]

RURAL ETHNORACIAL DIVERSITY AND INEQUITIES   91

Black people have also experienced long-term declines in land ownership in the rural South, including heir property for which there is no clear title trajectory.[76]

Perhaps surprising to some readers is that racial segregation is as much a reality in rural and small-town America as it is in the nation's large cities.[77] Owing to the history of residential exclusion discussed earlier, rural minoritized populations have often been relegated to the least desirable parts of town, inhabiting what have been characterized as "rural ghettos."[78] Living in communities with inadequate employment opportunities, schools, housing, and services compounds the effects of individual-level disadvantage and reduces the probability of upward mobility.[79] Though there were declines in racial residential segregation in the 1990s, rural Black people continue to be the most highly segregated group. While rural Hispanic people are less segregated overall, they are more segregated than their metropolitan counterparts, and segregation is often much higher in new rural Hispanic immigrant destinations than it is in other settings. Employers in such places sometimes provide temporary housing, such as trailers, to attract Hispanic migrant workers, though living conditions are often subpar, and such living arrangements can effectively isolate these residents from the rest of the community and make incorporation even more difficult.[80]

As we describe further in chapter 4, rural minoritized populations also generally have worse health outcomes, higher mortality rates, lower rates of health insurance coverage, and less access to health-care providers than both rural Whites and urban minoritized populations. Mortality rates among rural Black and American Indian people are especially high. Although Hispanics have lower mortality rates than Whites in urban and rural areas alike (a phenomenon referred to as the "Hispanic paradox"),[81] this advantage is largely driven by immigrants and the healthy migrant effect, and it disappears by the third generation. Nonetheless, Hispanic people have the lowest health insurance coverage rates of all ethnoracial groups. Health insurance coverage is especially low among rural

92   CHAPTER 3

Hispanics in new immigrant destinations, driven in part by the concentration of noncitizens in these places.[82]

Despite the many barriers to upward mobility and well-being discussed in this and the preceding section, it would be a misunderstanding to assume that all rural minoritized people are poor. As in rural America in general, the rural minoritized population is heterogeneous in their experiences and outcomes. Due to centuries of resistance and persistence, rural minoritized populations have experienced vast improvements in educational attainment, economic well-being, residential mobility, and entrepreneurship over time.

Most of this section has emphasized the "double jeopardy" of being rural and minoritized. The inequities associated with this intersection are stark. But this should not be interpreted to imply that rural White people are immune from economic hardship and exclusion. This too would be a misunderstanding. Indeed, of the 20 counties with the highest poverty rates in the late 2010s, half were rural Appalachian counties with populations that were over 90 percent White.[83] Inequality, place, and race intersect in unique ways for White people, with poor rural Whites often "othered" and derided in popular language (e.g., redneck, hillbilly, white trash, trailer trash) and media (e.g., *The Beverly Hillbillies, Here Comes Honey Boo Boo, Hillbilly Hand Fishin'*). This is not to draw false equivalencies to the centuries of structural racism and violence directed at rural minoritized groups, but it is evidence that poor rural Whites are not immune from barriers to full social and economic incorporation or from the stigma and marginalization associated with their intersecting race, class, and place identities.

CONCLUSION

The broad theme of this chapter is that the notion that rural America is homogenously White is a myth and misunderstanding. The rural United States has always been home to more ethnoracial minorities and has been more diverse than commonly presumed, and it is becoming increasingly so. Growing ethnoracial diversity in rural America is being driven by both immigration and natural increase among Hispanic and mixed-race people as well as by White population decline. Children, who represent a larger share of minoritized populations than White populations, are the vanguard of rural America's growing diversity. Increasing ethnoracial diversity will "be at the leading edge of major changes in rural community life as the nation moves toward becoming a majority-minority society" by the 2040s.[84]

At the same time, it would also be a misunderstanding to assume that all of rural America is ethnoracially diverse. Racial composition and its changes vary dramatically across different regions of the rural United States, with some places facing massive and rapid change and others remaining largely ethnoracially homogenous. Today's patterns of racial residential composition and increasing diversity reflect both historical processes and contemporary economic, political, and social shifts. The history of rural ethnoracial group settlement and its contemporary composition must be understood within the context of institutionalized systems of racial domination. Racism is not "reducible to the fading echoes of historical systems of domination."[85] Instead, racism continues to structure the economic, political, social, and civic institutions of rural communities; drives unequal and unjust economic, educational, housing, and health outcomes; and limits opportunities for upward mobility. Importantly, rural minoritized ethnoracial groups have historically resisted and persisted (and continue to do so) in the face of structural racism and its associated barriers, resulting in improvements in numerous arenas over time.

Increasing ethnoracial diversity has critical implications for rural communities, including for employment and economic incorporation, education and service needs, ethnoracial relations and conflict, cultural changes, and voting patterns. Yet these discussions are typically absent from current public policy debates, such as those about immigration. Minoritized populations have the potential to provide

94   CHAPTER 3

a demographic and economic lifeline to struggling rural communities. The concomitant forces of long-term youth outmigration from rural areas and White natural decrease have left many rural communities with dwindling populations, labor forces, and tax bases. Migrants from other places and natural increase among minoritized groups can help expand the labor force and tax base and spur economic development in such places.[86]

However, there are challenges to full incorporation and equity for rural America's minoritized populations. Despite substantial improvements in economic well-being and living conditions over the past several decades, rural minoritized groups continue to experience worse economic, housing, and health outcomes than both their rural White and urban minoritized counterparts. Importantly, while many cities are accustomed to dealing with the education, healthcare, housing, and other needs of minoritized populations, many rural and small-town communities are not. Especially in the case of the recency and rapid pace of Hispanic population growth in many rural areas, there is potential for intergroup avoidance and conflict rather than inclusion.

Ultimately, greater ethnoracial diversity is certain for rural America in the coming decades. It remains to be seen which places will embrace these changes and restructure their institutions and policies to facilitate upward social mobility for all groups and which will maintain existing and/or enact new barriers to full inclusion and opportunities to succeed for all of rural America's residents.

4 Rural Population Health and Health Disparities

There I am standing by the shore of a swiftly flowing river, and I hear the cry of a drowning man. So, I jump into the river, put my arms around him, pull him to shore and apply artificial respiration. Just when he begins to breathe, there is another cry for help. So, I jump into the river, reach him, pull him to shore, apply artificial respiration, and then just as he begins to breathe, another cry for help. So back in the river again, reaching, pulling, applying, breathing and then another yell. Again and again, without end, goes the sequence. You know, I am so busy jumping in, pulling them to shore, applying artificial respiration, that I have no time to see who the hell is upstream pushing them all in.

—Parable documented in McKinlay (1974)

Americans are dying too young. The United States performs worst on life expectancy of all high-income peer countries, and the relative disadvantage is even more pronounced for rural Americans. The *rural mortality penalty*—higher death rates in rural than in urban areas—is wide, persistent, and growing.[1] The rural health disadvantage is driven by many factors, including individuals' health behaviors and economic resources; availability and quality of health care; and social, built, and physical environments.

96   CHAPTER 4

Moreover, as alluded to in the preceding parable, broader upstream structural forces influence each of these downstream factors to affect health.

This chapter documents recent patterns and trends in rural health and mortality in the United States, with attention to within-rural variation, including the rural subgroups and places with the most troubling health profiles. The second part of the chapter summarizes the factors that contribute to the rural health and mortality disadvantage. We then close the chapter with a detailed exploration of two contemporary population health crises—the drug overdose epidemic and the COVID-19 pandemic—which have cut short the lives of millions of Americans across the rural-urban continuum in recent years but have also affected urban and rural areas in different ways.

PATTERNS AND TRENDS IN NONMETRO HEALTH AND MORTALITY

The rural health and mortality penalties are long-standing, large, and growing. However, it was not always the case that nonmetro areas had worse health profiles and higher mortality rates (deaths per 100,000 population) than metro areas. For most of U.S. history, health was worse and mortality rates were higher in metro than in nonmetro areas due to contaminated water; inadequate trash and sewage disposal; greater population density and crowding; and the rapid spread of contagious diseases, such as tuberculosis, diarrheal disease, and other infectious diseases, in cities.[2] Estimates suggest that the metro mortality rate was 50 percent higher than the non-metro rate in the 1880s.[3] Thanks to large-scale public works projects during the late 19th and early 20th centuries, cities benefited from massive improvements in water quality and sanitation.[4] Additional improvements in diet, shelter, and general living conditions, along with public health transformations, including mass vaccination, heath exams, and health education, improved U.S. life expectancy overall and helped eliminate the metro mortality penalty by the 1940s.[5] Metro and nonmetro mortality rates remained similar from the 1940s until the late 1980s.[6]

Contemporary Mortality Trends

The nonmetro mortality penalty emerged in the 1980s for males and in the 1990s for females, with especially large increases beginning in the mid-2000s (see figure 16). As of 2020, the nonmetro male mortality rate was 16.5 percent higher than the metro male rate, and the nonmetro female rate was 18.9 percent higher than the metro female rate. The statistics presented in figure 16 adjust for the differential age composition of metro versus nonmetro counties (i.e., the rates are age adjusted). As we saw in chapter 1, nonmetro populations are older than metro populations, driving up their overall mortality rates. However, as the figure makes clear, the rural mortality penalty persists even after controlling for age differences.

Figure 16 demonstrates that the increase in the nonmetro mortality penalty over the last four decades was due to larger metro mortality declines throughout the 1980s, 1990s, and 2000s, followed by nonmetro stagnation in the 2010s. The 2010s was a troubling decade for U.S. mortality. Even before the onset of the COVID-19 pandemic in 2020, the United States was performing poorly relative to both its own trends in prior decades and trends in other high-income countries. Mortality rates then jumped in 2020 and 2021 in metro and nonmetro areas alike due to the COVID-19 pandemic, with larger increases in nonmetro counties. COVID-19 was so devastating for rural America that the 2020 mortality rate among nonmetro males was higher than it had been since the 1990s, and among nonmetro females it was the highest it had been since the 1980s.

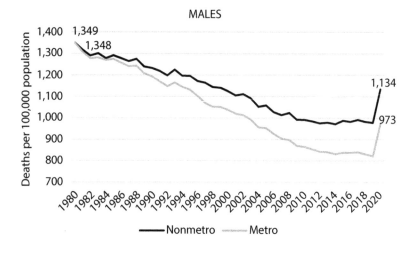

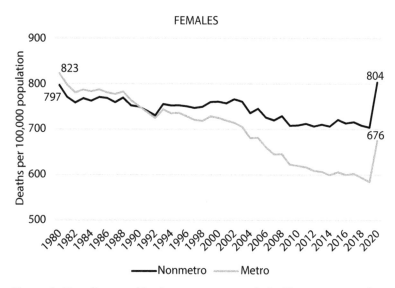

Figure 16. Mortality rates (deaths per 100,000 population) by metro status for males and females, 1980–2020. *Note*: Mortality rates are age adjusted. Start- and end-point values included on trend lines. *Source*: Author calculations using data from CDC WONDER, U.S. Centers for Disease Control and Prevention, 2022a, 2022b.

Causes of Death Contributing to Higher Nonmetro Mortality Rates

Which causes of death help explain why mortality rates are higher in nonmetro than in metro areas? The answer is—almost all of them. Figure 17 shows the top 10 causes of death in 2020 by metro status and for those ages 1 to 24, 25 to 64, and 65 and older. We separate by age group because people of different ages are at higher risk for different diseases. Across nearly every major cause of death and in all age groups, nonmetro mortality rates are higher than metro rates. The exceptions are drug overdoses and homicide, for which rates are higher in metro counties. Nonmetro counties have higher mortality rates from cancers, heart disease, infectious diseases (COVID-19, influenza, and pneumonia), chronic lower respiratory disease, Alzheimer's disease, stroke, diabetes, kidney disease, chronic liver disease and cirrhosis (alcohol induced), suicide, transport accidents, and congenital malformations. Additionally, nonmetro females have higher rates of maternal mortality than metro females,[7] and infant mortality rates are higher in nonmetro than in metro areas.[8] While nearly all causes of death contribute to the contemporary nonmetro disadvantage, cancer and heart disease are the largest contributors because they are the top causes of death in the U.S. population overall.

While figure 17 shows rates for one point in time (2020), differential changes in these rates in nonmetro versus metro areas have widened the mortality gap over time. For nearly all causes of death, rates have either declined less (e.g., cancers, heart disease) or increased more (e.g., suicide, alcohol-induced, diabetes, respiratory diseases) in nonmetro areas than in metro areas over the past three decades.[9]

That there is no single cause of death to blame for the large and widening nonmetro disadvantage clues us into the fact that there is no single explanation either. Instead, numerous factors at multiple levels have created the trends we observe today. We return to this point later in the chapter.

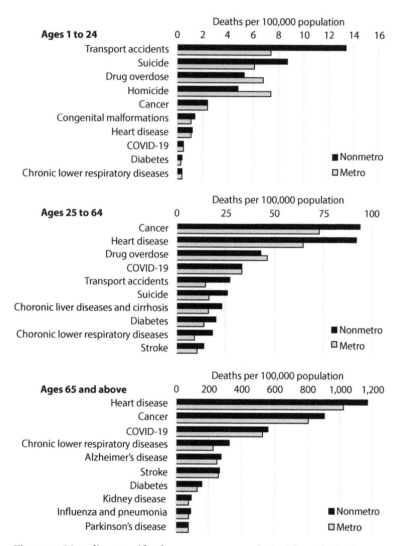

Figure 17. Mortality rates (deaths per 100,000 population) from the leading causes of death by metro status for ages 1–24, 25–64, and 65+, 2020. *Note:* Mortality rates are age adjusted within each age category. *Source:* Author calculations using data from CDC WONDER, U.S. Centers for Disease Control and Prevention, 2022b.

Metro Status Differences in Other Health Outcomes

Mortality is only one metric of population health. Not only do nonmetro residents die at higher rates than metro residents, but they also report worse self-rated health; have higher rates of heart disease, diabetes, stroke, cancer, obesity, functional limitations, disability, injury, pain, cognitive decline, and Alzheimer's disease and related dementias; and have worse oral health and mental health.[10]

Particularly concerning are high rates of obesity and poor cardiovascular health among rural children and young adults, with estimates suggesting that the average rural child has a 26 percent greater chance of being obese than the average urban child.[11] Childhood obesity has implications for health across the life course. Children who are obese are likely to be obese as adults, increasing their risk of cardiovascular disease, hypertension, type 2 diabetes, obstructive sleep apnea, asthma, and certain cancers.[12] Sociologists comparing cardiovascular health between metro and nonmetro young adults ages 24 to 34 found that, compared to young adults living in core metro communities, those living in rural communities were less likely to be in ideal cardiovascular health (7 percent versus 4 percent), more likely to have a BMI over 25 (31 percent versus 34 percent), and less likely to have ideal blood pressure (30 percent versus 26 percent).[13]

NONMETRO VARIATION IN HEALTH AND MORTALITY

As we emphasize throughout this book, nonmetro areas and populations are not homogenous, and it would be a misunderstanding to assume that all nonmetro areas and groups suffer from poor health and high mortality rates. For example, there is wide variation in mortality and other health outcomes by ethnoracial status. Figure 18 shows metro status differences in mortality rates from 1999 to 2020

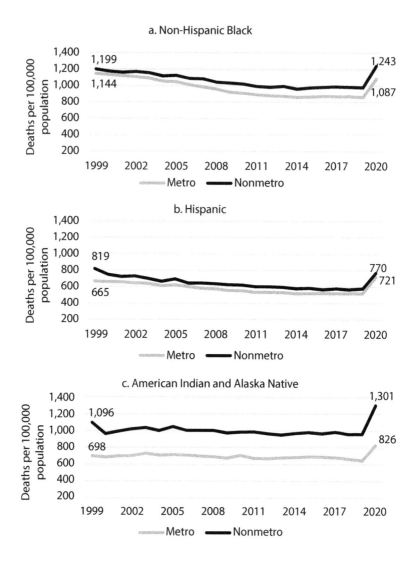

across different ethnoracial groups. Nonmetro rates are higher than metro rates for all ethnoracial groups, with an especially large gap for American Indians. In addition, nonmetro Black and American Indian populations have much higher mortality rates than nonmetro White, Hispanic, and Asian populations.[14]

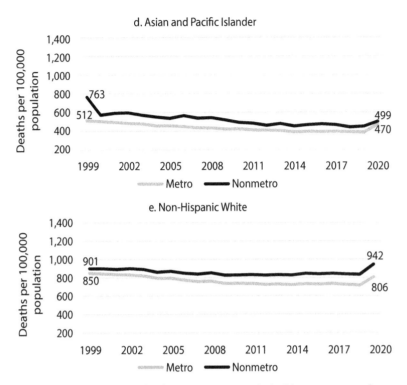

Figure 18. Mortality rates (deaths per 100,000 population) by metro status for (a) non-Hispanic Blacks, (b) Hispanics, (c) non-Hispanic American Indians and Alaska Natives, (d) non-Hispanic Asians and Pacific Islanders, and (e) non-Hispanic Whites, 1999–2020. *Note*: All racial groups are non-Hispanic. Hispanics are of any race. Mortality rates are age adjusted. Rates from pre-1999 (as in figure 16) not included because disaggregated rates by Hispanic ethnicity are not available in CDC WONDER for years prior to 1999. Start- and end-point values included on trend lines. *Source*: Author calculations using data from CDC WONDER, U.S. Centers for Disease Control and Prevention, 2022b.

In addition to higher mortality rates, nonmetro Black populations also have higher rates of obesity and several chronic diseases,[15] are less likely to have health insurance and a personal health-care provider, and are more likely to forgo seeing a health-care provider due to cost than nonmetro Whites.[16] In part, this is because nonmetro

Black people encounter health challenges that are faced by nonmetro residents generally, as well as disadvantaged socioeconomic status and disproportionate concentration in the U.S. South (a region with a particularly concerning health profile for all ethnoracial groups).[17] As discussed in chapter 3, nonmetro Black people also face unique disadvantages that are specific to their minoritized ethnoracial status, including the impacts of structural racism and environmental racism (e.g., the disproportionate siting of landfills, incinerators, hazardous waste, and polluting industries in communities of color).[18] However, it would be a misunderstanding to conclude that nonmetro Black people do worse on all health outcomes. Despite the disadvantages just listed, nonmetro Black populations do better than metro Black and nonmetro White populations on certain health behaviors and causes of mortality. For example, nonmetro Black people have lower rates of substance use, drug overdose, and suicide than metro Black and nonmetro White people.[19] In addition, nonmetro Black mortality rates declined quite dramatically throughout the 1990s and 2000s (though not as much as the decline in metro rates).[20] Much of this progress was due to declines in cardiovascular and cancer mortality. However, that progress stalled in the 2010s and was entirely wiped out in 2020 by the COVID-19 pandemic.

Nonmetro American Indian people have long had higher mortality rates than both their metro counterparts and nonmetro White and Hispanic people. The nonmetro American Indian mortality rate in 2020 was 38 percent higher than that for nonmetro White people and 57 percent higher than for metro American Indians (see figure 18). Nonmetro American Indians face challenges that are faced by nonmetro residents generally, including socioeconomic disadvantages and difficulty accessing health care and other services. However, like the nonmetro Black population, the nonmetro American Indian population also faces challenges that are unique to their minoritized status. Due to colonization, abuse and violence, forced resettlement and assimilation, and discrimination, American Indian communities in the United States have endured centuries of loss of their land, livelihoods, and cultures, resulting in a legacy of collective intergenerational trauma and grief. Not only is this history health harming, it also sometimes manifests in adverse coping behaviors (e.g., substance misuse) and physiological stress that "gets under the skin" to harm health.[21]

Nonmetro immigrants, who are predominantly Hispanic but include nonnegligible shares of Asian people as well, also face many challenges that can adversely affect health, including language barriers, cultural differences, health-care access barriers, and anti-immigrant sentiment and actions.[22] These challenges are even more pronounced for undocumented immigrants. Nonmetro Hispanic and Asian immigrants are also disproportionately represented in physically demanding jobs, such as agriculture and food processing, which expose them to risk of injury and chemicals that are harmful to their health.[23] Given these challenges and their comparatively disadvantaged socioeconomic status and low rates of insurance coverage (especially among Hispanics), it might be surprising to see relatively low mortality rates for nonmetro Hispanic and Asian populations. Rural Hispanic and Asian adults are also less likely than rural Black, American Indian, and White adults to report their health as fair or poor, engage in unhealthy behaviors such as smoking and binge drinking, or have activity limitations.[24] Some of this is driven by what is referred to as the *immigrant health paradox*.[25] Not only is it the case that healthier individuals are more likely than less healthy individuals to migrate (a phenomenon known in the social sciences as the "healthy migrant effect"), but it is also believed that cultural factors among immigrants, such as better health habits and stronger social support networks, contribute to lower rates of chronic disease and higher life expectancy. Over time, however, immigrants and their children tend to acculturate to the U.S. lifestyle of unhealthy diets and more sedentary behavior, and their health declines over generations.

Health and mortality outcomes are also worse in certain types of rural places compared with others. It is well established that rural counties with high poverty rates and low educational attainment

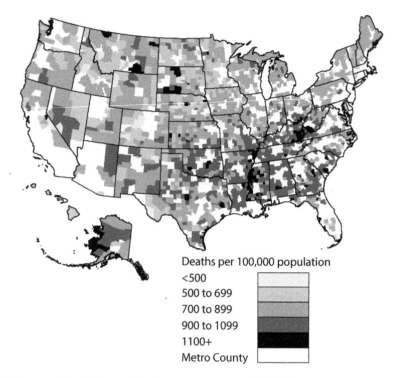

Figure 19. Mortality rates (deaths per 100,000 population) for nonmetro counties, 2017–2019. *Note*: Mortality rates are age adjusted. *Source*: U.S. Centers for Disease Control and Prevention, 2022c.

have high mortality rates, with the highest mortality rates found in high-poverty rural counties.[26] There are clusters of high mortality rates in the United States that have persisted despite changes to population composition, medical advancements, and policies aimed at reducing poverty.[27] Large regional differences can be seen in figure 19. Like the persistent poverty maps we saw in chapter 2, mortality rates are highest in rural counties in central Appalachia, parts of the South, and territories with large shares of American Indian residents in the upper Plains and Oklahoma. These places have long had higher mortality rates than the rest of the country,[28] a reality that points to the role of long-term structural disadvantages that have affected generations of residents.

However, not all of rural America is in dire straits. Prior to the COVID-19 pandemic, several rural regions were experiencing mortality declines, including parts of Texas, the Northeast, and counties along the southeast Atlantic and the Pacific coasts. In addition, rural counties characterized by larger shares of employment in recreation and services have lower mortality rates than rural counties dependent on other types of industries, especially mining.[29] The recreation county advantage is partly due to relatively healthy in-movers, including affluent retirees and amenity migrants, issues discussed in chapter 1.

EXPLANATIONS FOR THE RURAL HEALTH AND MORTALITY DISADVANTAGE

Explanations for the rural health and mortality penalties cross many dimensions and levels. Factors affecting health operate throughout the life course from gestation to death and can be classified into the micro, meso, and macro (structural) levels.[30]

The micro level includes factors proximate to the individual, such as health behaviors, socioeconomic status (SES), and health-care use. The meso level captures social relationships and intermediary community-level settings, such as family context, health care, workplaces, and built and physical environments. The macro level incorporates upstream institutions and structures, including macroeconomic changes, policies and politics, and structural racism. These upstream factors trickle down to affect the meso and micro levels and ultimately, health and death.

Micro-Level Factors

In terms of health behaviors, nonmetro areas have higher rates of tobacco use, poor diet, sedentary leisure time, and lower seat belt

108   CHAPTER 4

use.[31] For example, estimates suggest that 18.3 percent of rural adults ages 18–90 smoke cigarettes daily, compared to 13.4 percent of urban adults. A national study of young adults ages 24–34 found that nonmetro residents were less likely than metro residents to engage in at least five physical activity sessions and more likely to consume more than three sugar-sweetened beverages per week.[32]

Health behaviors, morbidity, and mortality are all strongly associated with SES, and the link between SES and health has grown stronger in recent decades. Health is better and mortality rates are lower among individuals with more education, income, and wealth. Sociologists Bruce Link and Jo Phelan long ago identified SES as a "fundamental cause" of health and health disparities because higher SES individuals have more access to resources (e.g., money, power, prestige, and social connections) that help them avoid diseases and their negative consequences.[33] This includes more knowledge about disease risks and how to prevent them; access to better housing, schools, food, and recreational opportunities; and the ability to afford costly high-quality health care that can save their lives when they do become sick. As we saw in chapter 2, rural residents have lower educational attainment and income than their urban peers. There is also evidence that poverty might have a stronger influence on harmful health behaviors in rural areas than in urban areas.[34] However, while SES clearly plays a key role, the rural mortality penalty cannot be entirely explained by socioeconomic factors,[35] meaning other important factors are also at play.

In terms of health-care use, rural residents are less likely to be insured, less likely to use health care, and more likely to delay seeking care than urban residents.[36] Much of this difference is due to inadequate access to health care in rural areas, but it is also the product of state policy choices, an issue we discuss more later.

Meso-Level Factors

Meso-level factors also contribute to health and mortality disparities. A long tradition of sociological research has identified the important link between social relationships and health through their influence on health behaviors, psychosocial well-being, and provision of financial and instrumental support (e.g., errands, chores).[37] There is some evidence that rural residents benefit from stronger social support networks and social cohesion than urban residents,[38] but more recent research suggests that rural-urban differences in social support are actually quite small.[39] There is also evidence that social capital–promoting institutions that are beneficial for health (e.g., creative, athletic, and entertainment venues; personal services; and social services) are less available in some types of rural communities.[40]

The family environment is critical for health across the life course. Children growing up in rural areas experience more adverse childhood experiences (ACEs) in the family environment than urban children, including economic hardship, witnessing household violence, and living with household substance misuse.[41] There is a strong link between ACEs and risky behaviors and poor mental and physical health in adulthood.[42] Family is also important in older age, with adult children being a critical source of primary support for their aging parents. However, rural older adults tend to live farther away from their adult children than do urban older adults.[43]

Built, employment, and physical environments include the characteristics of the places where we live, work, attend school, consume health care and other services, and engage in recreation. One type of built environment important for health is health-care infrastructure. Rural areas tend to have insufficient and declining health-care infrastructure, and residents must travel greater distances to receive care. This includes not only primary care, but also preventive and emergency care, dental care, pharmacies, mental health and substance use treatment services, aging and disability services, and sexual and reproductive health services.[44] Rural residents travel over twice the distance for health care as urban residents.[45] Nearly 60 percent of rural counties have no obstetricians.[46] And between 2005 and 2022, over 183 rural hospitals closed.[47] Although telehealth has

110 CHAPTER 4

been lauded as a potential way to fill the rural health-care gap, many rural residents have inadequate access to high-speed broadband and cellular service, limiting the potential for telehealth to reach them. We have seen from the COVID-19 pandemic how much access to health care and public health resources matter, and improvements in medical care over time have helped reduce deaths from certain causes, such as screenable cancers. However, evidence shows that medical care contributes little (estimates are as low as 3.5 percent)[48] to population health compared to the health behavior and SES factors discussed earlier and the structural factors discussed later. This is because while access to high-quality health care is critical for saving lives once people become sick or injured, health care does not *cause* most of the diseases or injuries that make people sick to begin with.

In addition to health care, the built environment includes infrastructure like roads, housing, recreation spaces, and food outlets. Rural areas tend to lack sidewalks and fitness facilities. Affordable housing shortages affect urban and rural areas alike, but the housing stock is older and is more likely to be substandard in rural areas. For example, while only 21.5 percent of the nation's occupied housing units are in rural areas, 30 percent of units that lack piped water are in rural communities, and in some American Indian communities the incidence of homes lacking basic plumbing is over 10 times the national average.[49] In terms of food environments, idyllic notions that small farms and bountiful gardens are commonplace is largely a myth. Many rural Americans are food insecure, defined by the USDA as "limited or uncertain availability of nutritionally adequate and safe foods."[50] This includes not only not having enough to eat, but also not having enough access to healthy (i.e., nutrient rich) foods and having too much access to unhealthy (i.e., processed, high fat, high sodium, added sugar) foods. Food insecurity contributes to reduced nutrient intake, diabetes, obesity, other chronic health conditions, and poor mental health. Rural residents must travel longer distances to grocery stores and emergency food pantries, and food tends to be more expensive in rural areas.[51] Food insecurity rates are higher among nonmetro White, Hispanic, and American Indian populations compared to their metro counterparts, and the nonmetro South has a disproportionately high rate of food insecurity.[52]

Work environments are also critical to health. Rural workers are more likely to be employed in manual labor occupations that expose them to wear and tear on their bodies, hazardous toxins, and injuries from accidents.[53] For example, coal extraction in Appalachia puts workers at risk of injury and respiratory diseases, such as coal workers' pneumoconiosis (CWP), commonly known as black lung disease, a problem that has been increasing since the mid-1990s.[54] Full-time workers in rural areas are also less likely than their urban counterparts to have access to paid sick leave, increasing the odds that they will go to work sick and expose coworkers to illness.[55]

Physical and natural environments also influence health. In some rural parts of the United States, the natural environment embodies features that are protective for health, such as fresh air and opportunities to engage in physical activity and commune with nature. But other parts of rural America have been referred to as "dumping grounds" for locally undesirable land uses (LULUs) that are harmful to both the environment and health, including air, soil, and water pollutants stemming from industrial production, agriculture (e.g., pesticides and concentrated animal feeding operations), energy resource development (e.g., mining, mountaintop removal, natural gas extraction, and petroleum drilling), and waste facility siting.[56] Coal production in Appalachia has been linked not only to chronic lung diseases, but also to cancers and birth defects. Unconventional oil and gas extraction (i.e., "fracking") releases chemicals associated with cancer and childhood leukemia.[57] Pesticides from agricultural production are known to contribute to cancer, endocrine and immune system disorders, respiratory diseases, skin irritation, stomach and liver illness, neurological decline, and reproductive problems,[58] with Hispanic populations most affected due to their disproportionately high exposure to these toxins.[59] Hazardous waste facilities, which have been linked to adverse reproductive outcomes, cancers, and diabetes

112   CHAPTER 4

among nearby residents,[60] are disproportionately located in rural Black communities in the South and on American Indian reservations.[61] In addition, although lead poisoning is a well-known problem in urban areas, it also affects rural areas due to their relatively old housing stock (with lead-based pipes and paint), contaminated well water, and pollutants that become embedded in the soil.[62]

The natural environment also harms health through climate change and natural disasters. Among the best-known environmental disasters in U.S. history is the Dust Bowl of the 1930s, when a severe drought, overfarming, and soil erosion led to the intense and prolonged destruction of the Great Plains. As captured by one description:

> Children died of dust pneumonia, and livestock suffocated on dirt, their insides packed with soil. Women hung wet sheets in windows, taped doors and stuffed cracks with rags. None of this really worked. Housecleaning, in this era, was performed with a shovel. As banks, churches and businesses closed, food became scarce.... Starving, they pickled tumbleweed, and ate yucca roots and roadkill.[63]

Many parts of rural America are more vulnerable than urban areas to the adverse effects of natural and human-made disasters because they have less robust and sometimes substandard infrastructure, training, and emergency services; are more geographically isolated and harder to reach; have larger coverage areas; and have less capacity to recover from hazards such as wildfires, tornados, droughts, and flooding (all of which have been increasing in frequency and severity in recent decades). Moreover, the historical patterns of structural racism discussed in chapter 3 and patterns of economic inequality discussed in chapter 2 mean that rural low income and minoritized populations are often residentially located in areas vulnerable to climate disasters. For example, approximately 19 million people live in places with high flood risk (such as river deltas and coastal wetlands), which are clustered in rural areas and in the South, have substantially higher percentages of mobile homes, and

RURAL POPULATION HEALTH AND DISPARITIES 113

are home to disproportionately high shares of Black and American Indian people.[64] It is no surprise then that rural communities have higher rates of flood-related mortality than urban communities.[65] Severe weather changes are also affecting rural livelihoods and recreation activities that depend on predictable weather, including agriculture and tourism (e.g., skiing).

Structural Factors

Although each of these factors contributes to the rural health and mortality penalties, they all miss the bigger picture illustrated by the parable that began this chapter. Here we can glean insights from sociological and political economy theories asserting that "to properly understand the U.S. mortality disadvantage, geographic research needs to 'scale up' and refocus on upstream political, economic, and policy drivers."[66] That is, we must look upstream at how our macroeconomic and policy environments affect the host of downstream factors that influence health.

Thinking first about macroeconomic conditions, many of the micro- and meso-level factors discussed earlier that are harmful to health stem from a long history of geographically uneven economic development that has been unkind to rural America. As discussed in chapter 2, deindustrialization moved many living-wage production jobs out of rural towns and small cities that depended on them.[67] This led to fewer and lower-wage employment opportunities, especially for individuals without a college degree. Many rural areas that were previously home to labor markets with decent-paying manufacturing and mining jobs are now dominated by precarious low-wage service work that does not provide health insurance, paid sick leave, and other benefits.[68] Reduced economic opportunities and population loss not only shrink the tax bases that fund health-promoting services but may also lead to unhealthy coping behaviors, such as smoking, substance use, unhealthy diet, and physical inactivity— behaviors that increase the risk of premature mortality.

114   CHAPTER 4

Policies also play a critical role in health because they shape opportunities and incentives for individuals to make healthy choices.[69] As Clare Bambra and her colleagues write, policies and political choices are "the *causes of the causes of the causes* of geographical inequalities in health."[70] Not only are U.S. policies in the areas of housing, income support, labor protections, and education (to name a few) less generous than those in other high-income countries, but these and other policies that influence health also vary dramatically across states.[71] Consider smoking. Although smoking is a behavioral risk factor for several diseases, smoking prevalence reflects more than individual choices. Geographic differences in smoking prevalence (and smoking-related mortality) reflect different state policy choices on tobacco control, including excise taxes and restrictions on smoking in public places. Unsurprisingly, states with higher excise taxes and more indoor smoking restrictions have lower smoking prevalence.[72]

While national and local policies are important, state policies are becoming increasingly important drivers of health due to the rapid decentralization of policymaking authority from the federal to state levels (i.e., devolution), as well as the increasing use of state preemption (i.e., states prohibiting cities and counties from enacting their own policies).[73] State policy environments have become more polarized over the last two decades (an issue we discuss further in chapter 5). While some states have enacted policies that improve health—such as Medicaid expansion under the Affordable Care Act (ACA), excise taxes on tobacco and alcohol, paid sick leave mandates, firearm restrictions, environmental impact reviews on new development, and more—other states have moved in the opposite direction. Research shows that states that have been more progressive on these types of policies have experienced larger increases in life expectancy and larger reductions in mortality among working-age adults over the last two decades than have states with more conservative policy orientations.[74]

Why does this matter for the rural mortality penalty? Policies tend to be more conservative, and are becoming increasingly so, in more

RURAL POPULATION HEALTH AND DISPARITIES 115

rural states. For example, rural states have been less likely than urban states to expand Medicaid under the ACA, resulting in higher rates of uninsurance among rural residents and rural hospital closures.[75] And through preemption, rural states have been more likely than urban states to ban their city and county governments from enacting local policies on things such as employer-paid sick leave, firearm restrictions, environmental protections, and food and nutrition policies.[76] The increasing polarization of state policy environments means that an increasing share of rural Americans are living in policy contexts that have been demonstrated to be *health harming* rather than *health promoting*. When we consider how our everyday lives are embedded in multiple policy contexts, we can start to think more critically about the many ways such contexts might be contributing to the rural mortality penalty through their downstream impacts.

CONTEMPORARY HEALTH CRISES: THE DRUG OVERDOSE EPIDEMIC AND COVID-19 PANDEMIC

With this overarching rural population health context in mind, we move to a discussion of two contemporary health crises that have garnered significant media and political attention and have cut short millions of American lives: the drug overdose epidemic and the COVID-19 pandemic.

The Drug Overdose Epidemic

The United States is now in its third decade of a devastating drug overdose crisis that has claimed over one million lives and shows no signs of abating. A common narrative about the overdose crisis, especially during the early coverage of opioid overdoses, was that it was hitting rural communities especially hard.[77] That coverage, while providing critical attention to disadvantaged rural areas, was a misrepresentation and misunderstanding of the geography of the

116   CHAPTER 4

overdose crisis, and it ignored substantial variation across different parts of rural America. The reality is that drug overdose rates were higher in nonmetro areas only during the late 2000s and early 2010s.[78] For most of the past 30 years, overdose rates have either been comparable between metro and nonmetro areas or higher in metro areas. Since the emergence of fentanyl (a highly potent synthetic opioid) in the late 2010s, overdoses have increased at a faster rate in metro areas.

However, broad metro versus nonmetro comparisons obscure substantial differences within rural America. While some rural areas have among the lowest overdose rates in the country (e.g., Mississippi Delta and Central Plains), others have among the highest (e.g., Appalachia and the Rust Belt).[79] Aggregating rural places into a single rate obscures important differences across different types of rural places.

From once vibrant manufacturing cities to coal country, what characterizes most of the places in the United States with the highest drug overdose rates is not metro status per se, but that they are places with a high degree of economic and social disadvantage. Indeed, research from Shannon Monnat and other sociologists shows that, in addition to drug supply, factors related to place-level distress, such as higher county-level poverty and unemployment rates, less education, and higher rates of marital breakdown, single-parent families, disability, and vacant housing, are associated with higher rates of drug overdoses.[80] Put simply, drug overdoses are more common in communities where a large share of the population is suffering.

McDowell County, West Virginia, and Scioto County, Ohio, are examples that epitomize many of the places with the highest drug overdose rates. For several decades, McDowell County was the world's largest coal producer. It was dotted with company towns— places where nearly all housing, stores, and services were owned by the mining company that was also the main employer. When the mines closed, the population plummeted from nearly 100,000 people in 1950 to fewer than 19,000 people today. As the coal companies closed, good-paying mining jobs were replaced with lower-paying service jobs as the main source of employment. But now even many of those jobs are long gone; Walmart closed its doors in 2016. Left jobless and hopeless and with untreated physical and psychological pain, many remaining residents turned to drugs and alcohol to cope. McDowell County was one of the canaries in the proverbial coal mine, with opioid overdoses surging there long before the rest of the country was paying attention to the coming crisis. And it still has among the highest fatal drug overdose rates in the United States (ranked 10th nationally for the period 2016–2020).[81]

In *Dreamland: The True Tale of America's Opiate Epidemic*,[82] Sam Quinones described the small city of Portsmouth in Scioto County, Ohio. At one time, Portsmouth boasted a thriving manufacturing economy anchored by shoe factories and steel mills. But because of U.S. policy choices that encouraged offshoring, by the 1990s those factories were long gone. The plants were replaced by big-box stores, check-cashing and rent-to-own services, pawn shops, and scrap yards. In today's Scioto County, median household income is far lower than the national average, and poverty, disability, and unemployment rates are high.[83] In Portsmouth, the emptying out of factories was followed by the emptying out of people and hope.[84] At the time Quinones published *Dreamland*, Portsmouth had the distinction of being the "pill mill capital of America," with more prescription opioids per capita than anywhere else in the country. Scioto County still has among the highest fatal overdose rates in the country (ranked fifth nationally for 2016–2020),[85] more recently driven by fentanyl and methamphetamine rather than prescription opioids and heroin.[86]

Places like McDowell and Scioto were primed to be vulnerable to opioids, drugs that temporarily numb both physical and psychological pain. Lax federal and state policies related to pharmaceutical distribution, marketing, and monitoring allowed pharmaceutical companies to exploit this pain by targeting these places with opioid overprescribing.

118   CHAPTER 4

Although drug overdose rates are high in many rural and urban areas alike, rural communities face unique challenges in contending with the crisis. Overdose deaths represent only a small fraction of people with substance use disorders, leaving many in need of mental health and substance use treatment and social services. Rural areas have less capacity and fewer resources than large urban hubs to provide these services.[87] Even when services are available, privacy concerns and stigma are significant barriers to rural residents seeking treatment.[88] Rural communities also do not have the infrastructure (e.g., beds, pretrial services, supervisory staff, and substance use treatment case managers) to absorb the rising number of drug-related arrestees. This means that individuals struggling with addiction languish in jail without treatment while they await trial. Local public health systems are also increasingly called upon to deal with the externalities of injection drug use, including HIV and hepatitis C virus (HCV) infection. Although this problem is not limited to rural areas, rural public health systems have fewer resources to prevent and contain outbreaks.

Finally, although opioids (primarily fentanyl) continue to be the main contributor to drug overdoses across the rural-urban continuum, the contributions of cocaine and methamphetamine (stimulants) have also increased dramatically in recent years, demonstrating that the problem is bigger than opioids alone. Indeed, we are now in a polysubstance phase of the drug overdose crisis. Both methamphetamine use and methamphetamine-involved overdose rates are higher in nonmetro than metro counties.[89] Methamphetamine has devastating effects on the physical and mental health of users, including anxiety, confusion, insomnia, hallucinations, paranoia, violent behavior, and severe tooth decay and skin sores, with many of these conditions leading to premature death that is not defined as an overdose.

The story of the contemporary U.S. drug overdose crisis illustrates how upstream structural drivers, including macro-level economic changes, corporate behaviors, and policy choices, laid the

RURAL POPULATION HEALTH AND DISPARITIES

groundwork for a population health crisis that has caused disproportionate harm in some areas of the United States, including parts of rural America.

The COVID-19 Pandemic

The COVID-19 pandemic began in the United States in January 2020. As of January 2024, there had been 1.17 million COVID-19 deaths in the United States. The number of cases is more difficult to nail down given early delays in testing, nonreports of positive cases from at-home tests used later in the pandemic, and the fact that people can become infected multiple times. Nonetheless, as of March 2023, when Johns Hopkins University stopped tracking cases, they estimated nearly 104 million U.S. cases since the start of the pandemic.[90]

Early on, some people predicted that rural areas might be spared the brunt of COVID-19 given their lower population density and lack of transportation hubs that facilitated quick spread. And initially the virus was concentrated in urban areas. However, rural scholars who understood the numerous risk factors facing rural areas were already raising alarms in March 2020 about COVID-19's potential impacts on rural America.[91]

From March 2020 to December 2020, aggregate case and death rates were higher in urban counties than in rural counties, but rural rates surpassed urban rates in December 2020 and have remained higher ever since (see figure 20). As of February 2023, nonmetro counties had a COVID-19 mortality rate that was over 40 percent higher than the metro rate (412 deaths per 100,000 among nonmetro counties, compared to 292 deaths per 100,000 among metro counties).[92]

Why did this happen? There are several characteristics of rural populations and communities that increased their risk of having higher rates of infection and death once COVID-19 spread across the United States. In terms of population vulnerabilities, rural

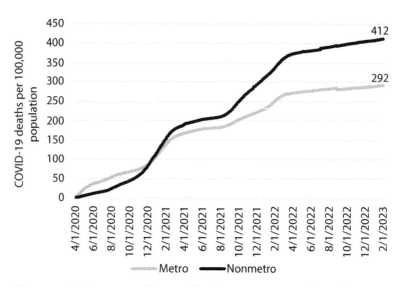

Figure 20. COVID-19 mortality rates (deaths per 100,000 population) for metro and nonmetro counties. *Note*: Mortality rates are current as of February 1, 2023. End-point values included on trend lines. *Source*: USA Facts, 2023.

populations on average are older and sicker than urban populations. Older adults and those with preexisting medical conditions, such as heart disease, cancer, respiratory diseases, and obesity, are at much higher risk of death should they become infected with the coronavirus. Poverty, low education, and lack of health insurance are also risk factors,[93] all of which are more prevalent among rural than urban residents.

Rural communities also face several meso-level disadvantages, such as weaker health care and public health infrastructures. Many rural communities have no hospitals at all, and where rural hospitals do exist, they have fewer personnel and less equipment (e.g., ventilators) and capacity to deal with surges in cases. Rural labor markets and working conditions may also place workers at risk. Rural workers were less likely to be able to work remotely during the pandemic,[94] partly due to the types of jobs that exist in rural places. Essential industries like food processing and agriculture are disproportionately located in rural areas.[95] Workers cannot do those jobs from home. Very few food processing facilities closed during the pandemic, and these facilities are known for the very conditions that are ideal for COVID-19 spread (i.e., crowded, damp, and cold).[96] Many of these facilities were also negligent in enacting safety measures, such as mandatory face masks and social distancing.[97]

Finally, it is now well-established that the U.S. government failed to respond effectively to COVID-19.[98] Some of these failures were long in the making, with plenty of blame attributable to prior federal administrations. However, as laid out in *Pandemic Politics: The Deadly Toll of Partisanship in the Age of COVID-19*, among the top reasons the United States performed so poorly in mitigating the pandemic relative to its peer nations was that then president Trump downplayed its severity, gutted the very agencies tasked with protecting against such a crisis, consistently undermined health experts, and politicized the pandemic in ways that negatively affected protective and preventive behaviors (e.g., mask wearing, social distancing, vaccine uptake) and influenced how state governors responded to the pandemic.[99] This proved to be fatal for large shares of Americans, but most of all in the rural and small-town communities from which Trump drew his strongest support. As we will see in chapter 5, rural residents are more likely to vote Republican than urban residents, and rural counties had much larger vote shares for Trump in both the 2016 and 2020 presidential elections. From early in the pandemic, Trump denied the severity of COVID-19, referring to it as a "fake news media conspiracy" and saying it was "like a flu" and "going to go away without a vaccine."[100] Given the overwhelming rural support for Trump, it should be no surprise that rural residents were more resistant to engaging in preventive behaviors, such as mask wearing, social distancing, and getting vaccinated.[101] Vaccine resistance and hesitancy have been identified as the primary contributors to lower rural vaccination rates, and partisanship and support for Trump have been identified as the primary predictors

122   CHAPTER 4

of vaccination status.[102] Relatedly, differences in state COVID-19 mitigation policies likely also played a role in higher rural mortality rates. Governors in more rural and Republican-leaning states were slower to enact state stay-at-home orders and physical distancing mandates, and once these were enacted, they lifted these measures much more quickly than governors in more urban and Democrat-leaning states.[103]

As with the drug overdose crisis, the case of COVID-19 illustrates the need to consider the upstream factors (e.g., policies and politics) that trickled downstream to affect meso-level conditions (such as health care and workplace conditions) and micro-level factors (such as protective and preventive behaviors) to lead to disproportionately high COVID-19 mortality rates in rural America.

CONCLUSION

This chapter demonstrates that rural areas in the United States have worse health and higher mortality rates than urban areas and that the gap is growing. Rural mortality rates are higher than urban rates for nearly every cause of death and across all age, ethnoracial, and sex groups. However, the idea that all rural places and populations suffer from poor health is a myth and misunderstanding. Some rural subpopulations and places have worse health and mortality profiles than others.

Explanations for the rural disadvantage in health and mortality involve multiple levels and dimensions of influence, including micro-level factors (e.g., health behaviors, SES, and health-care use), meso-level factors (e.g., family, built and physical environments), and structural factors (e.g., macroeconomic conditions, corporate behaviors, politics, and policies). While substantial attention has been given to the role of health care, and it is true that health care is less available in rural communities than in urban ones, health care is not the primary driver of poor health and mortality. Nor is it the primary driver of rural-urban health disparities. Far too often, the approach to population health in the United States has been to apply health-care and behavioral interventions to places with the worst health profiles. This approach has been costly and ineffective because it treats problems *after they arise* rather than *preventing their onset* in the first place. As illustrated by the parable at the beginning of this chapter, we must move our focus upstream to think about how our macroeconomic, corporate, and policy environments have influenced and continue to influence U.S. population health generally and the rural health and mortality penalties specifically.

The importance of structural drivers is illustrated by two population health crises that have claimed millions of American lives but that have unfolded in different ways between rural and urban America: the drug overdose epidemic and the COVID-19 pandemic. Drug overdose rates have been slightly higher in metro than in nonmetro counties overall for most of the past 30 years. But while some rural counties have among the lowest overdose rates in the country, other rural counties have among the very highest. Rather than metro status, what characterizes most of the places with the highest drug overdose rates is a high degree of economic and social disadvantage, community disintegration, and despair. These conditions are linked to federal and state policy choices and macroeconomic changes that have left some people and places behind. Rural communities also face unique challenges in contending with the drug overdose crisis, such as greater stigma related to drug use, less service capacity, and fewer resources than in large urban hubs.

In terms of COVID-19, while rural counties started out with lower case and death rates early in the pandemic, rural rates have been higher and have increased faster than urban rates since December 2020. The result is that COVID-19 has intensified the rural mortality penalty. While rural areas faced many preexisting conditions that made them vulnerable to higher COVID-19 mortality rates—an older age structure, higher rates of chronic conditions, lower SES, less robust health-care infrastructure, and a greater share of high-risk jobs—politics and related policy choices have been among the most important reasons many rural residents did not engage in the necessary behaviors to prevent virus spread and reduce the risk of death.

Ultimately, interventions aimed at improving the U.S. health profile overall, and reducing the rural mortality penalty specifically, will be ineffective if they focus only on health care and behavioral interventions. The large and growing rural health and mortality penalty has its roots in upstream macroeconomic, corporate, political, and policy forces that make their way downstream to influence community- and individual-level determinants of health.

5 Rural Politics and Policies

Red state, blue city: How the urban-rural divide
is splitting America

—*The Atlantic*

Revenge of the rural voter

—*Politico*

These headlines highlight a central theme in contemporary American politics: the rural-urban divide. Indeed, politics and governance in the United States are inherently spatial. Politicians represent people who live in places (e.g., precincts, districts, towns, cities, counties, and states), and levels of government are divided across spatial scales (e.g., local, state, and federal). Moreover, current trends in the United States toward decentralization and devolution—the transfer of government power and administrative responsibilities from the federal level to the state and local levels—have made spatial issues even more salient in recent years.

The events surrounding the 2016 and 2020 presidential elections provide ample examples of space and place concerns in politics and policy. In 2016, Hillary Clinton defeated Donald Trump by a wide margin (approximately 3 million votes) among the national electorate. However, Trump won because U.S. presidential elections are not determined by the popular vote, but by a subnational spatialized system called the Electoral College. And in 2020, when

126   CHAPTER 5

Joe Biden defeated Trump and unfounded accusations were leveled regarding voting irregularities (e.g., "Stop the Steal"), Trump and his allies focused their attention on particular states and local election boards (e.g., Maricopa County, Arizona; Fulton County, Georgia; Philadelphia County, Pennsylvania). They did so because it is this patchwork of entities, not a national body that manages elections, and because like-minded voters are often clustered in certain locales (i.e., fraud charges were only lodged against cities with high Democratic turnout; Trump's camp alleged no problems in areas he had carried). These elections highlight ways that space and place shape American politics.

This chapter explores issues related to rural politics and policies. It begins by tracing the rural-urban sectarian divide in American politics. We consider whether the 2016 presidential election of Donald Trump represented a "rural revolt" as well as whether rural and small-town America is a political monolith. Finally, the chapter contends with the conceptual question of person-based versus place-based policies and what a forward-facing policy framework aimed at enhancing well-being in the rural United States might look like.

THE RURAL-URBAN POLITICAL DIVIDE

In the wake of the 2016 and 2020 presidential elections, the media placed great focus on the rural-urban political divide in the United States. While journalists spun this story as something new and unique to Donald Trump, and some of the particulars were, there is also a long history of rural-urban sectarianism in American politics. Beginning in the late 1700s, in the nation's infancy, these dynamics influenced competing visions for the future of the fledgling democracy. Federalists, such as Alexander Hamilton, favored a strong central government, a national bank, and a manufacturing-based economy. In contrast, Democratic-Republicans, like Thomas Jefferson, argued for the principles of republicanism, the rights of states, and agrarianism. Fearing the more centralized model of the Federalists, Jefferson and his supporters promoted the ideal of rural farmers and plain folk (as opposed to urban bankers and industrialists) as the standard-bearers of American democracy. Jefferson's related animosity toward cities was plain. He wrote, "The mobs of great cities add just so much to the support of pure government, as sores do to the strength of the human body."[1] A life made from the land, it was argued, undergirded liberty and discouraged corruption; it was therefore farmers who possessed the virtues upon which the health of the new republic depended.[2] The Jeffersonian view has had enduring cultural power in American politics (despite the profound contradiction that much of the nation's agriculture at the time, including on Jefferson's own plantation, depended upon the labor of enslaved people).

The U.S. Civil War (1861–1865) also had rural-urban undercurrents that divided the North and South.[3] While not the primary cause of the Civil War, markedly uneven patterns of development and population settlement existed between the two regions on the eve of the conflict. As of 1860, the South was home to a population only two-thirds the size of that in the North, and the North-South ratio of urban residents was four-to-one. These differences had been set in motion in the early 19th century when the regions embarked on disparate development trajectories and related political economies: industrialization and urbanization in the North and plantation agriculture dependent on enslavement in the South. The question of slavery and its expansion westward ultimately led to southern secession and war.

In the late 19th century, the rise of the Populist Party demonstrated the continued resonance of Jeffersonian ideals. A particular force in the politics of the southern and western United States (e.g., Populist James Weaver carried four western states in the presidential election of 1892), the Populist platform advocated for a range of reforms aimed at advancing the interests of farmers and other marginalized groups amid capitalism in the Gilded Age. As opposed to

128   CHAPTER 5

urban financiers and railroad tycoons, "the Populists were agrarian fundamentalists who argued that, as producers of elemental goods and fillers of basic needs, they were superior to those who manipulated money," despite a power balance that favored the latter.[4]

In the 1930s, Franklin D. Roosevelt's New Deal drew widespread support from an American countryside reeling from the ravages of the Great Depression.[5] The New Deal included major policy initiatives to provide farm supports and bring roads, bridges, and electrification to rural areas. The New Deal coalition drew support from a variety of Democratic Party voting blocs: labor unions and blue-collar workers, minoritized ethnoracial groups and immigrants, and Whites in the rural South. In contrast, the Republican Party at the time garnered most of its support from the more affluent, business groups, and northern White Protestants. Working-class and minoritized populations were drawn to this version of Democratic politics because it promoted federal government intervention and redistribution to address the hardships of the Great Depression and aid the disadvantaged. The "Solid South" was already a Democratic stronghold, having been a one-party region since post–Civil War Reconstruction, efforts southerners linked to Republicans like Abraham Lincoln and Ulysses S. Grant. In fact, prior to the New Deal, Black voters tended to align with the Republican Party because it was Democrats who had erected and maintained the suppression of Black civil and political rights via Jim Crow segregation in the South. The joint appeal of the New Deal coalition to the working-class, ethnoracial minorities, and White southerners meant many rural voters favored Democrats through the middle of the 20th century.

But in the ensuing decades the rural-urban partisan tides began to turn. In the 1960s the Civil Rights Act and Voting Rights Act were steered through Congress primarily by northern Democrats (with substantial Republican support). Southern Democrats were broadly opposed to these measures, and the New Deal coalition began to splinter. Republicans were subsequently able to capitalize on White racial resentment, cultural conservatism, and distrust of federal

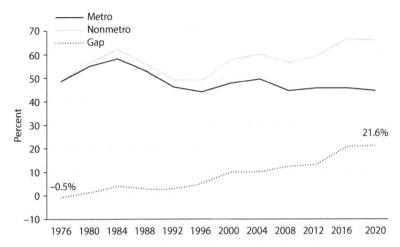

Figure 21. Percent of votes for the Republican presidential candidate in metro and nonmetro areas, 1976–2020. *Note:* Analysis limited to votes for either the Republican or Democratic candidate. Start- and end-point values included on gap trend line. *Source:* Adapted and extended from Albrecht, 2019.

overreach to flip the South from solidly Democrat to solidly Republican (i.e., the "Southern Strategy"). At the same time, many in the White working class nationwide, traditional supporters of Democrats, became disaffected with the Democratic Party, with those coined "Reagan Democrats" in the 1980s being emblematic. By the 2000s, when Republican vice-presidential candidate Sarah Palin began making appeals to rural voters in the "real America," a new iteration of rural-urban political sectarianism was well underway.[6]

Today, rural America is disproportionately a Republican stronghold.[7] Figure 21 shows the percentage of votes won by the Republican presidential candidate in nonmetro and metro counties, and the percentage point gap between the two, from 1976 to 2020. The data demonstrate two clear facts: (1) Republican presidential candidates have consistently garnered greater support from nonmetro voters than their metro counterparts, and (2) this gap has been steadily growing over the last four decades. In 1976, when Democrat

130   CHAPTER 5

Jimmy Carter defeated Republican Gerald Ford, differences in candidate preferences between nonmetro and metro voters were negligible (less than one percentage point). But in the 1980s and 1990s, a trend toward greater support for Republican candidates among nonmetro voters emerged. And since 2000 that gap has widened considerably. In the 1980 election, the nonmetro-metro difference in support of the Republican candidate was 1.6 percentage points; in 2000 it was 10.0 percentage points; and by 2020 it was a whopping 21.6 percentage points. Fully two-thirds of the nonmetro vote went to Republican Donald Trump in 2016 and 2020, while less than half of those in metro counties voted for Trump in those cycles (45.8 percent and 44.7 percent, respectively). Though not as dramatic as the trend toward a preference for Republican presidential candidates in nonmetro settings, it is also notable that no Republican candidate has captured more than 50 percent of the metro vote since George H. Bush in 1988.

Congressional elections follow a similar pattern. For example, an analysis of the 2018 congressional election cycle showed that of the 182 rural House districts in play that year, just 30 (16 percent) were home to an incumbent Democrat. Districts that were urban, on the other hand, leaned markedly in the other direction; of the 82 urban districts in play in 2018, Republicans held just 9 (11 percent). Not only was there a decided rural-urban party divide in incumbency, but few seats in either setting were competitive for challengers. In contrast, suburban districts were more varied in terms of party incumbency and more likely to be competitive.[8] Ultimately, the voting pattern in the 2018 congressional midterms showed that Democrats received their greatest support (67 percent of the vote) in counties at the urban core of metro areas of a million residents or more. Support for Democrats then gradually fell across the urban to rural continuum, reaching a low of just 32.5 percent of the vote in nonmetro counties that were not adjacent to a metro area and had no towns with a population over 10,000.[9] The rural-urban partisan divide is evident in U.S. Senate elections as well, as captured by the popular notion of "blue" (Democrat) and "red" (Republican) states, with blue states generally situated on the more urban East and West Coasts and red states in the more rural interior of the country and in the South. These spatial differences in contemporary voting behavior, of course, reflect people with disparate views on social and political issues. For example, national surveys by the Pew Research Center show widely divergent opinions between rural and urban residents on a range of questions. According to Pew, in 2018 a larger share of rural than urban residents agreed with the statements that growing numbers of newcomers from other countries threaten traditional American customs and values (57 percent versus 35 percent), government is doing too many things better left to businesses and individuals (49 percent versus 28 percent), it is an unfavorable thing that same-sex marriage is now legal (52 percent versus 35 percent), and abortion should be illegal in all or most cases (52 percent versus 36 percent).[10] These numbers suggest a major divergence of opinion on key issues; the average rural-urban difference across these items is nearly 20 points.

Another issue on which there is wide rural-urban disagreement is guns. When asked whether current gun laws should be stricter, 66 percent of urban residents agreed, compared to just 38 percent in rural areas—a 28-point difference. Similar patterns exist on questions about specific gun policies, such as banning assault-style weapons or expanding the right to carry concealed firearms.[11] Gun-specific views are shaped, in part, by spatial differences in gun ownership. Nearly six in ten rural Americans report having guns in their homes, while fewer than three in ten report the same in urban areas.[12]

Beyond gun ownership, why do rural and urban Americans hold such starkly different political positions? As covered in the preceding chapters, social processes generate uneven development and concentrate different types of people in rural versus urban places. These same considerations have implications for rural-urban political polarization.[13] Rural-urban differences related to economics, education, age, race and ethnicity, and other social statuses influence

132   CHAPTER 5

political differences. For example, White and older voters (who represent larger shares of the population in rural than urban areas) are more likely to favor conservative candidates than are non-White and younger voters.[14] Research also suggests that extractive industries (e.g., mining and logging), which tend to be located in rural areas, foster orientations that align with more conservative values.[15] Greater religious affiliation and religiosity—in particular the higher concentration of Protestant evangelical denominations in rural areas—and more general support for moral traditionalism among rural people are also at play.[16] Research shows that, on balance, social status differences between the people living in rural and urban areas account for the greatest variation in voting behavior, though all of the factors outlined earlier matter.[17] It has been argued that the politics of rural America may even be less conservative than it is anti-statist, representing a general rejection of government in a political economy perceived to treat rural people and places as an externality (i.e., the collateral damage of economic gains for urban global interests).[18]

The political scientist Katherine Cramer has pointed to "rural consciousness" as a critical lens through which people interpret politics. She argues that this place-based political orientation has three defining features: "(1) a belief that rural areas are ignored by decision makers, including policy makers, (2) a perception that rural areas do not get their fair share of resources, and (3) a sense that rural folks have fundamentally distinct values and lifestyles, which are misunderstood and disrespected by city folks."[19] These themes were captured by the reflections of the chair of the Democratic Party in a rural county Donald Trump won handily in 2020:

> I've come to believe it is because the national Democratic Party has not offered rural voters a clear vision that speaks to their lived experiences. The pain and struggle in my community is real, yet rural people do not feel it is taken seriously by the Democratic Party. My fear is that the Democrats will continue to blame rural voters for the red-sea electoral map and dismiss these voters as backward. . . .

For years, rural people have heard they are voting "against their own self-interest" when they elect Republicans, or that they vote the "wrong way" because they are uneducated. These are arrogant and damaging messages that are not easily forgotten. . . .

[There is] a perception that cities are where decisions are made, culture happens and resources flow, and that rural communities are not in control of their own futures. . . .

When people feel left behind, they look for a way to make sense of what is happening to them. There is a story to be told about rural America, yet Democrats are not telling it.[20]

Beyond attitudes and ideologies, it is also important to recognize that the structure of our system of government has a degree of rural-urban sectarianism baked in. At the national level, the U.S. Senate is composed of two senators from each state, giving primacy to geography over population size. Moreover, the use of the Electoral College in presidential elections, rather than the popular vote, again gives weight to geography alongside population (the number of electors in each state is equal to its total number of senators and representatives). And while the number of representatives a state receives in the U.S. House is determined by population (e.g., in 2020, California had 53 representatives, while seven states had only 1), it is primarily legislative partisans at the state level who draw the boundaries of congressional district maps. As of 2020, only 10 U.S. states relied on independent commissions for state and federal redistricting; in the other 40 states it was state lawmakers themselves who had this responsibility.[21] This is not to suggest that independent commissions themselves are apolitical; that would be naïve. But state legislators obviously have overt political agendas in how they draw district lines; namely, their own reelection and that of other members of their party. The result is that they produce maps to protect incumbency and majority party advantage rather than achieve true democratic representation.

The intentional manipulation of the boundaries of electoral districts is known as *gerrymandering*. In essence, the process involves

134   CHAPTER 5

politicians picking their voters, rather than voters picking their politicians, thus reducing political competition. The major parties use two complementary methods to accomplish this goal: "packing" and "cracking."[22] Packing refers to the segregation of certain types of people into a small number of districts, giving them overwhelming power but in only a few places. Cracking refers to the spread of certain types of people across many districts, thus diluting their voting power in each. Gerrymandering by party, race and ethnicity, and rural and urban residence helps to fuel political polarization and reduce moderation and pragmatism.

In U.S. politics, the rural-urban divide is further reinforced by reliance on geographic winner-take-all districts rather than more proportional forms of representation.[23] That is, the winner of the largest share of the vote in each geographic district (which can be less than a simple majority) is declared the exclusive winner of the contest, even when other candidates or parties receive substantial support. In such a system what matters most is not the number of votes cast, but how those votes are spatially distributed. This dynamic often results in rural constituencies having a greater voice than their urban counterparts in legislative bodies. Indeed, it is common in geographic winner-take-all frameworks for parties to achieve majority control of legislatures based on a minority share of the overall vote because the political geography plays in their favor. Both gerrymandering and geographic winner-take-all systems serve to amplify a party's power beyond what it earns by its vote share alone. These mechanisms are especially powerful when combined with other suppression tactics aimed at diminishing turnout among particular groups of voters (e.g., minoritized ethnoracial populations).

We have also seen increasing divergence in state policy orientations across a wide array of domains since the 1980s (and especially since 2000), with less urbanized states moving in a more conservative policy direction and more urbanized states moving in a more liberal policy direction. Figure 22 shows a clear divergence

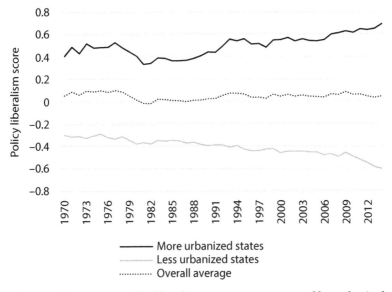

Figure 22. Average state policy liberalism scores among more and less urbanized states, 1970–2014. *Note*: The scale can range from −1.0 to +1.0. Larger positive values indicate more progressive policy scores indexed across 16 domains (i.e., abortion, campaign finance, civil rights/liberties, criminal justice, education, environment, health and welfare, housing and transportation, immigration, private sector labor, public sector labor, LGBT rights, marijuana, taxes, voting, and other) capturing 135 policies. Larger negative values indicate more conservative policy scores. The urbanization index, as calculated by Rakich, is based on American Community Survey data as the natural logarithm of the average number of people living within a five-mile radius of a given resident. We defined "more urbanized" states (N = 25) as those with an urbanization index greater than the national average (10.4). All other states (N = 25) are defined as "less urbanized." Washington, D.C., is excluded from both data sets. *Source*: Author calculations based on policy liberalism score data from Grumbach, 2018 and urbanization index data from Rakich, 2020.

136   CHAPTER 5

in average state policy liberalism scores (an index derived from 135 policies across 16 domains) in more urbanized versus less urbanized states from 1970 to 2014. In 1970, the difference in the average scores between more and less urbanized states was 0.71 point (on a scale with a maximum possible difference of 2 points). But by 2014, that difference had grown to 1.3 points. Divergence is observed across a wide array of policies. For example, New York (a Democrat-dominated state with a large urban population) invests $22,231 per pupil in K–12 education, has a $15/hour minimum wage, expanded Medicaid to cover health insurance for more low-income residents under the Affordable Care Act, charges a $4.35 excise tax per pack of cigarettes, and has among the strictest gun control laws in the nation. Conversely, Mississippi (a Republican-dominated state with a large rural population) invests $8,692 per pupil in K–12, does not have a state minimum wage, has not expanded Medicaid, charges $0.68 in excise taxes on a pack of cigarettes, and has few laws that control the sale or possession of firearms.[24] As these examples demonstrate, Americans in predominantly rural and urban states are living in increasingly different policy contexts.

A RURAL REVOLT FOR DONALD TRUMP?

In the wake of the 2016 presidential election in favor of Donald Trump, the (largely urban coastal) mass media establishment searched for reasons that the political punditry had erred so badly in its predictions of his defeat. A central journalistic storyline that grew out of this process was that a rural populist revolt had carried Trump to victory. Emblematic was a headline pronouncing 2016 the year that America experienced the *revenge of the rural voter*.[25]

This message was oversimplified. While it was true that the vote in rural America did overwhelmingly go to Trump and was important to his victory, the idea that this was something new and unforeseen was a misunderstanding. For starters, the rural vote numbers were simply not sufficient to swing the election in Trump's favor. The share of rural voters in 2016 was in line with the rural share of the general population (as established in the introduction, roughly 14 to 20 percent), meaning that in absolute numbers, most votes for Trump came from those in urban areas. And as covered earlier in this chapter, rural voters have increasingly been trending Republican in presidential elections for decades, so continued movement in that direction was predictable.

Research by Shannon Monnat and David Brown shows it was Trump's overperformance (and, conversely, Clinton's underperformance) in small cities in the industrial Midwest that tipped the Electoral College in his favor.[26] While Clinton won the national popular vote by a margin of millions, Trump won the Electoral College by fewer than 80,000 votes spread across just three states: Michigan (a margin of 10,704), Pennsylvania (a margin of 44,292), and Wisconsin (a margin of 22,748). In short, the idea that a rural revolt produced Trump's victory is a myth and misunderstanding.

That said, Monnat and Brown's research does point to a critical aspect of the rural Trump vote in 2016 that spans the rural-urban continuum: *landscapes of despair.* Trump consistently performed better than Clinton in both rural and urban counties with greater economic distress, worse health, more deaths due to suicide and substance misuse, lower educational attainment, and higher rates of marital breakdown (i.e., separation and divorce). As described in previous chapters, these are challenges that face many rural communities. Monnat and Brown conclude, "Trump's populist message may have been attractive to many long-term Democratic voters (and previous election abstainers) in these places who felt abandoned by a Democratic party that has failed to articulate a strong pro-working class message, [and] whose agendas often emphasize policies and programs to help the poor at what seems like the expense of the working-class."[27] Qualitative research has documented the sociocultural basis of this appeal, rooted in grievances related to economic anxiety and racial resentment.[28]

138   CHAPTER 5

IS RURAL AMERICA A POLITICAL MONOLITH?

While the increasing dominance of Republicans among rural voters is unmistakable, rural America is not a political monolith. First, just as there are millions of Republicans in cities who are routinely outvoted by their Democratic neighbors, there are also millions of Democrats in rural areas where Republican voters hold sway.[29] Moreover, while the rural-urban binary has utility for comparative purposes, it is an oversimplification of spatial social organization. That is, there is no clean break between what is rural and what is urban; life occurs on a continuum across and at the interface of urban, suburban, exurban, and rural settings. Research using a more nuanced rural-urban definition shows that the spatial "tipping point" in voting behavior happens at the suburban-exurban interface, with those in larger inner suburbs tending to align more closely with the preferences of voters in the urban core and those in the exurbs leaning more toward those in rural areas.[30]

It is also true that there are distinct enclaves of Democratic support in rural America (just as there are urban enclaves of Republicanism). For example, Democrats have pockets of strength in areas dominated by natural amenity recreation.[31] As discussed in chapter 1, these are settings that attract in-migrants, often originally from urban contexts, who in turn influence local political proclivities. In fact, sometimes this process can result in a social landscape characterized by ideological fault lines between old-timers and newcomers.[32] There are also examples like the rural state of Vermont electing a socialist to the U.S. Senate (Bernie Sanders) or the progressive history in rural Minnesota linked to the Farmer-Labor Party. And rural areas with significant minoritized ethnoracial populations consistently vote in the Democratic column: namely, the Black Belt, Delta, Lower Rio Grande Valley, and American Indian territories. In the 2020 presidential election, for instance, Trump won only three majority Black rural counties, and in the swing state of Arizona, Biden carried rural Apache County (over 70 percent Native

American) and rural Santa Cruz County (over 80 percent Hispanic) in landslides.[33] In short, while dominant trends are clear, the idea that rural America is a political monolith is an oversimplification.

PERSON- VERSUS PLACE-BASED POLICIES

The trends discussed earlier are driven in part by political reactions to the social challenges facing rural America, including those related to population loss, economic hardship, and health declines described in previous chapters. A perennial debate around policies to address these issues is whether to favor person-based or place-based policies. Broadly, the question is this: Is it better to invest in people's ability to relocate to more prosperous places or to invest in revitalizing distressed areas where people already live?[34] Economists have traditionally favored the first option, motivated by the principle of labor mobility as a critical input in capitalist economies. That is, most economists argue workers need to move to where new jobs are, or else the economy will suffer from a mismatch of jobs without workers in one labor market and workers without jobs in another. Labor mobility is essential for market functioning and firm-level productivity as well as a proven mechanism for workers to increase their earnings.[35] And the United States has many historical reference points of Americans moving to opportunity: the immigrant experience broadly, the push to "Go West," the Great Migration of Black people from the rural South to urban industrial centers in the North, and so on.

However, there are countervailing trends that work against the labor mobility assumption. Most notably, U.S. labor mobility has been steadily *falling* for the last 50 years. People are simply moving for jobs less than they used to. And despite high numbers of job exits during the COVID-19 pandemic—what some have called the Great Resignation—data indicate that Americans are continuing to move at historically low rates.[36] In fact, studies show that today, fully half

140 CHAPTER 5

of all U.S.-born adults live within 50 miles of their place of birth.[37] Research suggests that one reason for this is that "home attachment" or "rootedness"—people's desire to be near their families and friends and the social connections of community—is increasing.[38] This preference is strong among the young and old and the more and less educated alike. Of course, community attachment is not new. There is a robust sociological tradition of studies on this topic.[39] Most of us know that moving is hard and has high social and economic costs. In this context, relying only on people moving out of economically distressed areas seems both insufficient and impractical.

A different approach is to invest in communities to improve conditions. The economist Timothy Bartik puts the case for place-based policy simply: "Places matter for policy because places matter to people."[40] His research shows that the benefits of job creation in terms of spurring additional local employment are greater in economically distressed communities than in other places. Further, because legislators represent geographic constituencies, they are obviously interested in delivering place-based results.

It is also the case that local governments play an important, though frequently neglected, role in development efforts. Linda Lobao and Paige Kelly emphasize the role of local government in providing "the scaffolding needed for economic development as seen in local infrastructure, land-use planning, an educated and healthy labor force, and quality public services."[41] They researched county-level governments across the United States with attention to differences between rural and urban areas. Overall, they found active, savvy, and collaborative efforts by local officials, but also revealed systematic rural-urban differences. They show that governmental capacity—the administrative and fiscal resources available to local officials—differs significantly between rural and urban counties, with increasing rurality accompanied by lesser capacity. Rural county governments had fewer professional staff, grant writers, and specialists devoted to development and land-use concerns. Relatedly, rural counties were less likely than their urban counterparts

RURAL POLITICS AND POLICIES 141

to employ traditional business attraction strategies (e.g., tax abatements and recruiting) or alternative development strategies (e.g., local entrepreneurship, small business development, worker training). Rural county governments also generally provided fewer public services, with notable gaps for mental health and substance use disorders. They conclude that "local governments are, in many respects, the unsung heroes behind rural development," but that disparities in resource capacity put rural officials at a considerable disadvantage. "As the fates of local governments and their communities are intertwined, it is important to consider how to improve local governments' future effectiveness. The trick is to realize what can be done at the local level and what needs broader systemic intervention."[42] State preemption laws that forbid local governments from enacting their own policies represent an increasing threat to the ability of local governments to act on behalf of their constituents. The use of such policies has accelerated in recent years, limiting local authority in various policy domains.[43]

Finally, analysts note that nostalgic views of the past and the restoration of "the way things used to be" have often motivated rural policy. Indeed, it continues to be the case that many view *farm policy* as synonymous with *rural policy*. This is a myth and misunderstanding. Not only do most rural people not make a living from farming, but social change abounds in rural America. Moreover, it is often the case that memories of the "way things used to be" are biased by rosy retrospection. A fair reading of history shows that the good old days were not all good; they were filled with both problems and promise, much as things are today.

FUTURE-FACING RURAL POLICY

In his essay "Megatrends and Implications for Rural Development Policy," Jose Enrique Garcilazo, head of the Regional and Rural Unit of the Organisation for Economic Co-operation and Development

142   CHAPTER 5

(OECD), outlines major considerations for rural policy in the 21st century.[44] He calls attention to a series of megatrends as providing critical context—including demographic change, globalization, digitalization, and climate change—that successful rural policy must consider. If today's politics are reflective of the notion of rural people and places being left behind, policy must aim to bridge the gap to the future. Garcilazo notes that the absence of agglomeration economies in rural regions, an issue covered in chapter 2, creates higher costs for getting goods and services to larger markets, a smaller market base for local services, and higher marginal costs for the delivery of public goods like education and health. However, despite these challenges, all rural places are also endowed with assets. The key for good policy is to figure out how to leverage existing assets in the context of the social transformations being driven by broad megatrends. Doing so will require using regional networks and collaboration to create economies of scale and scope. Moreover, strategies will need to move beyond commodity-based policy (e.g., agriculture and energy) to center enhanced rural well-being more broadly.

The challenges associated with demographic change and globalization, articulated in previous sections of this book, call for forward-facing rural policy. In addition, Garcilazo argues that digitalization and the remote working it allows—issues spotlighted during the COVID-19 pandemic—provide new opportunities for rural and small-town America if accompanied by strategic public policy. This requires attention to improving broadband access and affordability, as well as investment in digital skills for workers and information and information technology capacity for businesses, especially small and medium-sized firms. As we transition to a lower-carbon economy to mitigate climate change, problems and prospects are many for rural America. Garcilazo contends that because rural areas constitute most of the land mass in OECD countries, they "have an essential role to play in a low-carbon economy. . . . [They] contain natural resources, and offer biodiversity and ecosystem services to sustain our lives. They produce food and energy, clean the air, detoxify the waste, clear the water and sequester the carbon."[45] In some cases the lower-carbon transition will mean "reshoring" manufacturing activities (i.e., returning production facilities to a company's country of origin, the opposite of "offshoring"), which could benefit rural areas. If policy recognizes the pivotal capacity of rural and small-town places in the effort to fight and adapt to climate change, and it does so within a framework that expressly considers other megatrends, real progress is possible on the challenges facing contemporary rural America.

All this also requires policy flexibility that acknowledges that rural America is not a monolith; it is diverse and changing rapidly. Policies at both the federal and state levels tend to be written with place-neutral intent, without considering how they might affect rural places differently than urban places. Instead, policies must consider the unique needs of rural places, including how those needs vary across different regional, economic, and demographic contexts. One-size-fits-all approaches will not best position rural people and places to thrive and prosper in the 21st century.

CONCLUSION

The overarching theme of this chapter has been to think about the intersection of the rural-urban continuum with questions of politics and policies. A key idea is that politics and governance in the United States are inherently spatial. In addition, this chapter explored the conceptual question of person-based versus place-based policies and what a future-facing rural policy framework might look like.

Rural-urban political sectarianism dates to the founding of the nation and continues to operate as a critical dimension of U.S. politics to this day. In contemporary America, rural areas are an unmistakable Republican stronghold, and rural residents are living in increasingly conservative policy environments. However, the media characterization of Donald Trump's 2016 presidential election as a

144   CHAPTER 5

"rural revolt" is an oversimplification, as is thinking about rural and small-town America as a political monolith. In short, we need to take a nuanced view of dominant political trends.

Finally, it is critical to understand that *farm* policy and *rural* policy are not synonymous. Failure to do so is to subscribe to a myth and misunderstanding about contemporary rural America. Place-based policies targeted at rural areas that allow for flexibility in serving the diversity of rural people and places hold promise for enhancing well-being. Providing a strategic policy framework for resourcing regional collaborations to leverage local assets and address local challenges in the context of demographic change, globalization, digitalization, and climate change has the potential to boost rural prosperity in the 21st century.

Conclusion

At the outset of this book, we noted that the contemporary United States is decidedly urban centric, and that modern American sociology reflects this tendency with a disproportionate focus on urban life. We posed two questions in this context. Why should we pay attention to rural areas and sociological issues therein? What sociological lessons are there to learn from focusing on social, economic, and demographic changes in, and the problems and prospects facing, rural America?

Our overarching objective has been to answer these questions and in doing so contribute to a fuller understanding of the United States as a whole. We approached this task by painting a social scientific portrait of rural and small-town America focused on changes, challenges, and opportunities. Throughout, we assessed the ways conventional wisdom is often inaccurate or oversimplified and can lead to myths and misunderstandings about rural America. The book's central theme has been that, despite popular notions to the contrary, rural America is no paragon of stability. Social change abounds,

146   CONCLUSION

accompanied by new challenges for rural people and places. Our points of focus elaborating on this theme included changes in population size and composition, economies and livelihoods, ethnoracial diversity and inequities, population health and health disparities, and politics and policies.

SUMMARY OF KEY POINTS

While the United States is primarily an urban and urbanizing nation, rural America continues to be home to a substantial number of people. In 2020, roughly 14 to 20 percent of the U.S. population—46 to 66 million people—were living in nonmetro counties and rural areas, respectively. By either definition, that is more people than resided in any single U.S. state or made up most major ethnoracial groups nationally. Moreover, rural America accounts for far more of the country's land area than cities do. It is the primary source of our natural resources and natural amenities, including the most basic inputs that sustain our lives, like food, water, and energy. Rural America also occupies a prominent place in our history and contemporary culture.

In chapter 1 we highlighted that population change in rural America has been profound. Over its history, the United States has transformed from a rural agrarian colony into a majority-urban society. As the share of the U.S. population residing in urban centers has grown, so too have the number of cities and the proportion of territory classified as urban. But urbanization has not always proceeded in a single direction. The 1970s and 1990s, for instance, saw rural rebounds when population growth outpaced that of metro areas. The most recent decade was not one of those periods. Between 2010 and 2020, rural America lost population for the first time in history. This unprecedented outcome was the product of a diminishing number of births barely exceeding a rising number of deaths, as well as more people moving out than in.

CONCLUSION 147

A considerable social challenge in rural America is the "demographic paradox," a divide between demographic "winners" (places experiencing growing populations and economies but urbanizing as a result) and demographic "losers" (places experiencing population loss and economic decline). This highlights an important misconception: it is a myth and misunderstanding that all rural communities are losing people and fading away. Indeed, many rural areas are demographically and economically vibrant and growing, such as those endowed with attractive natural amenities. But it is also true that sustained population growth is only possible for so long before rural communities transition to urban. If the absence of sustained population growth is a social problem, it implicates rurality itself. A more balanced view requires the development of paths to social and economic vitality for rural America that do not necessarily prescribe an urban future.

Key compositional changes in the population of rural America include aging and immigration. Population aging—driven in part by the out-migration of young adults and their reproductive potential—creates special challenges for local economies (e.g., lower labor force participation due to retirement) and services (e.g., health care). New immigrant destinations in rural America represent a population lifeline for aging communities, while also raising difficult issues around integration, inclusion, and equity for newcomers.

In chapter 2 we emphasized that change has also been the watchword for rural economies and livelihoods. Contrary to popular stereotypes of bucolic settings where most people make a living from the land, processes such as the agrarian-industrial-postindustrial transition and globalization have fundamentally transformed rural America. Today, the notion that farming dominates the economy of the rural United States is a myth and misunderstanding. Over the last century, the employment share in agriculture has steadily fallen, and it currently accounts for a very small segment of rural employment. And while factories and plants are often associated with cities, today manufacturing represents a larger share of employment

148   CONCLUSION

in rural than in urban America. The nationwide trend toward deindustrialization presents a considerable social problem in many small communities. Losing a plant in a large and economically diversified metropolis is painful, but it can be downright devastating when it is the main employer in town.

We also brought attention to the fact that economic hardship is not exclusive to rural or urban settings. Both underemployment and poverty are pressing social problems in rural America. Diversified economies provide communities protection from dislocation and hardship. But a vexing challenge in rural America is that achieving economic diversity is extremely difficult. Small populations and the absence of agglomeration benefits for firms limit the ability to develop a diverse mix of employers and jobs in rural areas. The dominant economic paradigm in American society is to achieve prosperity through growth. But again, sustained growth often means crossing the threshold to urban. A critical challenge in rural America is finding a balance between economic vitality and rurality. If growth is the only path, then rurality itself is once more implicated as a social problem.

In chapter 3 we spotlighted that growing ethnoracial diversity is another major trend in rural America. We stressed that the common notion that rural America is composed of a homogeneously White population is a myth and misunderstanding. The rural United States is and has been more ethnoracially diverse than is often presumed, and it is becoming increasingly so. These changes have important implications for rural communities, including those related to employment and economic incorporation, education and service needs, ethnoracial relations and conflict, and culture and politics. We emphasized that the patterns of ethnoracial settlement and inequities in today's rural America are rooted in institutionalized systems of racial domination. But we also underscored that minoritized ethnoracial groups—and the growing rural Hispanic population in particular—have the potential to provide a demographic and economic lifeline to struggling rural communities. Ultimately, increasing ethnoracial diversity is certain for rural America in the coming decades. What remains to be seen is which parts of rural America will embrace these changes and restructure their institutions and policies to facilitate greater inclusion and opportunity for all groups and which will erect barriers to incorporation.

In chapter 4 we turned to the issue of rural population health and health disparities. The main point was that rural America has worse health and higher mortality rates than urban areas and that the gap is growing. Indeed, rural mortality rates are higher than urban rates for nearly every cause of death. At the same time, however, there are important differences within and across rural areas; some rural subpopulations (e.g., Black and American Indian people) and places (e.g., Appalachia) have worse health and mortality profiles than others (e.g., high natural amenity areas).

We stressed that the rural disadvantages in health and mortality are driven by social forces at the micro level (e.g., health behaviors, SES, and health-care use), meso level (e.g., family, built and physical environments), and structural level (e.g., macroeconomic conditions, politics, and policies). Special importance was placed on the need to focus upstream on how macroeconomic and policy environments shape U.S. population health generally and rural population health specifically. As examples, we drew on two population health crises that have led to the deaths of millions of Americans, but with different dynamics in rural and urban areas: the drug overdose epidemic and the COVID-19 pandemic.

In chapter 5 we called attention to the rural-urban divide in contemporary American politics. Rural-urban sectarianism is not new. It has extended through the nation's entire history, though the specific issues shaping the dynamic have changed over time. Today, rural America is a clear Republican stronghold, and rural residents are living in increasingly conservative policy environments. However, the idea that rural America is a political monolith is an oversimplification. Distinct enclaves of Democratic support exist in rural areas dominated by attractive natural amenities and minoritized ethnoracial populations.

150   CONCLUSION

Finally, we underscored that farm policy is not rural policy. Certainly most farming does take place in rural areas, and we could not sustain our lives without the food and fiber the sector produces. But *rural* and *farm* are not synonymous. Place-based policies that extend beyond commodities to focus on the broader needs of rural America and that allow flexibility to serve the diversity of people and places that comprise it hold promise for promoting prosperity and well-being. This is especially true when they are crafted with express consideration of the broad megatrends of demographic change, globalization, digitalization, and climate change.

THE FUTURE OF RURAL AMERICA

What does all of this portend for the future of rural and small-town America? We have no crystal ball. Nevertheless, we can be sure that profound social, economic, and demographic changes will persist, giving rise to complex social challenges that call for innovative solutions. The issues documented in this book will continue to evolve, requiring steadfast attention from social scientists, policymakers, and other stakeholders. These are not only the concerns of rural scholarship, rural policy, and rural people. They are the concerns of all those who wish to understand and address the social challenges of the nation. In many respects, rural and urban people and places have never been more interconnected and interdependent than they are today.[1] The flows of people, capital, goods, services, and information back and forth across the rural-urban continuum are ceaseless and growing. The boundaries between rural and urban are increasingly blurry. And a tremendous amount of social and economic life occurs at the interface. Ultimately, the destiny of rural and urban America is a shared one. After all, "rural and urban are flip sides of the same coin."[2]

Current megatrends—demographic change, globalization, digitalization, and climate change—are not rural *or* urban, they are

CONCLUSION   151

rural *and* urban. All include spatialized interrelationships and interdependencies. All encompass both rural and urban people and places, as well as the connections between them. Rural-urban demographic change, the focus of this book, is inherently relational. Globalization—the increasing transnational interconnectedness of people, business, and government—is geographically all encompassing. Digitalization can reduce spatial opportunity costs, but rural-urban inequality is also central to the "digital divide." And climate change is a global challenge with localized dynamics. We cannot achieve a full understanding of these megatrends by treating rural and urban separately or by ignoring the differences across and within rural and urban places.

In the final analysis, the future (or futures) of the rural United States remains an open question. But there are at least two conclusions of which we can be certain. The first is that change will be constant and carry implications for the entire nation. The second is that by holding myths and misunderstandings up to empirical evidence from the social sciences, we all stand to gain a better understanding of the context, composition, and complexities of rural and small-town America.

Notes

INTRODUCTION

Epigraph: Lefebvre [1956] 2016, 67.

1. Brown and Schafft (2019) raise similar points. See also Bailey, Jensen, and Ransom 2014; Lichter and Brown 2011; Slack and Jensen 2020.

2. U.S. Census Bureau 2021b. The terminology around ethnoracial groupings is fraught. While some advocate for the use of the term *people of color*, others find that descriptor offensive given the Americas' history of colorism and the pejorative use of the term *colored people*. At present, the descriptors "historically marginalized" or "historically minoritized" are often used to center how "systemic inequalities, oppression, and marginalization place individuals into 'minority' status rather than their own characteristics" (Sotto-Santiago 2019, 74). Throughout this book, we typically invoke the term *minoritized*, but sometimes use *non-White* for clarity and brevity, particularly when we are summarizing U.S. Census data. In each case, we are referring to individuals and groups who have been systemically marginalized and minoritized because of their race and/or ethnicity. The terms we use, while simplistic, are intended to be inclusive of all groups and capture all people.

153

154 NOTES TO CHAPTER 1

3. U.S. Census Bureau 2017; U.S. Department of Agriculture 2020.
4. Bailey et al. 2014; Brown and Schafft 2011, 2019; Lichter and Brown 2011; Lichter and Ziliak 2017.
5. Snipp 1989.
6. Rutherford 2017.
7. Truesdell 1949.
8. Gibson 2012.
9. Durkheim [1893] 1984.
10. Tönnies [1887] 1940.
11. Du Bois [1903] 1989; see also Jakubek and Wood 2018.
12. Jakubek and Wood 2018.
13. Du Bois [1899] 1973.
14. Sorokin and Zimmerman 1929.
15. Larson and Zimmerman 2003.
16. Johnson and Lichter 2020.
17. Laughlin 2016.
18. Monnat and Brown 2017.
19. Bell 1992; Halfacree 1993.
20. U.S. Department of Agriculture 2019a.
21. U.S. Census Bureau 2022a.
22. U.S. Census Bureau 2021a.
23. Office of Management and the Budget 2023.
24. U.S. Census Bureau 2021a.
25. Johnson and Lichter 2020.

1. RURAL POPULATION CHANGE

1. Van Dam 2019.
2. Johnson and Lichter 2019; Peters 2019; Thiede et al. 2017.
3. Brooks, Mueller, and Thiede 2020; Fuguitt, Heaton, and Lichter 1988; Johnson and Lichter 2020; Lichter, Brown, and Parisi 2021.
4. Barrington-Leigh and Millard-Ball 2015.
5. Fuguitt 1985; Johnson, Nucci, and Long 2005.
6. Johnson and Lichter 2020.
7. Brooks et al. 2020; Johnson and Lichter 2020; Van Dam 2019.
8. Ely and Hamilton 2018.
9. Rural Health Information Hub 2022.
10. Ely and Hamilton 2018.
11. Brooks and Voltaire 2020; Brown 2019.

NOTES TO CHAPTER 1 155

12. Johnson 2020; Thiede et al. 2017.

13. As we progress through this book, some information is presented as "age adjusted." Age adjusting accounts for differences in the age composition across different populations, places, and times. By age adjusting, we control for the effects of differences in the age composition across groups when making comparisons.

14. Life expectancy is the length of life for a hypothetical cohort assumed to be exposed from birth to death to the mortality rates observed in the year they were born.

15. Abrams, Myrskylä, and Mehta 2021.

16. Cosby et al. 2019; Cossman et al. 2010; Monnat 2020a.

17. Ely, Driscoll, and Matthews 2017; Monnat 2020a; Vierboom, Preston, and Hendi 2019.

18. Sun, Cheng, and Monnat 2021.

19. Monnat 2020a.

20. Johnson 2020.

21. Johnson et al. 2005.

22. Johnson 2022.

23. Golding and Winkler 2020.

24. Johnson 2022.

25. Johnson and Winkler 2015.

26. Carr and Kefalas 2009; Mills and Hazarika 2001; Von Reichert, Cromartie, and Arthun 2014.

27. Carr and Kefalas 2009.

28. Brown et al. 2008.

29. Lekies et al. 2015; Qin 2016.

30. Petersen and Winkler 2022.

31. Carr, Lichter, and Kefalas 2012; Lichter and Johnson 2020.

32. Johnson 2022.

33. Dobis et al. 2021.

34. Johnson 2022.

35. Johnson 2022.

36. Johnson et al. 2005.

37. Baechtel 2000.

38. Johnson and Lichter 2020.

39. U.S. Department of Agriculture 2022a.

40. Pilgeram 2021; Sherman 2021a, 2021b; Smith and Krannich 2000; Ulrich-Schad 2018; Ulrich-Schad and Qin 2018; Winkler 2013; Winkler et al. 2007.

156　NOTES TO CHAPTER 2

41. Ulrich-Schad 2018, 45.
42. Pilgeram 2021; Sherman 2021a, 2021b; Winkler 2013.
43. Smith and Trevelyan 2019. See also Glasgow and Berry 2013.
44. Domina 2006; Mills and Hazarika 2001.
45. Johnson and Lichter 2019.
46. Brown et al. 2008; Glasgow and Brown 2012.
47. Brown et al. 2019; Slack and Jensen 2008; Slack and Rizzuto 2013; Thiede et al. 2017; Warner, Homsy, and Morken 2017.
48. Kebede et al. 2021; Lichter 2012.
49. Sharp and Lee 2017.
50. Johnson and Lichter 2022.
51. Hall 2013; Massey and Capoferro 2008.
52. Broadway 2007; Kandel and Parrado 2005.
53. Johnson and Lichter 2016; Lichter and Johnson 2020.
54. Johnson and Lichter 2008.
55. Johnson and Lichter 2008.

2. RURAL ECONOMIES AND LIVELIHOODS

Epigraph: Sherman 2009, 46–47, 49.
1. Slack 2014; Thiede and Slack 2017.
2. Schumpeter 1942.
3. Lobao and Meyer 2001, 103.
4. Dimitri, Effland, and Conklin 2005.
5. Dimitri et al. 2005; Lobao and Meyer 2001.
6. Dimitri et al. 2005. These numbers include only those working in agriculture directly. Not included are people working in closely related fields, such as food processing.
7. PBS n.d.
8. Lobao and Meyer 2001.
9. Laughlin 2016.
10. Laughlin 2016.
11. Harris 2020.
12. Slack 2014; Thiede and Slack 2017.
13. Goodman and Steadman 2002.
14. U.S. Bureau of Labor Statistics 2021.
15. Kalleberg 2011.
16. McLaughlin and Coleman-Jensen 2008.
17. U.S. Department of Agriculture 2019b. See also Mueller 2021.
18. Curtis et al. 2019, 56.

NOTES TO CHAPTER 2 157

19. Freudenburg 1992; Krannich et al. 2014; Mueller 2021; Perdue and Pavela 2012; Stedman, Parkins, and Beckley 2005.

20. Mueller 2022; Sherman 2021a, 2021b; Ulrich-Schad and Qin 2018; Winkler 2013.

21. Jensen et al. 1999; Slack 2010, 2014; Slack and Jensen 2002, 2004; Thiede and Slack 2017; Thiede, Lichter, and Slack 2018.

22. Carr and Kefalas 2009.

23. Domina 2006; McLaughlin and Perman 1991.

24. Carr and Kefalas 2009.

25. Slack, Thiede, and Jensen 2020.

26. Clogg 1979; Clogg and Sullivan 1983; Hauser 1974; Sullivan 1978.

27. According to the U.S. Bureau of Labor Statistics (2021), the labor force is defined as the sum of those employed and unemployed. People with formal jobs are *employed*. People who are jobless, looking for a job, and available for work are *unemployed*. People who are neither employed nor unemployed are *not in the labor force*.

28. Slack et al. 2020.

29. Sherman 2009.

30. Jensen, McLaughlin, and Slack 2003; Sherman 2014; Tickamyer, Sherman, and Warlick 2017.

31. Weber and Miller 2017.

32. President's National Advisory Commission on Rural Poverty 1967.

33. U.S. Department of Agriculture 2022b.

34. Billings and Blee 2000; Duncan 1999; Duncan and Ulrich-Schad 2021; Fontenot et al. 2010; Gaventa 1980; Lyson and Falk 1993; Maril 1989; O'Connell 2012; Slack et al. 2009; Slack and Myers 2012; Snipp 1996.

35. Slack et al. 2009.

36. Billings and Blee 2000; Duncan 1999; Gaventa 1980; Lyson and Falk 1993; Maril 1989; O'Connell 2012; Slack et al. 2009; Snipp 1996.

37. Nolan, Waldfogel, and Wimer 2017; Pacas and Rothwell 2020; Weber and Miller 2017.

38. Nolan et al. 2017; Pacas and Rothwell 2020; Weber and Miller 2017.

39. See Pacas and Rothwell 2020; Mueller, Brooks, and Pacas 2022.

40. Hawk 2013.

41. Schoceht 2019.

42. Swendener et al. 2023.

43. Pilgeram 2021; Sherman 2021b.

44. Slack and Jensen 2010, 185–186.

45. Castells and Portes 1989.

158   NOTES TO CHAPTER 3

46. Marcelli, Williams, and Joassart 2010; Portes, Castells, and Benton 1989; Williams and Windebank 1998.

47. Portes et al. 1989, 1.

48. Jensen, Tickamyer, and Slack 2019; Nelson and Smith 1999; Slack et al. 2017.

49. Nelson and Smith 1999; Slack et al. 2017.

50. Granovetter 1985.

51. Portes 1994.

52. Jensen, Cornwell, and Findeis 1995; Slack 2007a, 2007b; Slack and Jensen 2010.

53. Beggs, Haines, and Hurlbert 1996.

54. Jensen et al. 2019.

55. Ratner 2000.

56. Warlick 2017.

57. Zhao et al. 2019.

58. Warlick 2017.

59. Swendener et al. 2023.

60. Slack and Myers 2012.

61. Warlick 2017.

62. Center on Budget and Policy Priorities 2021.

63. Lichter and Jayakody 2002.

64. National Association of Area Agencies on Aging 2021.

65. Rhubart et al. 2020.

3. RURAL ETHNORACIAL DIVERSITY AND INEQUITIES

Epigraph: Adapted from Lay 2017, 193.

1. Lichter et al. 2007a.

2. Snipp 1989.

3. Saenz and Torres 2003.

4. Lichter 2012.

5. Iceland 2014, 140.

6. Harvey 2017, 144.

7. In 2023 the U.S. Office of Management and Budget proposed changes to how it would measure race and ethnicity in federal surveys, including the U.S. Census. If the proposed changes are approved, race and ethnicity would be combined into a single question. For more on the proposed changes, see U.S. Office of Management and Budget 2023.

8. Iceland 2014.

9. Noe-Bustamante, Mora, and Lopez 2020.

NOTES TO CHAPTER 3   159

10. Brown and Schafft 2011; Saenz 2012; Summers 1991.

11. Author calculations using data from the 1990 and 2020 Censuses.

12. Author calculations using data from the 1990 and 2020 Censuses.

13. U.S. Department of Health and Human Services 2022.

14. Dewess and Marks 2017.

15. Johnson and Lichter 2022.

16. Johnson and Lichter 2022.

17. Johnson and Lichter 2022, 1.

18. Author calculations using data from the 1990 Census and U.S. Census Bureau 2021d.

19. Lichter 2012.

20. Dewess and Marks 2017.

21. Harvey 2017.

22. Lichter 2012.

23. Johnson and Lichter 2022.

24. Harvey 2017, 144.

25. U.S. Department of the Interior 2022, 63.

26. Harvey 2017.

27. Dunbar-Ortiz 2015.

28. Snipp 2003.

29. U.S. Census Bureau 2021c.

30. U.S. Census Bureau 2022b.

31. Dewess 2014.

32. Dewess 2014.

33. U.S. Department of Health and Human Services 2022.

34. Dewess 2014; U.S. Census Bureau 2021c.

35. Dewess and Marks 2017.

36. Library of Congress n.d.-a.

37. Lichter 2012.

38. Iceland 2014.

39. Green 2014.

40. Harvey 2017.

41. Loewen 2005; O'Connell 2019.

42. Kelly 2014.

43. Iceland 2014, 147.

44. Du Bois 1899.

45. Harvey 2017.

46. Iceland 2014.

47. National Research Council 2006.

48. Harvey 2017, 152.

160 NOTES TO CHAPTER 3

49. Blakemore 2019.
50. Martin, Fix, and Taylor 2006.
51. Centro de Los Derechos del Migrante 2020.
52. Jensen 2006; Kandel and Cromartie 2004; Lichter and Johnson 2006.
53. Population Reference Bureau 2007.
54. Gouveia and Saenz 2000; Kandel and Parrado 2005.
55. Johnson and Lichter 2013; Nelson, Lee, and Nelson 2009.
56. Population Reference Bureau 2007.
57. Durand, Massey, and Charvet 2000; Johnson and Lichter 2022; Massey 2008.
58. Marrow 2005; National Academies of Sciences, Engineering, and Medicine 2016.
59. U.S. Department of State, Office of the Historian, n.d.
60. Martin et al. 2006.
61. U.S. Department of State, Office of the Historian, n.d.
62. Yeung and Hu-DeHart 2004.
63. Library of Congress, n.d.-b.
64. Snipp 1996, 127.
65. De Jong 2003; Dunbar-Ortiz 2015; King et al. 2018; Smith 1991.
66. Wright 2020.
67. Jakubek and Wood 2018.
68. Snipp et al. 1993.
69. Dewess 2014.
70. Lichter, Sanders, and Johnson 2015.
71. Burton et al. 2013.
72. Taylor and Kalt 2005.
73. Slack, Thiede, and, Jensen 2020.
74. Lichter et al. 2015, 209.
75. Oliver and Shapiro 2019.
76. Gilbert, Sharp, and Felin 2002.
77. Duncan 1999; Lichter et al. 2007a; Lichter et al. 2007b; Lichter, Parisi, and Taquino 2012.
78. Lichter et al. 2012.
79. Harvey 2017.
80. Population Reference Bureau 2007.
81. Markides and Coreil 1986.
82. Monnat 2017.
83. Author calculation using data from U.S. Census Bureau 2021d and Appalachian Regional Commission n.d.

NOTES TO CHAPTER 4   161

84. Lichter 2012, 3.

85. Harvey 2017, 142.

86. Johnson and Lichter 2008; Lichter 2012.

4. RURAL POPULATION HEALTH AND HEALTH DISPARITIES

Epigraph: Documented by McKinlay 1974.

1. Cosby et al. 2019; Cossman et al. 2007; Cossman et al. 2010; Elo et al 2019; James, Cossman, and Wolf 2018; Monnat 2020a; Vierboom et al. 2019.

2. Haines 2001.

3. Higgs 1973.

4. Cutler and Miller 2005.

5. Haines 2001.

6. Cosby et al. 2008.

7. Cross, Califf, and Warraich 2021.

8. Ely, Driscoll, and Matthews 2017; U.S. Centers for Disease Control and Prevention 2022.

9. Elo et al. 2019; Monnat 2020a; NASEM 2021; Singh and Siahpush 2014.

10. Anderson et al. 2015; Befort, Nazir, and Peri 2012; Glasgow, Morton, and Johnson 2004; Glauber 2022; Harp and Borders 2019; Jones 2010; Lawrence, Hummer, and Harris 2017; Monnat and Pickett 2011; Rafferty et al. 2021; Rahman et al. 2021; Rhubart and Monnat 2022; Vargas, Dye, and Hayes 2002; von Reichert and Berry 2020; Zhao et al. 2019.

11. Johnson and Johnson 2015.

12. Dietz 1998.

13. Lawrence et al. 2017.

14. This includes both American Indian and Alaska Native populations.

15. Cohen et al. 2022; Mainous et al. 2004.

16. James et al. 2017.

17. Probst et al. 2011.

18. Bell and Owens-Young 2020; Grundy and Prusaczyk 2022; Kozhimannil and Henning-Smith 2018; Nuriddin, Mooney, and White 2020; Rhubart and Engle 2017.

19. Ivey-Stephenson et al. 2017; James et al. 2017; Rudd et al. 2016.

20. NASEM 2021.

21. Brave Heart, Yellow Horse, and DeBruyn 1998; Rose 2022.

22. Cristancho et al. 2008; Monnat 2017.

23. U.S. Department of Agriculture 2017.

NOTES TO CHAPTER 4

24. James et al. 2017.

25. Markides and Coreil 1986.

26. Cosby et al. 2019.

27. Cossman et al. 2007.

28. James 2014; James and Cossman 2017; James et al. 2018; Murray et al. 2006.

29. Monnat 2020a.

30. NASEM 2021.

31. Agunwamba et al. 2017; Blackwell, Lucas, and Clarke 2014; Eberhardt and Pamuk 2004; Hartley 2004; Roberts et al. 2017.

32. Lawrence et al. 2017.

33. Link and Phelan 1995.

34. Roberts et al. 2017.

35. Cosby et al. 2019.

36. Caldwell et al. 2016.

37. House, Landis, and Umberson 1988; Umberson and Montez 2010.

38. Amato 1993; Beggs, Haines, and Hurlbert 1996; Hofferth and Iceland 1998.

39. Beaudoin and Thorson 2004; Sørensen 2016.

40. Rhubart et al. 2022.

41. Crouch et al. 2022.

42. Monnat and Chandler 2015.

43. Clark, Lawrence, and Monnat 2022.

44. Brown et al. 2019; Burrows, Suh, and Hamann 2012; Capriotti, Pearson, and Dufour 2020; Pendergrast and Rhubart 2022.

45. Akinlotan et al. 2021.

46. Ostmo and Rosencrans 2022.

47. Cecil G. Sheps Center 2022.

48. McKinlay, McKinlay, and Beaglehole 1989.

49. National Rural Housing Coalition n.d.

50. U.S. Department of Agriculture 2022c.

51. Coleman-Jensen and Steffen 2017.

52. Coleman-Jensen and Steffen 2017.

53. Myers et al. 2022; Rural Health Information Hub 2019.

54. Blackley, Halldin, and Laney 2018.

55. Henning-Smith et al. 2022.

56. Lichter and Brown 2011; Rhubart and Engle 2017.

57. Clark et al. 2022.

58. EPA 2022; Harrison 2008.

59. Carolan 2016.

NOTES TO CHAPTER 4   163

60. Choi et al. 2006; Kouznetsova et al. 2007; Vrijheid et al. 2002.
61. Bullard 2000; Hanson 2001.
62. Aelion and Davis 2019; Wiener and Jurevic 2016.
63. Royte 2005 (review of Timothy Egan's *The Worst Hard Time*).
64. Tate et al. 2021.
65. Berko et al. 2014.
66. Bambra, Smith, and Pearce 2019.
67. Bailey, Jensen, and Ransom 2014; Brown and Swanson 2003; Lobao 2014; Smith and Tickamyer 2011.
68. Berry 2014; Burton et al. 2013; Slack 2014.
69. Montez et al. 2020.
70. Bambra et al. 2019, 37–38.
71. Montez et al. 2020.
72. Farrelly et al. 2013.
73. Montez et al. 2020.
74. Montez et al. 2020; Montez et al. 2022.
75. American Hospital Association 2022; Rhubart and Engle 2017.
76. Author calculations using data from Grassroots Change 2021.
77. Noonan 2017; Runyon 2017; van Vlaanderen 2018.
78. Monnat 2023.
79. Monnat 2020b; Rigg, Monnat, and Chavez 2018.
80. Monnat 2019; Monnat et al. 2019; Peters et al. 2020.
81. Author calculations based on data from the U.S. Centers for Disease Control and Prevention 2022b.
82. Quinones 2015.
83. U.S. Census Bureau 2022c.
84. Arnade 2017.
85. Author calculations based on data from the U.S. Centers for Disease Control and Prevention 2022b.
86. Quinones 2021.
87. Borders and Booth 2007.
88. Pullen and Oser 2014.
89. Ellis, Kasper, and Cicero 2021 (methamphetamine use rates); author calculations based on data from the U.S. Centers for Disease Control and Prevention 2022b (methamphetamine-involved overdose rates).
90. Johns Hopkins University 2023.
91. Monnat 2020b; Kaiser Health News 2020.
92. Author calculations based on data from USA Facts 2023.
93. Gong et al. 2019.
94. Brooks et al. 2021; Callaghan et al. 2021.

164 NOTES TO CHAPTER 5

95. Hooks and Sawyer 2020; Peters 2020; Taylor, Boulos, and Almond 2020.

96. Paschal 2020; Reuben 2020; Smith-Nonini and Paschal 2020.

97. Paschal 2020; Smith-Nonini and Paschal 2020.

98. Gadarian, Goodman, and Pepinsky 2021, 2022.

99. Gadarian et al. 2022.

100. Doggett 2022; Lovelace 2020.

101. Callaghan et al. 2021; Haischer et al. 2020; Kaiser Family Foundation 2021; Sun and Monnat 2022; Ulrich-Schad, Givens, and Beacham 2022.

102. Gadarian et al. 2022; Kirzinger et al. 2021; Kirzinger, Munan, and Brodie 2021.

103. Adolph et al. 2021; Lin et al. 2021.

5. RURAL POLITICS AND POLICIES

Epigraphs: Kron 2012; Evich 2016.

1. Jefferson 1785.

2. Danbom 1995.

3. Towers 2019.

4. Danbom 1995, 158.

5. Danbom 1995, 158.

6. Packer 2021.

7. Albrecht 2019; Rodden 2019.

8. Montgomery 2018.

9. Johnson and Scala 2020.

10. Parker et al. 2018.

11. Pew Research Center 2021.

12. Parker et al. 2017. See also Scala and Johnson 2017.

13. See also Bishop 2008.

14. Fisher 2014.

15. Bell and York 2010; Cramer 2016; Hochschild 2016; Sherman 2009; Wuthnow 2018.

16. Gimpel and Karnes 2006; Lichter and Brown 2011; Scala and Johnson 2017.

17. Kelly and Lobao 2019.

18. Ashwood 2018.

19. Cramer 2016, 12.

20. Hogseth 2020.

21. National Conference of State Legislatures 2021.

NOTES TO CONCLUSION   165

22. Princeton Gerrymandering Project 2022.
23. Rodden 2019.
24. Montez, Hayward, and Zajacova 2021.
25. Evich 2016.
26. Monnat and Brown 2017.
27. Monnat and Brown 2017, 234.
28. Cramer 2016; Hochschild 2016; Sherman 2009; Wuthnow 2018.
29. Krebs 2016.
30. Scala and Johnson 2017.
31. Scala and Johnson 2017; Ulrich-Schad and Duncan 2018.
32. Sherman 2021a.
33. Benzow 2020.
34. Bartik 2020; Florida 2019.
35. Azzopardi et al. 2020.
36. Frey 2021.
37. Zabek 2019.
38. Coate and Magnum 2021.
39. See, for example, Kasarda and Janowitz 1974.
40. Bartik 2020, 122.
41. Lobao and Kelly 2021, 83.
42. Lobao and Kelly 2021, 88–89.
43. Montez 2020.
44. Garcilazo 2021.
45. Garcilazo 2021, 24.

CONCLUSION

1. Bailey, Jensen, and Ransom 2014; Brown and Schafft 2019; Lichter and Brown 2011.
2. Lichter and Ziliak 2017, 8.

References

Abrams, Leah R., Mikko Myrskylä, and Neil K. Mehta. 2021. "The Growing Rural-Urban Divide in US Life Expectancy: Contribution of Cardiovascular Disease and Other Major Causes of Death." *International Journal of Epidemiology* 50 (6): 1970–1978.

Adolph, Christopher, Kenya Amano, Bree Bang-Jensen, Nancy Fullman, and John Wilkerson. 2021. "Pandemic Politics: Timing State-Level Social Distancing Responses to COVID-19." *Journal of Health Politics, Policy and Law* 46 (2): 211–233.

Aelion, C. M., and H. T. Davis. 2019. "Blood Lead Levels in Children in Urban and Rural Areas: Using Multilevel Modeling to Investigate Impacts of Gender, Race, Poverty, and the Environment." *Science of the Total Environment* 694: 133783.

Agunwamba, Amenah A., Ichiro Kawachi, David R. Williams, Lila J. Finney Rutten, Patrick M. Wilson, and Kasisomayajula Viswanath. 2017. "Mental Health, Racial Discrimination, and Tobacco Use Differences across Rural-Urban California." *Journal of Rural Health* 33 (2): 180–189.

Akinlotan, Marvellous, Kristin Primm, Nima Khodakarami, Jane Bolin, and Alva Ferdinand. 2021. "Rural-Urban Variations in Travel Burdens

168 REFERENCES

for Care: Findings from the 2017 National Household Travel Survey." *Southwest Rural Health Research Center.* Accessed October 28, 2022. https://www.ruralhealthresearch.org/publications/1441.

Albrecht, Don E. 2019. "The Nonmetro Vote and the Election of Donald Trump." *Journal of Rural Social Sciences* 34 (1): 1–32.

Amato, Paul R. 1993. "Urban-Rural Differences in Helping Friends and Family Members." *Social Psychology Quarterly* 56 (4): 249–262.

American Hospital Association. 2022. "Rural Hospital Closures Threaten Access: Solutions to Preserve Care in Local Communities." Accessed May 24, 2023. https://www.aha.org/system/files/media/file/2022/09/rural-hospital-closures-threaten-access-report.pdf.

Anderson, Timothy J., Daniel M. Saman, Martin S. Lipsky, and M. Nawal Lutfiyya. 2015. "A Cross-Sectional Study on Health Differences between Rural and Non-Rural U.S. Counties Using the County Health Rankings." *BMC Health Services Research* 15: 441.

Appalachian Regional Commission. n.d. "Appalachian Counties Served by ARC." Accessed May 24, 2023. https://www.arc.gov/appalachian-counties-served-by-arc/.

Arnade, Chris. 2017. "'The Pill Mill of America': Where Drugs Mean There Are No Good Choices, Only Less Awful Ones." *Guardian.* Accessed November 1, 2022. https://www.theguardian.com/society/2017/may/17/drugs-opiod-addiction-epidemic-portsmouth-ohio.

Ashwood, Loka. 2018. *For-Profit Democracy: Why the Government Is Losing the Trust of Rural America.* New Haven, CT: Yale University Press.

Azzopardi, Damien, Fozan Fareed, Mikkel Hermansen, Patrick Lenain, and Douglas Sutherland. 2020. "The Decline in Labor Mobility in the United States: Insights from New Administrative Data." OECD Working Paper. Accessed February 19, 2022. https://www.oecd.org/official documents/publicdisplaydocumentpdf/?cote=ECO/WKP(2020)52&doc Language=En.

Baechtel, Mark. 2000. "Dead Center America." *Washington Post*, January 16.

Bailey, Conner, Leif Jensen, and Elizabeth Ransom, eds. 2014. *Rural America in a Globalizing World: Problems and Prospects for the 2010s.* Morgantown: West Virginia University Press.

Bambra, Clare, Katherine E. Smith, and Jamie Pearce. 2019. "Scaling up: The Politics of Health and Place." *Social Science & Medicine* 232: 36–42.

Barrington-Leigh, Christopher, and Adam Millard-Ball. 2015. "A Century of Sprawl in the United States." *Proceedings of the National Academy of Sciences* 112 (27): 8244–8249.

REFERENCES 169

Bartik, Timothy J. 2020. "Using Place-Based Jobs Policies to Help Distressed Communities." *Journal of Economic Perspectives* 34 (3): 99–127.

Beaudoin, Christopher E., and Esther Thorson. 2004. "Social Capital in Rural and Urban Communities: Testing Differences in Media Effects and Models." *Journalism & Mass Communication Quarterly* 81 (2): 378–399.

Befort, Christie A., Niaman Nazir, and Michael G. Perri. 2012. "Prevalence of Obesity among Adults from Rural and Urban Areas of the United States: Findings from NHANES (2005-2008)." *Journal of Rural Health* 28 (4): 392–397.

Beggs, John J., Valerie A. Haines, and Jeanne S. Hurlbert. 1996. "Revisiting the Rural-Urban Contrast: Personal Networks in Nonmetropolitan and Metropolitan Settings." *Rural Sociology* 61 (2): 306–325.

Bell, Caryn N., and Jessica L. Owens-Young. 2020. "Self-Rated Health and Structural Racism Indicated by County-Level Racial Inequalities in Socioeconomic Status: The Role of Urban-Rural Classification." *Journal of Urban Health* 97 (1): 52–61.

Bell, Michael M. 1992. "The Fruit of Difference: The Rural-Urban Continuum as a System of Identity." *Rural Sociology* 57 (1): 65–82.

Bell, Shannon Elizabeth, and Richard York. 2010. "Community Economic Identity: The Coal Industry and Ideology Construction in West Virginia." *Rural Sociology* 75 (1): 111–143.

Benzow, August. 2020. "Rural America Is Not All Trump Country: A Closer Look at the Rural Counties Biden Won." Economic Innovation Group. Accessed February 19, 2022. https://eig.org/news/rural-america-is-not-all-trump-country.

Berko, Jeffrey, Deborah D. Ingram, Shubhayu Saha, and Jennifer D. Parker. 2014. "Deaths Attributed to Heat, Cold, and Other Weather Events in the United States, 2006–2010." *National Health Statistics Reports* 76: 1–15.

Berry, E. Helen. 2014. "Thinking about Rural Health" In *Rural America in a Globalizing World: Problems and Prospects for the 2010s*, edited by C. Bailey, L. Jensen, and E. Ransom, 661–676. Morgantown: West Virginia University Press.

Billings, Dwight B., and Kathleen M. Blee. 2000. *The Road to Poverty: The Making of Wealth and Hardship in Appalachia*. Cambridge, UK: Cambridge University Press.

Bishop, Bill. 2008. *The Big Sort: Why the Clustering of Like-Minded America Is Tearing Us Apart*. Boston: Houghton Mifflin.

170 REFERENCES

Blackley, David J., Cara N. Halldin, and A. Scott Laney. 2018. "Continued Increase in Prevalence of Coal Workers' Pneumoconiosis in the United States, 1970–2017." *American Journal of Public Health* 108 (9): 1220–1222.

Blackwell, Debra L., Jacqueline W. Lucas, and Tainya C. Clarke. 2014. "Summary Health Statistics for U.S. Adults: National Health Interview Survey, 2012." *Vital and Health Statistics* 10 (260). Accessed June 10, 2016. http://www.cdc.gov/nchs/data/series/sr_10/sr10_260.pdf.

Blakemore, Erin. 2019. "The Largest Mass Deportation in American History." History. Accessed December 27, 2022. https://www.history.com/news/operation-wetback-eisenhower-1954-deportation.

Borders, Tyrone F., and Brenda M. Booth. 2007. "Research on Rural Residence and Access to Drug Abuse Services: Where Are We and Where Do We Go?" *Journal of Rural Health* 23 (s1): 79–83.

Brave Heart, Maria Yellow Horse, and Lemyra M. DeBruyn. 1998. "The American Indian Holocaust: Healing Historical Unresolved Grief." *American Indian and Alaska Native Mental Health Research* 8 (2): 56–78.

Broadway, Michael. 2007. "Meatpacking and the Transformation of Rural Communities: A Comparison of Brooks, Alberta and Garden City, Kansas." *Rural Sociology* 72 (4): 560–582.

Brooks, Matthew M., J. Tom Mueller, and Brian C. Thiede. 2020. "County Reclassifications and Rural–Urban Mortality Disparities in the United States (1970–2018)." *American Journal of Public Health* 110 (12): 1814–1816.

Brooks, Matthew M., J. Tom Mueller, and Brian C. Thiede. 2021. "Rural-Urban Differences in the Labor-Force Impacts of COVID-19 in the United States." *Socius* 7: 1–12.

Brooks, Matthew M., and Sabrina T. Voltaire. 2020. "Rural Families in the U.S.: Theory, Research, and Policy." In *Rural Families and Communities in the United States: Facing Challenges and Leveraging Opportunities*, edited by Jennifer E. Glick, Susan M. McHale, and Valerie King, 253–268. Cham, Switzerland: Springer.

Brown, David L. 2019. "A Quarter Century of Trends and Changes in the Demographic Structure of American Families." In *The Family in Rural Society*, edited by Raymond T. Coward and William M. Smith, 9–25. New York: Routledge.

Brown, David L., Nina Glasgow, Laszlo J. Kulcsar, Benjamin C. Bolender, and Marie-Joy Agruillas. 2008. *Rural Retirement Migration*. Dordrecht: Springer.

REFERENCES

Brown, David L., Nina Glasgow, Laszlo J. Kulcsar, Scott Sanders, and Brian C. Thiede. 2019. "The Multi-Scalar Organization of Aging-Related Services in US Rural Places." *Journal of Rural Studies* 68: 219–229.

Brown, David L., and Kai A. Schafft. 2011. *Rural People and Communities in the 21st Century: Resilience & Transformation.* 1st ed. Malden, MA: Polity Press.

Brown, David L., and Kai A. Schafft. 2019. *Rural People and Communities in the 21st Century: Resilience & Transformation.* 2nd ed. Medford, MA: Polity Press.

Brown, David L., and Louis E. Swanson, eds. 2003. *Challenges for Rural America in the Twenty-First Century.* University Park: Pennsylvania State University Press.

Bullard, Robert Doyle. 2000. *Dumping in Dixie: Race, Class, and Environmental Quality.* Vol 3. Boulder, CO: Westview Press.

Burrows, Elizabeth, Ryung Suh, and Danielle Hamann. 2012. "Health Care Workforce Distribution and Shortage Issues in Rural America." *National Rural Health Association Policy Brief* (January). Accessed November 1, 2022. https://www.ruralhealth.us/getattachment /Advocate/Policy-Documents/HealthCareWorkforceDistributionand ShortageJanuary2012.pdf.aspx?lang=en-US.

Burton, Linda M., Daniel T. Lichter, Regina S. Baker, and John M. Eason. 2013. "Inequality, Family Processes, and Health in the 'New' Rural America." *American Behavioral Scientist* 57 (8): 1128–1151.

Caldwell, Julia T., Chandra L. Ford, Steven P. Wallace, May C. Wang, and Lois M. Takahashi. 2016. "Intersection of Living in a Rural Versus Urban Area and Race/Ethnicity in Explaining Access to Health Care in the United States." *American Journal of Public Health* 106 (8): 1463–1469.

Callaghan, Timothy, Jennifer A. Lueck, Kristin Lunz Trujillo, and Alva O. Ferdinand. 2021. "Rural and Urban Differences in COVID-19 Prevention Behaviors." *Journal of Rural Health* 37 (2): 287–295.

Capriotti, Theresa, Tiffany Pearson, and Lillian Dufour. 2020. "Health Disparities in Rural America: Current Challenges and Future Solutions." Clinical Advisor. Accessed October 31, 2022. https://www .clinicaladvisor.com/home/topics/practice-management-information -center/health-disparities-in-rural-america-current-challenges-and -future-solutions/.

Carolan, Michael. 2016. *The Sociology of Food and Agriculture.* 2nd ed. London: Routledge.

172 REFERENCES

Carr, Patrick J., and Maria J. Kefalas. 2009. *Hollowing Out the Middle: The Rural Brain Drain and What It Means for America*. Boston: Beacon Press.

Carr, Patrick J., Daniel T. Lichter, and Maria J. Kefalas. 2012. "Can Immigration Save Small-Town America? Hispanic Boomtowns and the Uneasy Path to Renewal." *The Annals of the American Academy of Political and Social Science* 641 (1): 38–57.

Castells, Manuel, and Alejandro Portes. 1989. "World Underneath: The Origins, Dynamics, and Effects of the Informal Economy." In *The Informal Economy: Studies in Advanced and Less Developed Countries*, edited by Alejandro Portes, Manuel Castells, and Lauren A. Benton, 11–37. Baltimore, MD: Johns Hopkins University Press.

Cecil G. Sheps Center for Health Services Research. 2022. "183 Rural Hospital Closures Since January 2005." Accessed October 28, 2022. https://www.shepscenter.unc.edu/programs-projects/rural-health /rural-hospital-closures/.

Center on Budget and Policy Priorities. 2021. "Policy Basics: Temporary Assistance for Needy Families." Accessed October 11, 2021. https:// www.cbpp.org/research/family-income-support/temporary-assistance -for-needy-families.

Centro de Los Derechos del Migrante, Inc. 2020. "Ripe for Reform: Abuses of Agricultural Workers in the H-2A Visa Program." Baltimore, MD. Accessed May 9, 2023. https://cdmigrante.org/ripe-for -reform/.

Choi, Hannah S., Youn K. Shim, Wendy E. Kaye, and P. Barry Ryan. 2006. "Potential Residential Exposure to Toxics Release Inventory Chemicals during Pregnancy and Childhood Brain Cancer." *Environmental Health Perspectives* 114 (7): 1113–1118.

Clark, Cassandra J., Nicholaus P. Johnson, Mario Soriano Jr., Joshua L. Warren, Keli M. Sorrentino, Nina S. Kadan-Lottick, James E. Saiers, Xiaomei Ma, Nicole C. Deziel. 2022. "Unconventional Oil and Gas Development Exposure and Risk of Childhood Acute Lymphoblastic Leukemia: A Case-Control Study in Pennsylvania, 2009–2017." *Environmental Health Perspectives* 130 (8): 1–12.

Clark, Shelley, Elizabeth Lawrence, and Shannon Monnat. 2022. "Support from Adult Children and Parental Health in Rural America." *Journal of Rural Social Sciences* 37 (1): article 2.

Clogg, Clifford C. 1979. *Measuring Underemployment: Demographic Indicators for the United States*. New York: Academic Press.

Clogg, Clifford C., and Teresa A. Sullivan. 1983. "Labor Force Composition and Underemployment Trends, 1969–1980." *Social Indicators Research* 12 (2): 117–152.

Coate, Patrick, and Kyle Mangum. 2021. "Fast Locations and Slowing Mobility." Federal Reserve Bank of Philadelphia Working Paper. Accessed February 19, 2022. https://www.philadelphiafed.org/-/media/frbp/assets/working-papers/2019/wp19-49.pdf.

Cohen, Steven A., Caitlin C. Nash, Erin N. Byrne, Lauren E. Mitchell, and Mary L. Greaney. 2022. "Black/White Disparities in Obesity Widen with Increasing Rurality: Evidence from a National Survey." *Health Equity* 6 (1): 178–188.

Coleman-Jensen, Alisha, and Barry Steffen. 2017. "Food Insecurity and Housing Insecurity." In *Rural Poverty in the United States*, edited by Ann R. Tickamyer, Jennifer Sherman, and Jennifer Warlick, 257–298. Morgantown: West Virginia University Press.

Cosby, Arthur G., M. Maya McDoom-Echebiri, Wesley James, Hasna Khandekar, Willie Brown, and Heather L. Hanna. 2019. "Growth and Persistence of Place-Based Mortality in the United States: The Rural Mortality Penalty." *American Journal of Public Health* 109 (1): 155–162.

Cosby, Arthur G., Tonya T. Neaves, Ronald E. Cossman, Jeralynn S. Cossman, Wesley L. James, Neal Feierabend, David M. Mirvis, Carol A. Jones, and Tracey Farrigan. 2008. "Preliminary Evidence for an Emerging Nonmetropolitan Mortality Penalty in the United States." *American Journal of Public Health* 98 (8): 1470–1472.

Cossman, Jeralynn S., Ronald E. Cossman, Wesley L. James, Carol R. Campbell, Troy C. Blanchard, and Arthur G. Cosby. 2007. "Persistent Clusters of Mortality in the United States." *American Journal of Public Health* 97 (12): 2148–2150.

Cossman, Jeralynn S., Wesley L. James, Arthur G. Cosby, and Ronald E. Cossman. 2010. "Underlying Causes of the Emerging Nonmetropolitan Mortality Penalty." *American Journal of Public Health* 100 (8): 1417–1419.

Cramer, Katherine J. 2016. *The Politics of Resentment: Rural Consciousness in Wisconsin and the Rise of Scott Walker.* Chicago: University of Chicago Press.

Cristancho, Sergio, D. Marcela Garces, Karen E. Peters, and Benjamin C. Mueller. 2008. "Listening to Rural Hispanic Immigrants in the Midwest: A Community-Based Participatory Assessment of Major Barriers to Health Care Access and Use." *Qualitative Health Research* 18 (5): 633–646.

174   REFERENCES

Cromartie, John. 2017. "Rural America at a Glance: 2017 Edition." *Economic Information Bulletin* 182 (November). U.S. Department of Agriculture, Economic Research Service.

Cromartie, John. 2020. "Modest Improvement in Nonmetro Population Change During the Decade Masks Larger Geographic Shifts." *Amber Waves*, July. U.S. Department of Agriculture, Economic Research Service.

Cromartie, John, Elizabeth A. Dobis, Thomas P. Krumel, Jr., David McGranahan, and John Pender. 2020. "Rural America at a Glance: 2020 Edition." *Economic Information Bulletin* 221 (December). U.S. Department of Agriculture, Economic Research Service.

Cross, Sarah H., Robert M. Califf, and Haider J. Warraich. 2021. "Rural-Urban Disparity in Mortality in the US from 1999 to 2019." *JAMA* 325 (22): 2312–2314.

Crouch, Elizabeth, Sylvia Shi, Katherine Kelly, Alexander McLain, Jan Eberth, Janice Probst, Monique Brown, Melinda Merrell, and Kevin Bennett. 2022. "Rural-Urban Differences in Adverse and Positive Childhood Experiences: Results from the National Survey of Children's Health." Rural Health Research Gateway. Accessed October 26, 2022. ruralhealthresearch.org/ publications/1474.

Curtis, Katherine J., Junho Lee, Heather A. O'Connell, and Jun Zhu. 2019. "The Spatial Distribution of Poverty and the Long Reach of the Industrial Makeup of Places: New Evidence on Spatial and Temporal Regimes." *Rural Sociology* 84 (1): 28–65.

Cutler, David, and Grant Miller. 2005. "The Role of Public Health Improvements in Health Advances: The Twentieth-Century United States." *Demography* 42 (1): 1–22.

Danbom, David B. 1995. *Born in the Country: A History of Rural America.* Baltimore, MD: Johns Hopkins University Press.

de Jong, Greta. 2003. *A Different Day: African American Struggles for Justice in Rural Louisiana, 1990-1970.* Chapel Hill: University of North Carolina Press.

Dewess, Sarah. 2014. "Native Nations in a Changing Global Economy." In *Rural America in a Globalizing World: Problems and Prospects for the 2010s,* edited by Conner Bailey, Leif Jensen, and Elizabeth Ransom, 471–488. Morgantown: West Virginia University Press.

Dewess, Sarah, and Benjamin Marks. 2017. "Twice Invisible: Understanding Rural Native America." *Research Note* 2 (April). First Nations Development Institute. Accessed December 26, 2022. https://www

.usetinc.org/wp-content/uploads/bvenuti/WWS/2017/May%202017 /May%208/Twice%20Invisible%20-%20Research%20Note.pdf.

Dietz, William H. 1998. "Health Consequences of Obesity in Youth: Childhood Predictors of Adult Disease." *Pediatrics* 101 (Supp. 2): 518–525.

Dimitri, Carolyn, Anne Effland, and Neilson Conklin. 2005. "The 20th Century Transformation of U.S. Agriculture and Farm Policy." *Economic Information Bulletin* 3 (June). U.S. Department of Agriculture, Economic Research Service.

Dobis, Elizabeth A., Thomas P. Krumel, Jr., John Cromartie, Kelsey L. Conley, Austin Sanders, and Ruben Ortiz. 2021. "Rural America at a Glance: 2021 Edition." *Economic Information Bulletin* 230 (November). U.S. Department of Agriculture, Economic Research Service.

Doggett, Lloyd. 2022. "Timeline of Trump's Coronavirus Response" (blog post). Accessed October 20, 2022. https://doggett.house.gov/media /blog-post/timeline-trumps-coronavirus-responses.

Domina, Thurston. 2006. "What Clean Break? Education and Nonmetropolitan Migration Patterns, 1989–2004." *Rural Sociology* 71 (3): 373–398.

Du Bois, W. E. B. 1899. "The Negro in the Black Belt: Some Social Sketches." *Bulletin of the Department of Labor* 22 (40): 1–17.

Du Bois, W. E. B. [1899] 1973. *The Philadelphia Negro.* Millwood, NY: Kraus-Thompson.

Du Bois, W. E. B. [1903] 1989. *The Souls of Black Folk.* New York: Bantam.

Dunbar-Ortiz, Roxanne. 2015. *An Indigenous Peoples' History of the United States.* Boston: Beacon Press.

Duncan, Cynthia, and Jessica D. Ulrich-Schad. 2021. "Marginalization of Rural Communities in the U.S." In *Investing in Rural Prosperity,* edited by Andrew Dumont and Daniel Paul Davis, 47–65. St. Louis, MO: Federal Reserve Bank of St. Louis and the Board of Governors of the Federal Reserve System.

Duncan, Cynthia M. 1999. *Worlds Apart: Why Poverty Persists in Rural America.* New Haven, CT: Yale University Press.

Durand, Jorge, Douglas S. Massey, and Fernando Charvet. 2000. "The Changing Geography of Mexican Immigration to the United States: 1910–1996." *Social Science Quarterly* 81 (1): 1–15.

Durkheim, Émile. [1893] 1984. *The Division of Labor in Society.* Translated by W. D. Halls. New York: Free Press.

Eberhardt, Mark S., and Elsie R. Pamuk. 2004. "The Importance of Place of Residence: Examining Health in Rural and Nonrural Areas." *American Journal of Public Health* 94 (10): 1682–1686.

Ellis, Matthew S., Zachary A. Kasper, and Theodore J. Cicero. 2021. "Polysubstance Use Trends and Variability among Individuals with Opioid Use Disorder in Rural versus Urban Settings." *Preventive Medicine* 152 (2): 106729.

Elo, Irma T., Arun S. Hendi, Jessica Y. Ho, Yara C. Vierboom, and Samuel H. Preston. 2019. "Trends in Non-Hispanic White Mortality in the United States by Metropolitan-Nonmetropolitan Status and Region, 1990–2016." *Population and Development Review* 45 (3): 549–583.

Ely, Danielle M., and Brady E. Hamilton. 2018. "Trends in Fertility and Mother's Age at First Birth among Rural and Metropolitan Counties: United States, 2007–2017." *National Center for Health Statistics Data Brief*, no. 323.

Ely, Danielle M., Anne K. Driscoll, and T. J. Matthews. 2017. "Infant Mortality Rates in Rural and Urban Areas in the United States, 2014." *National Center for Health Statistics Data Brief*, no. 285.

Environmental Protection Agency (EPA). 2022. "Nutrient Pollution—The Effects: Human Health." Accessed October 31, 2022. https://www.epa.gov/nutrientpollution/effects-human-health.

Evich, Helena B. 2016. "Revenge of the Rural Voter." *Politico*, November 13.

Farrelly, Matthew C., Brett R. Loomis, Beth Han, Joe Gfroerer, Nicole Kuiper, G. Lance. Couzens, Shanta Dube, and Ralph S. Caraballo. 2013. "A Comprehensive Examination of the Influence of State Tobacco Control Programs and Policies on Youth Smoking." *American Journal of Public Health* 103 (3): 549–555.

Fisher, Patrick. 2014. *Demographic Gaps in American Political Behavior.* Boulder, CO: Westview Press.

Florida, Richard. 2019. "Don't Move People Out of Distressed Places: Instead, Revitalize Them." Bloomberg CityLab, September 12. Accessed February 17, 2022. https://www.bloomberg.com/news/articles/2019-09-12/focus-economic-policy-on-places-not-just-people.

Fontenot, Kayla, Joachim Singelmann, Tim Slack, Carlos Siordia, Dudley L. Poston, Jr., and Rogelio Saenz. 2010. "Understanding Falling Poverty in the Poorest Places: An Examination of the Experience of the Texas Borderland and Lower Mississippi Delta, 1990–2000." *Journal of Poverty* 14 (2): 216–236.

Freudenburg, William R. 1992. "Addictive Economies: Extractive Industries and Vulnerable Localities in a Changing World Economy." *Rural Sociology* 57 (3): 305–332.

Frey, William H. 2021. "Despite the Pandemic Narrative, Americans Are Moving at Historically Low Rates." Brookings. Accessed February 16,

2022. https://www.brookings.edu/research/despite-the-pandemic
-narrative-americans-are-moving-at-historically-low-rates/.

Fuguitt, Glenn V. 1985. "The Nonmetropolitan Population Turnaround." *Annual Review of Sociology* 11 (1): 259–280.

Fuguitt, Glenn V., Tim B. Heaton, and Daniel T. Lichter. 1988. "Monitoring the Metropolitanization Process." *Demography* 25 (1): 115–128.

Gadarian, Shana Kushner, Sara Wallace Goodman, and Thomas B. Pepinsky. 2021. "Partisanship, Health Behavior, and Policy Attitudes in the Early Stages of the COVID-19 Pandemic." *PLoS ONE* 16 (4): e0249596.

Gadarian, Shana Kushner, Sara Wallace Goodman, and Thomas B. Pepinsky. 2022. *Pandemic Politics: The Deadly Toll of Partisanship in the Age of COVID-19.* Princeton, NJ: Princeton University Press.

Gamble, Vanessa Northington. 1997. "Under the Shadow of Tuskegee: African Americans and Health Care." *American Journal of Public Health* 87 (11): 1773–1778.

Garcilazo, Jose Enrique. 2021. "Megatrends and Implications for Rural Development Policy." In *Investing in Rural Prosperity*, edited by Andrew Dumont and Daniel Paul Davis, 15–27. St. Louis, MO: Federal Reserve Bank of St. Louis and the Board of Governors of the Federal Reserve System.

Gaventa, John. 1980. *Power and Powerlessness: Quiescence and Rebellion in an Appalachia Valley.* Urbana: University of Illinois Press.

Gibson, Campbell. 2012. "American Demographic History Chartbook: 1790 to 2010." Accessed August 31, 2020. https:/www.demographic chartbook.com.

Gibson, Campbell, and Kay Jung. 2006. "Historical Census Statistics on the Foreign-Born Population of the United States: 1850 to 2000." U.S. Census Bureau Population Division Working Paper No. 81. Accessed December 23, 2022. https://www.census.gov/content/dam/Census /library/working-papers/2006/demo/POP-twps0081.pdf.

Gilbert, Jess, Gwen Sharp, and M. Felin. 2002. "The Loss and Persistence of Black-Owned Farms and Farmland: A Review of the Research Literature and Its Implications." *Journal of Rural Social Sciences* 18 (2): article 1.

Gimpel, James G., and Kimberly A. Karnes. 2006. "The Rural Side of the Urban-Rural Gap." *Political Science and Politics* 39 (3): 467–472.

Glasgow, Nina, and E. Helen Berry, eds. 2013. *Rural Aging in 21st Century America.* New York: Springer.

Glasgow, Nina, and David L. Brown. 2012. "Rural Ageing in the United States: Trends and Contexts." *Journal of Rural Studies* 28 (4): 422–431.

178 REFERENCES

Glasgow, Nina, Lois Wright Morton, and Nan E. Johnson, eds. 2004. *Critical Issues in Rural Health*. Ames, IA: Blackwell Publishing.

Glauber, Rebecca. 2022. "Rural Depopulation and the Rural-Urban Gap in Cognitive Functioning among Older Adults." *Journal of Rural Health* 38 (4): 696–704.

Golding, Shaun A., and Richelle L. Winkler. 2020. "Tracking Urbanization and Exurbs: Migration across the Rural-Urban Continuum, 1990–2016." *Population Research and Policy Review* 39 (5): 835–859.

Gong, Gordon, Scott G. Phillips, Catherine Hudson, Debra Curti, and Billy U. Philips. 2019. "Higher US Rural Mortality Rates Linked to Socioeconomic Status, Physician Shortages, and Lack of Health Insurance." *Health Affairs* 38 (12): 2003–2010.

Goodman, Bill, and Reid Steadman. 2002. "Services: Business Demand Rivals Consumer Demand in Driving Job Growth." *Monthly Labor Review* 125 (4): 3–16.

Gouveia, Lourdes, and Rogelio Saenz. 2000. "Global Forces and Latino Population Growth in the Midwest: A Regional and Subregional Analysis." *Great Plains Research* 10: 305–328.

Granovetter, Mark. 1985. "Economic Action and Social Structure: The Problem of Embeddedness." *American Journal of Sociology* 91 (3): 481–510.

Grassroots Change. 2021. "Preemption Watch." Accessed November 1, 2022. https://grassrootschange.net/preemption-watch/#/category.

Green, John. 2014. "The Status of African Americans in the Rural United States." In *Rural America in a Globalizing World: Problems and Prospects for the 2010s*, edited by Conner Bailey, Leif Jensen, and Elizabeth Ransom, 435–452. Morgantown: West Virginia University Press.

Grumbach, Jacob M. 2018. "From Backwaters to Major Policymakers: Policy Polarization in the States, 1970–2014." *Perspectives on Politics* 16 (2): 416–435.

Grundy, Stacy, and Beth Prusaczyk. 2022. "The Complex Intersection of Race and Rurality: The Detrimental Effects of Race-Neutral Rural Health Policies." *Health Equity* 6 (1): 334–337.

Haines, Michael R. 2001. "The Urban Mortality Transition in the United States, 1800–1940." *Annales de Démographie Historique* 101 (1): 33–64.

Haischer, Michael H., Rachel Beilfuss, Meggie Rose Hart, Lauren Opielinski, David Wrucke, Gretchen Zirgaitis, Toni D. Uhrich, and Sandra K. Hunter. 2020. "Who Is Wearing a Mask? Gender-, Age-, and

Location-Related Differences during the COVID-19 Pandemic." *PLoS ONE* 15 (10): e0240785.

Halfacree, K.H. 1993. "Locality and Social Representation: Space, Discourse, and Alternative Definitions of the Rural." *Journal of Rural Studies* 9 (1): 23–37.

Hall, Matthew. 2013. "Residential Integration on the New Frontier: Immigrant Segregation in Established and New Destinations." *Demography* 50 (5): 1873–1896.

Hanson, Randel D. 2001. "Half Lives of Reagan's Indian Policy: Marketing Nuclear Waste to American Indians." *American Indian Culture and Research Journal* 25 (1): 21–44.

Harp, Kathi, and Tyrone F. Borders. 2019. "Suicidal Thoughts, Plans, and Attempts by Non-Metropolitan and Metropolitan Residence." Rural and Underserved Health Research Center. Accessed October 28, 2022. https://ruhrc.uky.edu/publications/suicidal-thoughts-plans-and -attempts-by-non-metropolitan-and-metropolitan-residence/.

Harris, Katelynn. 2020. "Forty Years of Falling Manufacturing Employment." *Beyond the Numbers: Employment and Unemployment* 9 (16).

Harrison, Jill. 2008. "Lessons Learned from Pesticide Drift: A Call to Bring Production Agriculture, Farm Labor, and Social Justice Back into Agrifood Research and Activism." *Agriculture and Human Values* 25 (2): 163–167.

Hartley, David. 2004. "Rural Health Disparities, Population Health, and Rural Culture." *American Journal of Public Health* 94 (10): 1675–1678.

Harvey, Mark H. 2017. "Racial Inequalities and Poverty in Rural America." In *Rural Poverty in the United States*, edited by Ann R. Tickamyer, Jennifer Sherman, and Jennifer Warlick, 141–167. New York: Columbia University Press.

Hauser, Philip M. 1974. "The Measurement of Labor Utilization." *Malayan Economic Review* 19 (1): 1–17.

Hawk, William. 2013. "Expenditures of Urban and Rural Households in 2011." *Beyond the Numbers* 2 (5). Accessed March 28, 2022. https://www.bls.gov/opub/btn/volume-2/expenditures-of-urban-and -rural-households-in-2011.htm#:~:text=Urban%20households%20had %20higher%20expenditures,%2C%20health%20care%2C%20and %20entertainment.

Henning-Smith, Carrie, Janette Dill, Arianne Baldomero, and Katy Backes Kozhimannil. 2022. "Rural/Urban Differences in Access to

180 REFERENCES

Paid Sick Leave among Full-Time Workers." *Journal of Rural Health* 39 (3) 676–685.

Higgs, Robert. 1973. "Mortality in Rural America, 1870–1920: Estimates and Conjectures." *Exploration in Economic History* 10 (2): 177–195.

Hochschild, Arlie R. 2016. *Strangers in Their Own Land: Anger and Mourning on the American Right.* New York: New Press.

Hofferth, Sandra L., and John Iceland. 1998. "Social Capital in Rural and Urban Communities." *Rural Sociology* 63 (4): 574–598.

Hogseth, Bill. 2020. "Why Democrats Keep Losing Rural Counties Like Mine." *Poltico*, December 1. Accessed June 13, 2022. https://www.politico.com/news/magazine/2020/12/01/democrats-rural-vote-wisconsin-441458.

Hooks, Gregory, and Wendy Sawyer. 2020. "Mass Incarceration, COVID-19, and Community Spread." Prison Policy Initiative. Accessed June 18, 2021. https://www.prisonpolicy.org/reports/covidspread.html.

House, James S., Karl R. Landis, and Debra Umberson. 1988. "Social Relationships and Health." *Science* 241 (4865): 540–545.

Iceland, John. 2014. *A Portrait of America: The Demographic Perspective.* 1st ed. Oakland: University of California Press.

Ivey-Stephenson, Asha Z., Alex E. Crosby, Shane P. D. Jack, Tadesse Haileyesus, and Marcie-Jo Kresnow-Sedacca. 2017. "Suicide Trends among and within Urbanization Levels by Sex, Race/Ethnicity, Age Group, and Mechanism of Death—United States, 2001–2015." *MMWR Surveillance Summaries* 66 (18): 1–16.

Jakubek, Joseph, and Spencer D. Wood. 2018. "Emancipatory Empiricism: The Rural Sociology of W. E. B. Du Bois." *Sociology of Race and Ethnicity* 4 (1): 14–34.

James, Cara V., Ramal Moonesinghe, Shondelle M. Wilson-Frederick, Jeffrey E. Hall, Ana Penman-Aguilar, and Karen Bouye. 2017. "Racial/Ethnic Health Disparities among Rural Adults—United States, 2012–2015." *MMWR Surveillance Summaries* 66 (23): 1–9.

James, Wesley. 2014. "All Rural Places Are Not Created Equal: Revisiting the Rural Mortality Penalty in the United States." *American Journal of Public Health* 104 (11): 2122–2129.

James, Wesley, and Jeralynn Cossman. 2017. "Long Term Trends in Black and White Mortality in the Rural United States: Evidence of a Race-Specific Rural Mortality Penalty." *Journal of Rural Health* 33 (1): 21–31.

James, Wesley, Jeralynn Cossman, and Julia Kay Wolf. 2018. "Persistence of Death in the United States: The Remarkably Different Mortality

Patterns between America's Heartland and Dixieland." *Demographic Research* 39: 897–910.

Jefferson, Thomas. 1785. *Notes on the State of Virginia*. Boston: Lilly and Wait.

Jensen, Leif. 2006. "New Immigrant Settlements in Rural America: Problems, Prospects, and Policies." The Carsey School of Public Policy at the Scholars' Repository 17. Accessed December 23, 2022. https://scholars.unh.edu/carsey/17.

Jensen, Leif, Gretchen T. Cornwell, and Jill L. Findeis. 1995. "Informal Work in Nonmetropolitan Pennsylvania." *Rural Sociology* 60 (1): 91–107.

Jensen, Leif, Jill L. Findeis, Wan-Ling Hsu, and Jason P. Schacter. 1999. "Slipping into and out of Underemployment: Another Disadvantage for Nonmetropolitan Workers?" *Rural Sociology* 64 (3): 417–438.

Jensen, Leif, Diane K. McLaughlin, and Tim Slack. 2003. "Rural Poverty: The Persisting Challenge." In *Challenges for Rural America in the Twenty-First Century*, edited by David L. Brown and Louis E. Swanson, 118–131. University Park: Pennsylvania State University Press.

Jensen, Leif, Ann R. Tickamyer, and Tim Slack. 2019. "Rural-Urban Variation in Informal Work Activities in the United States." *Journal of Rural Studies* 68: 276–284.

Johns Hopkins University. 2023. "COVID-19 Dashboard." Center for Systems Science and Engineering. Accessed March 10, 2023. https://coronavirus.jhu.edu/map.html.

Johnson, James Allen, and Asal Mohamadi Johnson. 2015. "Urban-Rural Differences in Childhood and Adolescent Obesity in the United States: A Systematic Review and Meta-Analysis." *Childhood Obesity* 11 (3): 233–241.

Johnson, Kenneth M. 2020. "As Births Diminish and Deaths Increase, Natural Decrease Becomes More Widespread in Rural America." *Rural Sociology* 85 (4): 1045–1058.

Johnson, Kenneth M. 2022. "Rural America Lost Population over the Past Decade for First Time in History." *Carsey Research National Issue Brief*, no. 160.

Johnson, Kenneth M., and Daniel T. Lichter. 2008. "Natural Increase: A New Source of Population Growth in Emerging Hispanic Destinations in the United States." *Population and Development Review* 34 (2): 327–346.

Johnson, Kenneth M., and Daniel T. Lichter. 2013. "Rural Retirement Destinations: Natural Decrease and the Shared Demographic Destinies of Elderly and Hispanics." In *Rural Aging in 21st Century*

America, edited by Nina Glasgow and E. Helen Berry, 275–294. New York: Springer.

Johnson, Kenneth M., and Daniel T. Lichter. 2016. "Diverging Demography: Hispanic and Non-Hispanic Contributions to U.S. Population Redistribution and Diversity." *Population Research and Policy Review* 35 (5): 705–725.

Johnson, Kenneth M., and Daniel T. Lichter. 2019. "Rural Depopulation: Growth and Decline Processes over the Past Century. *Rural Sociology* 84 (1): 3–27.

Johnson, Kenneth M., and Daniel T. Lichter. 2020. "Metropolitan Reclassification and the Urbanization of Rural America." *Demography* 57 (5): 1929–1950.

Johnson, Kenneth M., and Daniel T. Lichter. 2022. "Growing Racial Diversity in Rural America: Results from the 2020 Census." *Carsey Research National Issue Brief*, no. 163.

Johnson, Kenneth M., Alfred Nucci, and Larry Long. 2005. "Population Trends in Metropolitan and Nonmetropolitan America: Selective Deconcentration and the Rural Rebound." *Population Research and Policy Review* 24 (5): 527–542.

Johnson, Kenneth M., and Dante J. Scala. 2020. "Voting Attitudes along the Red Rural–Blue Urban Continuum." *Carsey Research National Issue Brief*, no. 152.

Johnson, Kenneth M., and Richelle L. Winkler. 2015. "Migration Signatures across the Decades: Net Migration by Age in U.S. Counties, 1950–2010. *Demographic Research* 32 (38): 1065–1080.

Jones, Carol. 2010. "Rural Populations Have Higher Rates of Chronic Disease." USDA Economic Research Service. Accessed October 27, 2022. https://www.ers.usda.gov/amber-waves/2010/june/rural-populations-have-higher-rates-of-chronic-disease/.

Kaiser Family Foundation. 2021. "Does the Public Want to Get a COVID-19 Vaccine? When?" KFF COVID-19 Vaccine Monitor Dashboard. Accessed June 18, 2021. https://www.kff.org/coronavirus-covid-19/dashboard/kff-covid-19-vaccine-monitor-dashboard/.

Kaiser Health News. 2020. "Coronavirus Threatens Rural Hospitals." *U.S. News*, March 23. Accessed October 20, 2022. https://www.usnews.com/news/healthiest-communities/articles/2020-03-23/covid-19-threatens-rural-hospitals-already-stretched-to-breaking-point.

Kalleberg, Arne L. 2011. *Good Jobs, Bad Jobs: The Rise of Polarized and Precarious Employment Systems in the United States, 1970s to 2000s.* New York: Russell Sage Foundation.

REFERENCES   183

Kandel, William, and John Cromartie. 2004. "New Patterns of Hispanic Settlement in Rural America." *Rural Development Research Report*, no. 99. Accessed December 23, 2022. https://www.ers.usda.gov /publications/pub-details/?pubid=47091.

Kandel, William, and Emilio A. Parrado. 2005. "Restructuring of the US Meat Processing Industry and New Hispanic Migrant Destinations." *Population and Development Review* 31 (3): 447–471.

Kasarda, John D., and Morris Janowitz. 1974. "Community Attachment in Mass Society." *American Sociological Review* 39 (3): 328–339.

Kebede, Maraki, Annie Maselli, Kendra Taylor, and Erica Frankenberg. 2021. "Ethnoracial Diversity and Segregation in US Rural School Districts." *Rural Sociology* 86 (3): 494–522.

Kelly, Kate. 2014. "The Green Book: The First Travel Guide for African-Americans Dates to the 1930s." *Huffington Post*, January 6. Accessed December 23, 2022. https://www.huffpost.com/entry/the-green-book -the-first_b_4549962.

Kelly, Paige, and Linda Lobao. 2019. "The Social Bases of Rural-Urban Political Divides: Social Status, Work, and Sociocultural Beliefs." *Rural Sociology* 84 (4): 669–705.

King, Katrina Quisumbing, Spencer Wood, Jess Gilbert, and Marilyn Sinkewicz. 2018. "Black Agrarianism: The Significance of African American Landownership in the Rural South." *Rural Sociology* 83(3): 677–699.

Kirzinger, Ashley, Audrey Kearney, Liz Hamel, and Mollyann Brodie. 2021. "KFF COVID-19 Vaccine Monitor: The Increasing Importance of Partisanship in Predicting COVID-19 Vaccination Status." Kaiser Family Foundation. Accessed October 20, 2022. https://www.kff.org /coronavirus-covid-19/poll-finding/importance-of-partisanship -predicting-vaccination-status/.

Kirzinger, Ashley, Cailey Munana, and Mollyann Brodie. 2021. "Vaccine Hesitancy in Rural America." Kaiser Family Foundation. Accessed June 21, 2021. https://www.kff.org/coronavirus-covid-19/poll-finding /vaccine-hesitancy-in-rural-america/.

Kouznetsova, Maria, Xiaoyu Huang, Jing Ma, Lawrence Lessner, and David O. Carpenter. 2007. "Increased Rate of Hospitalization for Diabetes and Residential Proximity of Hazardous Waste Sites." *Environmental Health Perspectives* 115 (1): 75–79.

Kozhimannil, Katy B., and Carrie Henning-Smith. 2018. "Racism and Health in Rural America." *Journal of Health Care for the Poor and Underserved* 29 (1): 35–43.

184   REFERENCES

Krannich, Richard S., Brian Gentry, A. E. Luloff, and Peter G. Robertson. 2014. "Resource Dependency in Rural America: Continuities and Change." In *Rural America in a Globalizing World: Problems and Prospects for the 2010s*, edited by Conner Bailey, Leif Jensen, and Elizabeth Ransom, 208–225. Morgantown: West Virginia University Press.

Krebs, Justin. 2016. *Blue in a Red State: The Survival Guide to Life in the Real America*. New York: The New Press.

Kron, Josh. 2012. "Red State, Blue City: How the Urban-Rural Divide Is Splitting America." *Atlantic*, November 30.

Larson, Olaf F., and Julie N. Zimmerman. 2003. *Sociology in Government: The Galpin-Taylor Years in the U.S. Department of Agriculture, 1919–1953*. University Park: Pennsylvania State University Press.

Laughlin, Lynda. 2016. "Beyond the Farm: Rural Industry Workers in America." U.S. Census Bureau. Accessed October 8, 2021. https://www.census.gov/newsroom/blogs/random-samplings/2016/12/beyond_the_farm_rur.html.

Lawrence, Elizabeth, Robert A. Hummer, and Kathleen Mullan Harris. 2017. "The Cardiovascular Health of Young Adults: Disparities along the Urban-Rural Continuum." *The ANNALS of the American Academy of Political and Social Science* 672 (1): 257–281.

Lay, J. Celeste. 2017. "Case Study: Immigration and New Rural Residents." In *Rural Poverty in the United States*, edited by Ann R. Tickamyer, Jennifer Sherman, and Jennifer Warlick, 193–196. New York: Columbia University Press.

Lefebvre, Henri. [1956] 2016. "The Theory of Ground Rent and Rural Sociology." Translated by Matthew Dennis. *Antipode* 48 (1): 67–73.

Leicht, Kevin T., and J. Craig Jenkins. 2007. "New and Unexplored Opportunities: Developing a Spatial Perspective for Political Sociology." In *The Sociology of Spatial Inequality*, edited by Linda M. Lobao, Gregory Hooks, and Ann R. Tickamyer, 63–84. Albany: State University of New York Press.

Lekies, Kristi S., David Matarrita-Cascante, Rebecca Schewe, and Richelle Winkler. 2015. "Amenity Migration in the New Global Economy: Current Issues and Research Priorities." *Society and Natural Resources* 28 (10): 1144–1151.

Levin, Marc, and Michael Haugen. 2018. "Open Roads and Overflowing Jails: Addressing High Rates of Rural Pretrial Incarceration." Texas Public Policy Foundation. Accessed January 5, 2022. https://files.texaspolicy.com/uploads/2018/08/16104511/2018-04-RR-Rural-Pretrial-Incarceration-CEJ-Levin-Haugen-1.pdf.

REFERENCES 185

Library of Congress. n.d.-a. "U.S. History Primary Source Timeline." Accessed December 27, 2022. https://www.loc.gov/classroom-materials /united-states-history-primary-source-timeline/.

Library of Congress. n.d.-b. "Immigration and Relocation in U.S. History: Japanese." Accessed May 10, 2023. https://www.loc.gov/classroom -materials/immigration/japanese/.

Lichter, Daniel T. 2012. "Immigration and the New Racial Diversity in Rural America." *Rural Sociology* 77 (1): 3–35.

Lichter, Daniel T., and David L. Brown. 2011. "Rural America in an Urban Society: Changing Spatial and Social Boundaries." *Annual Review of Sociology* 37: 565–592.

Lichter, Daniel T., David L. Brown, and Domenico Parisi. 2021. "The Rural–Urban Interface: Rural and Small Town Growth at the Metropolitan Fringe." *Population, Space and Place* 27 (3): e2415.

Lichter, Daniel T., and Rukmalie Jayakody. 2002. "Welfare Reform: How Do We Measure Success?" *Annual Review of Sociology* 28: 117–141.

Lichter, Daniel T., and Kenneth M. Johnson. 2006. "Emerging Rural Settlement Patterns and the Geographic Redistribution of America's New Immigrants." *Rural Sociology* 71 (1): 109–131.

Lichter, Daniel T., and Kenneth M. Johnson. 2020. "A Demographic Lifeline? Immigration and Hispanic Population Growth in Rural America." *Population Research and Policy Review* 39 (5): 785–803.

Lichter, Daniel T., Kenneth M. Johnson, Richard N. Turner, and Allison Churilla. 2012. "Hispanic Assimilation and Fertility in New U.S. Destinations." *International Migration Review* 46 (4): 767–791.

Lichter, Daniel T., Domenico Parisi, Steven Michael Grice, and Michael Taquino. 2007a. "Municipal Underbounding: Annexation and Racial Exclusion in Small Southern Towns." *Rural Sociology* 72 (1): 47–68.

Lichter, Daniel T., Domenico Parisi, Steven Michael Grice, and Michael Taquino. 2007b. "National Estimates of Racial Segregation in Rural and Small-Town America." *Demography* 44 (3): 563–581.

Lichter, Daniel T., Domenico Parisi, and Michael C. Taquino. 2012. "The Geography of Exclusion: Race, Segregation, and Concentrated Poverty." *Social Problems* 59 (3): 364–388.

Lichter, Daniel T., Scott R. Sanders, and Kenneth M. Johnson. 2015. "Hispanics at the Starting Line: Poverty among Newborn Infants in Established Gateways and New Destinations." *Social Forces* 94 (1): 209–235.

Lichter, Daniel T., and James P. Ziliak. 2017. "The Rural-Urban Interface: New Patterns for Spatial Interdependence and Inequality in America."

The Annals of the American Academy of Political and Social Science 672 (1): 6–25.

Lin, Ge, Tonglin Zhang, Ying Zhang, and Quanyi Wang. 2021. "Statewide Stay-at-Home Directives on the Spread of COVID-19 in Metropolitan and Nonmetropolitan Counties in the United States." *Journal of Rural Health* 37 (1): 222–223.

Link, Bruce G., and Jo Phelan. 1995. "Social Conditions as Fundamental Causes of Disease." *Journal of Health and Social Behavior*, extra issue: 80–94.

Lobao, Linda. 2014. "Economic Change, Structural Forces and Rural America: Shifting Fortunes across Communities." In *Rural America in a Globalizing World: Problems and Prospects for the 2010s*, edited by Conner Bailey, Leif Jensen, and Elizabeth Ransom, 543–555. Morgantown: West Virginia University Press.

Lobao, Linda M., and Gregory Hooks. 2007. "Advancing the Sociology of Spatial Inequality: Spaces, Places, and the Subnational Scale." In *The Sociology of Spatial Inequality*, edited by Linda M. Lobao, Gregory Hooks, and Ann R. Tickamyer, 29–61. Albany: State University of New York Press.

Lobao, Linda M., Gregory Hooks, and Ann R. Tickamyer, eds. 2007. *The Sociology of Spatial Inequality*. Albany: State University of New York Press.

Lobao, Linda, and Paige Kelly. 2021. "Local Governments across Rural America: Status, Challenges and Positioning for the Future." In *Investing in Rural Prosperity*, edited by Andrew Dumont and Daniel Paul Davis, 81–91. St. Louis, MO: Federal Reserve Bank of St. Louis and the Board of Governors of the Federal Reserve System.

Lobao, Linda, and Katherine Meyer. 2001. "The Great Agricultural Transition: Crisis, Change, and Social Consequences of Twentieth Century Farming." *Annual Review of Sociology* 27: 103–124.

Loewen, James W. 2005. *Sundown Towns: A Hidden Dimension of American Racism*. New York: The New Press.

Lovelace, Berkeley, Jr. 2020. "Trump Claims the Worsening U.S. Coronavirus Outbreak is a 'Fake News Media Conspiracy' Even as Hospitalizations Rise." *CNBC*. Accessed October 20, 2022. https://www.cnbc.com /2020/10/26/coronavirus-trump-claims-the-worsening-us-outbreak-is-a -fake-news-media-conspiracy-even-as-hospitalizations-rise.html.

Low, Sarah A. 2017. "Rural Manufacturing Survival and Its Role in the Rural Economy." *Amber Waves*, October. U.S. Department of Agriculture, Economic Research Service.

REFERENCES   187

Lyson, Thomas A., and William W. Falk, eds. 1993. *Forgotten Places: Uneven Development in Rural America*. Lawrence: University Press of Kansas.

Mainous, Arch G., Dana E. King, David R. Garr, and William S. Pearson. 2004. "Race, Rural Residence, and Control of Diabetes and Hypertension." *The Annals of Family Medicine* 2 (6): 563–568.

Marcelli, Enrico, Colin C. Williams, and Pascale Joassart, eds. 2010. *Informal Work in Developed Nations*. New York: Routledge.

Maril, Robert L. 1989. *The Poorest of Americans: The Mexican-Americans of the Lower Rio Grande Valley of Texas*. Notre Dame, IN: University of Notre Dame Press.

Markides, Kyriakos S., and Jeannine Coreil. 1986. "The Health of Hispanics in the Southwestern United States: An Epidemiologic Paradox." *Public Health Reports* 101 (3): 253–265.

Marrow, Helen B. 2005. "New Destinations and Immigrant Incorporation." *Perspectives on Politics* 3 (4): 781–799.

Martin, Philip, Michael Fix, and J. Edward Taylor. 2006. *The New Rural Poverty: Agriculture and Immigration in California*. Washington, DC: The Urban Institute.

Massey, Douglas S., ed. 2008. *New Faces in New Places: The Changing Geography of American Immigration*. New York: Russell Sage Foundation.

Massey, Douglas S., and Chiara Capoferro. 2008. "The Geographic Diversification of American Immigration." In *New Faces in New Places: The Changing Geography of American Immigration*, edited by Douglas S. Massey, 25–50. New York: Russell Sage.

McKinlay, John B. 1974. "A Case for Refocusing Upstream: The Political Economy of Illness." In *Applying Behavioral Science to Cardiovascular Risk*, edited by the American Heart Association, 87–96. Dallas, TX: American Heart Association.

McKinlay, John B., Sonja M. McKinlay, and Robert Beaglehole. 1989. "A Review of the Evidence Concerning the Impact of Medical Measures on Recent Mortality and Morbidity in the United States." *International Journal of Health Services* 19 (2): 181–208.

McLaughlin, Diane K., and Alicia Coleman-Jensen. 2008. "Nonstandard Employment in the Nonmetropolitan United States." *Rural Sociology* 73 (4): 631–659.

McLaughlin, Diane K., and Lauri Perman. 1991. "Returns vs. Endowments in the Earnings Attainment Process for Metropolitan and Nonmetropolitan Men and Women." *Rural Sociology* 56 (3): 339–365.

188 REFERENCES

Mills, Bradford, and Gautam Hazarika. 2001. "The Migration of Young Adults from Non-Metropolitan Counties." *American Journal of Agricultural Economics* 83 (2): 329–340.

Monnat, Shannon M. 2017. "The New Destination Disadvantage: Disparities in Hispanic Health Insurance Coverage Rates in Metropolitan and Nonmetropolitan New and Established Destinations." *Rural Sociology* 82 (1): 3–43.

Monnat, Shannon M. 2019. "The Contributions of Socioeconomic and Opioid Supply Factors to U.S. Drug Mortality Rates: Urban-Rural and Within-Rural Differences." *Journal of Rural Studies* 68: 319–335.

Monnat, Shannon M. 2020a. "Trends in US Working-Age Non-Hispanic White Mortality: Rural-Urban and Within-Rural Differences." *Population Research and Policy Review* 39 (5): 805–834.

Monnat, Shannon M. 2020b. "Opioid Crisis in the Rural U.S." In *Rural Families and Communities in the United States*, edited by Jennifer E. Glick, Susan M. McHale, and Valerie King, 117–143. New York: Springer.

Monnat, Shannon M. 2020c. "Why Coronavirus Could Hit Rural Areas Harder." *Lerner Center Population Health Research Brief*, no. 16. Accessed October 24, 2022. https://surface.syr.edu/lerner/60.

Monnat, Shannon M. 2023. "Demographic and Geographic Variation in Fatal Drug Overdose Rates in the United States, 1999–2020." *ANNALS of the American Academy of Political and Social Science* 703 (1): 50–78.

Monnat, Shannon M., and David Brown. 2017. "More Than a Rural Revolt: Landscapes of Despair and the 2016 Presidential Election." *Journal of Rural Studies* 55 (1): 227–236.

Monnat, Shannon M., and Raeven Faye Chandler. 2015. "Long-Term Physical Health Consequences of Adverse Childhood Experiences." *The Sociological Quarterly* 56 (4): 723–752.

Monnat, Shannon M., and Raeven Faye Chandler. 2017. "Immigration and Immigrant Poverty in Rural America." In *Rural Poverty in the United States*, edited by Ann R. Tickamyer, Jennifer Sherman, and Jennifer Warlick, 168–201. New York: Columbia University Press.

Monnat, Shannon M., David J. Peters, Mark Berg, and Andrew Hochstetler. 2019. "Using Census Data to Understand County-Level Differences in Overall Drug Mortality and Opioid-Related Mortality by Opioid Type." *American Journal of Public Health* 109: 1084–1091.

Monnat, Shannon M., and Camille Beeler Pickett. 2011. "Rural/Urban Differences in Self-Rated Health: Examining the Roles of County Size and Metropolitan Adjacency." *Health & Place* 17: 311752–319752.

Montez, Jennifer Karas. 2020. "US State Polarization, Policymaking Power, and Population Health." *Milbank Quarterly* 98 (4): 1033–1052.

Montez, Jennifer Karas, Jason Beckfield, Julene Kemp Cooney, Jacob M. Grumbach, Mark D. Hayward, Huseyin Zeyd Koytak, Steven H. Woolf, and Anna Zajacova. 2020. "US State Policies, Politics, and Life Expectancy." *The Milbank Quarterly* 98 (3): 668–699.

Montez, Jennifer Karas, Mark D. Hayward, and Anna Zajacova. 2021. "Trends in U.S. Population Health: The Central Role of Policies, Politics, and Profits." *Journal of Health and Social Behavior* 62 (3): 286–301.

Montez, Jennifer Karas, Nader Mehri, Shannon M. Monnat, Jason Beckfield, Derek Chapman, Jacob M. Grumbach, Mark D. Hayward, Steven H. Woolf, and Anna Zajacova. 2022. "U.S. State Policy Contexts and Mortality of Working-Age Adults." *PLoS ONE* 17 (10): e0275466.

Montgomery, David. 2018. "In These Outlier Congressional Districts, Density Doesn't Equal Democrats." Bloomberg CityLab, November 1. Accessed January 19, 2022. https://www.bloomberg.com/news/articles /2018-11-01/outliers-in-congress-urban-republicans-rural-democrats.

Mueller, J. Tom. 2021. "Defining Dependence: The Natural Resource Community Typology." *Rural Sociology* 86 (2): 260–300.

Mueller, J. Tom. 2022. "Natural Resource Dependence and Rural American Economic Prosperity from 2000 to 2015." *Economic Development Quarterly* 36 (3): 160–176.

Mueller, J. Tom, Matthew M. Brooks, and José D. Pacas. 2022. "Cost of Living Variation, Nonmetropolitan America, and Implications for the Supplemental Poverty Measure." *Population Research and Policy Review* 41: 1501–1523.

Murray, Christopher J., Sandeep C. Kulkarni, Catherine Michaud, Niels Tomijima, Maria T. Bulzacchelli, Terrell J. Iandiorio, and Majid Ezzati. 2006. "Eight Americas: Investigating Mortality Disparities across Races, Counties, and Race-Counties in the United States." *PLoS Medicine* 3 (9): e260.

Myers, Andrew, Arin Leopold, Catherine Ipsen, and Bryce Ward. 2022. "America at a Glance: Occupational Injuries among Rural Workers." The University of Montana Rural Institute for Inclusive Communities. Accessed November 1, 2022. https://scholarworks.umt.edu/ruralinst _employment/47.

National Academies of Sciences, Engineering, and Medicine (NASEM). 2016. *The Economic and Fiscal Consequences of Immigration.* Washington, DC: National Academies Press. Accessed December 27, 2022.

https://nap.nationalacademies.org/catalog/23550/the-economic-and
-fiscal-consequences-of-immigration.

National Academies of Sciences, Engineering, and Medicine (NASEM).
2021. *High and Rising Mortality Rates among Working-Age Adults.*
Washington, DC: National Academies Press. Accessed October 27,
2022. https://nap.nationalacademies.org/catalog/25976/high-and
-rising-mortality-rates-among-working-age-adults.

National Association of Area Agencies on Aging. 2021. "Meeting the
Needs of Older Living in Rural Communities: The Roles of Area
Agencies on Aging." Data Brief. Accessed July 6, 2022. https://www
.usaging.org/Files/AAA-DB-Rural-508.pdf.

National Conference of State Legislatures. 2021. "Redistricting Commissions: Congressional Plans." Accessed January 21, 2022. https://www
.ncsl.org/research/redistricting/redistricting-commissions
-congressional-plans.aspx#Primary.

National Research Council. 2006. *Multiple Origins, Uncertain Destinies:
Hispanics and the American Future.* Washington, DC: The National
Academies Press.

National Rural Housing Coalition. n.d. "Housing Need in Rural America."
Accessed November 1, 2022. https://ruralhousingcoalition.org
/overcoming-barriers-to-affordable-rural-housing/.

Nelson, Margaret K., and Joan Smith. 1999. *Working Hard and Making
Do: Surviving in Small Town America.* Berkeley: University of
California Press.

Nelson, Peter B., Ahn Wei Lee, and Lise Nelson. 2009. "Linking Baby
Boomer and Hispanic Migration Streams into Rural America: A
Multi-Scaled Approach." *Population, Place, and Space* 15: 277–293.

Noe-Bustamante, Luis, Lauren Mora, and Mark Hugo Lopez. 2020.
"About One-in-Four U.S. Hispanics Have Heard of Latinx, but Just 3%
Use It." Pew Research Center. Accessed January 8, 2023. https://www
.pewresearch.org/hispanic/2020/08/11/about-one-in-four-u-s
-hispanics-have-heard-of-latinx-but-just-3-use-it/.

Nolan, Laura B., Jane Waldfogel, and Christopher Wimer. 2017. "Long-
Term Trends in Rural and Urban Poverty: New Insights Using a
Historical Supplemental Poverty Measure." *The Annals of the Ameri-
can Academy of Political and Social Science* 672 (1): 123–142.

Noonan, Rita. 2017. "Rural America in Crisis: The Changing Opioid
Overdose Epidemic." Centers for Disease Control and Prevention.
Accessed January 5, 2022. https://blogs.cdc.gov/publichealthmatters
/2017/11/opioids/.

REFERENCES 191

Nuriddin, Ayah, Graham Mooney, and Alexandre I. R. White. 2020. "Reckoning with Histories of Medical Racism and Violence in the USA." *Lancet* 396 (10256): 949–951.

O'Connell, Heather A. 2012. "The Impact of Slavery on Racial Inequality in Poverty in the Contemporary US South." *Social Forces* 90 (3): 713–734.

O'Connell, Heather A. 2019. "Historical Shadows: The Links between Sundown Towns and Contemporary Black-White Inequality." *Sociology of Race and Ethnicity* 5 (3): 311–325.

Office of Management and the Budget. 2023. *Revised Delineations of Metropolitan Statistical Areas, Micropolitan Statistical Areas, and Combined Statistical Areas, and Guidance on Uses of the Delineations of These Areas*. OMB Bulletin No. 23-01. Washington, DC.

Oliver, Melvin L., and Thomas M. Shapiro. 2019. "Disrupting the Racial Wealth Gap." *Contexts* 18 (1): 16–21.

Ostmo, Per, and Jessica Rosencrans. 2022. "Maternal Health Disparities: An Intersection of Race and Rurality." *Rural Health Research RECAP*. Rural Health Research Gateway. Accessed October 31, 2022. https://www.ruralhealthinfo.org/resources/19573.

Pacas, José D., and David W. Rothwell. 2020. "Why Is Poverty Lower in the Rural America According to the Supplemental Poverty Measure? An Investigation of the Geographic Adjustment." *Population Research and Policy Review* 39 (5): 941–975.

Packer, George. 2021. "The Four Americas." *Atlantic*, July/August 2021, 64–78.

Parker, Kim, Juliana Menasce Horowitz, Anna Brown, Richard Fry, D'Vera Cohn, and Ruth Igielnik. 2018. "What Unites and Divides Urban, Suburban and Rural Communities: Amid Widening Gaps in Politics and Demographics, Americans in Urban, Suburban and Rural Areas Share Many Aspects of Community Life." Pew Research Center. Accessed October 12, 2022. https://www.pewresearch.org/social-trends/2018/05/22/what-unites-and-divides-urban-suburban-and-rural-communities/www.pewresearch.org.

Parker, Kim, Juliana Menasce Horowitz, Ruth Igielnik, J. Baxter Oliphant, and Anna Brown. 2017. "America's Complex Relationship with Guns: An In-Depth Look at the Attitudes and Experiences of U.S. Adults." Pew Research Center. Accessed October 12, 2022. https://www.pewresearch.org/social-trends/2017/06/22/americas-complex-relationship-with-guns/.

Paschal, Olivia. 2020. "Covid-19 Pounded Arkansas Poultry Workers as Government and Industry Looked On." *Daily Yonder*, August 28.

Accessed October 22, 2020. https://dailyyonder.com/covid-19-pounded-arkansas-poultry-workers-as-government-and-industry-looked-on/2020/08/28/.

Pendergrast, Claire, and Danielle Rhubart. 2022. "Socio-Spatial Disparities in County-Level Availability of Aging and Disability Services Organizations." *Journal of Rural Social Sciences* 37 (1): article 3.

Perdue, Robert T., and Gregory Pavela. 2012. "Addictive Economies and Coal Dependency: Methods of Extraction and Socioeconomic Outcomes in West Virginia, 1997–2009." *Organization & Environment* 25 (4): 368–384.

Peters, David J. 2019. "Community Resiliency in Declining Small Towns: Impact of Population Loss on Quality of Life over 20 years." *Rural Sociology* 84 (4): 635–668.

Peters, David J. 2020. "Community Susceptibility and Resiliency to COVID-19 across the Rural-Urban Continuum in the United States." *Journal of Rural Health* 36 (3): 446–456.

Peters, David. J., Shannon M. Monnat, Andrew Hochstetler, and Mark Berg. 2020. "The Opioid Hydra: Understanding Mortality Epidemics and Pandemics across the Rural-Urban Continuum." *Rural Sociology* 85 (3): 589–622.

Petersen, Julia, and Richelle L. Winkler. 2022. "Rural America Gets a Boost from Migration Changes During the COVID-19 Pandemic." Rural Population Research Network, Brief 2022-10.

Pew Research Center. 2021. "Amid a Series of Mass Shootings in the U.S., Gun Policy Remains Deeply Divisive: Declining Support among Republicans for Ban on Assault-Style Weapons, National Gun Registry." Accessed October 12, 2022. https://www.pewresearch.org/politics/2021/04/20/amid-a-series-of-mass-shootings-in-the-u-s-gun-policy-remains-deeply-divisive/.

Pilgeram, Ryanne. 2021. *Pushed Out: Contested Development and Rural Gentrification in the West.* Seattle: University of Washington Press.

Population Reference Bureau. 2007. "Hispanic Segregation in America's New Rural Boomtowns." Accessed December 27, 2022. https://www.prb.org/resources/hispanic-segregation-in-americas-new-rural-boomtowns/.

Portes, Alenjandro. 1994. "The Informal Economy and Its Paradoxes." In *The Handbook of Economic Sociology,* edited by Neil J. Smelser and Richard Swedberg, 426–449. Princeton, NJ: Princeton University Press.

REFERENCES

Portes, Alejandro, Manuel Castells, and Lauren A. Benton, eds. 1989. *The Informal Economy: Studies in Advanced and Less Developed Countries.* Baltimore, MD: Johns Hopkins University Press.

President's National Advisory Committee on Rural Poverty. 1967. *The People Left Behind.* Washington, DC: U.S. Government Printing Office.

Princeton Gerrymandering Project. 2022. "Gerrymandering Project." Accessed January 21, 2022. https://gerrymander.princeton.edu/info/.

Probst, Janice C., Jessica D. Bellinger, Katrina M. Walsemann, James Hardin, and Saundra H. Glover. 2011. "Higher Risk of Death in Rural Blacks and Whites Than Urbanites Is Related to Lower Incomes, Education, and Health Coverage." *Health Affairs* 30 (10): 1872–1879.

Public Broadcasting Service (PBS). n.d. "Surviving the Dust Bowl: Mass Exodus from the Plains." Accessed May 20, 2023. https://www.pbs.org/wgbh/americanexperience/features/surviving-the-dust-bowl-mass-exodus-plains/.

Pullen, Erin, and Carrie Oser. 2014. "Barriers to Substance Abuse Treatment in Rural and Urban Communities: Counselor Perspectives." *Substance Use & Misuse* 49 (7): 891–901.

Qin, Hua. 2016. "Newcomers and Oldtimers: Do Classification Methods Matter in the Study of Amenity Migration Impacts in Rural America? *Population and Environment* 38 (1): 101–114.

Quinones, Sam. 2015. *Dreamland: The True Tale of America's Opiate Epidemic.* New York: Bloomsbury Press.

Quinones, Sam. 2021. *The Least of Us: True Tales of America and Hope in the Time of Fentanyl and Meth.* New York: Bloomsbury Press.

Rafferty, Ann P., Huabin Luo, Kathleen L. Egan, Ronny A. Bell, N. Ruth Gaskins Little, and Satomi Imai. 2021. "Rural, Suburban, and Urban Differences in Chronic Pain and Coping Among Adults in North Carolina: 2018 Behavioral Risk Factor Surveillance System." *Preventing Chronic Disease* 18: 200352.

Rahman, Momotazur, Elizabeth M. White, Caroline Mills, Kali S. Thomas, and Eric Jutkowitz. 2021. "Rural-Urban Differences in Diagnostic Incidence and Prevalence of Alzheimer's Disease and Related Dementias." *Alzheimer's & Dementia* 17 (7): 1213–1230.

Rakich, Nathaniel. 2020. "How Urban or Rural Is Your State? And What Does That Mean for the 2020 Election?" FiveThirtyEight. Accessed August 22, 2022. https://fivethirtyeight.com/features/how-urban-or-rural-is-your-state-and-what-does-that-mean-for-the-2020-election/.

Ratner, Shanna. 2000. *The Informal Economy in Rural Community Economic Development.* Accessed March 10, 2005. http://www.rural.org/publications/Ratner00-03.

Reuben, Anthony. 2020. "Coronavirus: Why Have There Been So Many Outbreaks in Meat Processing Plants?" *BBC News,* June 22. Accessed December 4, 2020. https://www.bbc.com/news/53137613.

Rhubart, Danielle C., and Elyzabeth W. Engle. 2017. "The Environment and Health." In *Rural Poverty in the United States,* edited by Ann R. Tickamyer, Jennifer Sherman, and Jennifer Warlick, 299–321. New York: Columbia University Press.

Rhubart, Danielle, and Shannon M. Monnat. 2022. "Self-Rated Physical Health among Working-Aged Adults along the Rural-Urban Continuum—United States, 2021." *Morbidity and Mortality Weekly Report* 71 (5).

Rhubart, Danielle C., Shannon M. Monnat, Leif Jensen, and Claire Pendergast. 2020. "The Unique Impacts of U.S. Social and Health Policies on Rural Population Health and Aging." *Public Policy Aging Report* 31 (1): 24–29.

Rhubart, Danielle, Yue Sun, Claire Pendergrast, and Shannon Monnat. 2022. "Sociospatial Disparities in 'Third Place' Availability in the United States." *Socius* 8: 1–11.

Rigg, Khary K., Shannon M. Monnat, and Melody N. Chavez. 2018. "Opioid-Related Mortality in Rural America: Geographic Heterogeneity and Intervention Strategies." *International Journal of Drug Policy* 57:119–129.

Roberts, Megan E., Nathan J. Doogan, Cassandra A. Stanton, Amanda J. Quisenberry, Andrea C. Villanti, Diann E. Gaalema, Diana R. Keith, et al. 2017. "Rural Versus Urban Use of Traditional and Emerging Tobacco Products in the United States, 2013–2014." *American Journal of Public Health* 107 (10): 1554–1559.

Rodden, Jonathan. 2019. *Why Cities Lose: The Deep Roots of the Urban-Rural Political Divide.* New York: Basic Books.

Rose, Margaret. 2022. "Native American Mental Health: Adding Culture to the Conversation." *Lerner Center Population Health Research Brief Series,* no. 58. Accessed October 31, 2022. https://surface.syr.edu/lerner/189.

Royte, Elizabeth. 2005. "Review of *The Worst Hard Time,* by Timothy Egan." *New York Times,* December 25. Accessed May 20, 2023. https://www.nytimes.com/2005/12/25/books/review/the-antijoads.html.

Rudd, Rose A., Puja Seth, Felicita David, and Lawrence Scholl. 2016. "Increases in Drug and Opioid-Involved Overdose Deaths—United

States, 2010–2015." *Morbidity and Mortality Weekly Report* 65 (50–51): 1445–1452.

Runyon, Luke. 2017. "Why Is the Opioid Epidemic Hitting Rural America Especially Hard?" NPR Illinois, January 4. Accessed January 5, 2022. https://www.nprillinois.org/health-harvest/2017-01-04/why-is-the-opioid-epidemic-hitting-rural-america-especially-hard.

Rural Health Information Hub. 2019. "Rural Agriculture Health and Safety." Accessed November 1, 2022. https://www.ruralhealthinfo.org/topics/agricultural-health-and-safety.

Rural Health Information Hub. 2022. Rural Health Information Hub home page. Accessed June 3, 2022. https://www.ruralhealthinfo.org/.

Rutherford, Adam. 2017. "A New History of the First Peoples in the Americas." *Atlantic*, October 3.

Sáenz, Rogelio. 2012. "Rural Race and Ethnicity." In *International Handbook of Rural Demography*, edited by László J. Kulcsár and Katherine J. Curtis, 207–223. Dordrecht, Netherlands: Springer.

Sáenz, Rogelio, and Cruz C. Torres. 2003. "Latinos in Rural America." In *Challenges for Rural America in the Twenty-First Century*, edited by David L. Brown and Louis E. Swanson, 57–70. University Park: Pennsylvania State University Press.

Scala, Dante J., and Kenneth M. Johnson. 2017. "Political Polarization along the Rural-Urban Continuum? The Geography of the Presidential Vote, 2000–2016." *Annals of the American Academy of Political and Social Science* 672 (1): 162–184.

Schneider, Gregory S., and Laura Vozzella. 2018. "With Blue Cities and Red Rural Areas, the Suburbs are the New Political Battleground." *Washington Post*, November 7.

Schochet, Leila. 2019. "5 Facts to Know about Child Care in Rural America." Accessed March 28, 2022. https://www.americanprogress.org/article/5-facts-know-child-care-rural-america/.

Schumpeter, Joseph A. 1942. *Capitalism, Socialism, and Democracy*. New York: Harper and Brothers.

Sharp, Gregory, and Barrett A. Lee. 2017. "New Faces in Rural Places: Patterns and Sources of Nonmetropolitan Ethnoracial Diversity Since 1990." *Rural Sociology* 82 (3): 411–443.

Sherman, Jennifer. 2009. *Those Who Work, Those Who Don't: Poverty, Morality, and Family in Rural America*. Minneapolis: University of Minnesota Press.

Sherman, Jennifer. 2014. "Rural Poverty: The Great Recession, Rising Unemployment, and the Under-Utilized Safety Net." In *Rural America in a Globalizing World: Problems and Prospects for the 2010s*, edited by Conner Bailey, Leif Jensen, and Elizabeth Ransom, 523–539. Morgantown: West Virginia University Press.

Sherman, Jennifer. 2021a. *Dividing Paradise: Rural Inequality and the Diminishing American Dream*. Oakland: University of California Press.

Sherman, Jennifer. 2021b. "'Please Don't Take This': Rural Gentrification, Symbolic Capital, and Housing Insecurity." *Social Problems* 70 (2): 491–510.

Singh, Gopal K., and Mohammad Siahpush. 2014. "Widening Rural– Urban Disparities in All-Cause Mortality and Mortality from Major Causes of Death in the USA, 1969–2009." *Journal of Urban Health* 91 (2): 272–292.

Slack, Tim. 2007a. "The Contours and Correlates of Informal Work in Rural Pennsylvania." *Rural Sociology* 72 (1): 69–89.

Slack, Tim. 2007b. "Work, Welfare, and the Informal Economy: Toward an Understanding of Household Livelihood Strategies." *Community Development* 38 (1): 26–42.

Slack, Tim. 2010. "Working Poverty across the Metro-Nonmetro Divide: A Quarter-Century in Perspective, 1979–2003." *Rural Sociology* 75 (3): 363–387.

Slack, Tim. 2014. "Work in Rural America in the Era of Globalization." In *Rural America in a Globalizing World: Problems and Prospects for the 2010s*, edited by Conner Bailey, Leif Jensen, and Elizabeth Ransom, 573–590. Morgantown: West Virginia University Press.

Slack, Tim, Michael R. Cope, Leif Jensen, and Ann R. Tickamyer. 2017. "Social Embeddedness, Formal Labor Supply, and Participation in Informal Work." *International Journal of Sociology and Social Policy* 37 (3–4): 248–264.

Slack, Tim, and Leif Jensen. 2002. "Race, Ethnicity, and Underemployment in Nonmetropolitan America: A 30-Year Profile." *Rural Sociology* 67 (2): 208–233.

Slack, Tim, and Leif Jensen. 2004. "Employment Adequacy in Extractive Industries: An Analysis of Underemployment, 1974–1998." *Society and Natural Resources* 17: 129–146.

Slack, Tim, and Leif Jensen. 2008. "Employment Hardship among Older Workers: Does Residential and Gender Inequality Extend into Older Age?" *Journals of Gerontology: Series B* 63 (1): S15–S24.

Slack, Tim, and Leif Jensen. 2010. "Informal Work in Rural America: Theory and Evidence." In *Informal Work in Developed Nations*, edited by Enrico Marcelli, Colin C. Williams, and Pascale Joassart, 177–191. New York: Routledge.

Slack, Tim, and Leif Jensen. 2020. "The Changing Demography of Rural and Small-Town America." *Population Research and Policy Review* 39 (5): 775–783.

Slack, Tim, and Candice A. Myers. 2012. "Understanding the Geography of Food Stamp Program Participation: Do Space and Place Matter?" *Social Science Research* 41 (2): 263–275.

Slack, Tim, and Tracey E. Rizzuto. 2013. "Aging and Economic Well-Being in Rural America: Exploring Income and Employment Challenges." In *Rural Aging in 21st Century America*, edited by Nina Glasgow and E. Helen Berry, 57–75. New York: Springer.

Slack, Tim, Joachim Singelmann, Kayla Fontenot, Dudley L. Poston, Rogelio Saenz, and Carlos Siordia. 2009. "Poverty in the Texas Borderland and Lower Mississippi Delta: A Comparative Analysis of Differences by Family Type." *Demographic Research* 20: 353–376.

Slack, Tim, Brian C. Thiede, and Leif Jensen. 2020. "Race, Residence, and Underemployment: Fifty Years in Comparative Perspective, 1968–2017." *Rural Sociology* 85 (2): 275–315.

Smith, Amy Symens, and Edward Trevelyan. 2019. "The Older Population in Rural America: 2012–2016." *American Community Survey Reports* (ACS-41), U.S. Census Bureau.

Smith, John P. 1991. "Cultural Preservation of the Sea Island Gullah: A Black Social Movement in the Post-Civil Rights Era." *Rural Sociology* 56 (2): 284–298.

Smith, Kristin E., and Ann R. Tickamyer, eds. 2011. *Economic Restructuring and Family Well-Being in Rural America*. University Park: Pennsylvania State University Press.

Smith, Michael D., and Richard S. Krannich. 2000. "'Culture Clash' Revisited: Newcomer and Longer-Term Residents' Attitudes Toward Land Use, Development, and Environmental Issues in Rural Communities in the Rocky Mountain West." *Rural Sociology* 65 (3): 396–421.

Smith-Nonini, Sandy, and Olivia Paschal. 2020. "As Covid-19 Hit Georgia Meatpacking Counties, Officials and Industry Shifted Blame." *Daily Yonder*, September 15. Accessed October 22, 2020. https://dailyyonder .com/as-covid-19-hit-georgia-meatpacking-counties-officials-and -industry-shifted-blame/2020/09/15/.

Snipp, C. Matthew. 1989. *American Indians: The First of this Land*. New York: Russell Sage Foundation.

198   REFERENCES

Snipp, C. Matthew. 1996. "Understanding Race and Ethnicity in Rural America." *Rural Sociology* 61 (1): 125–142.

Snipp, C. Matthew. 2003. "Racial Measurement in the American Census: Past Practices and Implications for the Future. *Annual Review of Sociology* 29: 563–588.

Snipp, C. Matthew, Hayward D. Horton, Leif Jensen, Joane Nagel, and Refugio Rochin. 1993. "Persistent Rural Poverty and Racial and Ethnic Minorities." In *Persistent Poverty in Rural America*, edited by the Rural Sociological Society Task Force on Persistent Rural Poverty, 173–199. Boulder, CO: Westview Press.

Sørensen, Jens F. L. 2016. "Rural-Urban Differences in Bonding and Bridging Social Capital." *Regional Studies* 50 (3): 391–410.

Sorokin, Pitirim, and Carle C. Zimmerman. 1929. *Principles of Rural-Urban Sociology*. New York: Henry Holt.

Sotto-Santiago, Sylk. 2019. "Time to Reconsider the Word Minority in Academic Medicine." *Journal of Best Practices in Health Professions Diversity* 12 (1): 72–78.

Stedman, Richard C., John R. Parkins, and Thomas M. Beckley. 2005. "Forest Dependence and Community Well-Being in Rural Canada: Variation by Forest Sector and Region." *Canadian Journal of Forest Research* 35 (1): 215–220.

Storper, Michael, and Richard Walker. 1989. *The Capitalist Imperative: Territory, Technology and Industrial Growth*. New York: Basil Blackwell.

Sullivan, Teresa A. 1978. *Marginal Workers, Marginal Jobs: Under-utilization of the U.S. Work Force*. Austin: University of Texas Press.

Summers, Gene F. 1991. "Minorities in Rural Society." *Rural Sociology* 56 (2):177–188.

Sun, Yue, Kent Jason G. Cheng, and Shannon M. Monnat. 2021. "Rural-Urban and Within-Rural Differences in COVID-19 Mortality Rates." *Journal of Rural Social Sciences* 37 (2): 1–45.

Sun, Yue, and Shannon M. Monnat. 2022. "Rural-Urban and Within-Rural Differences in COVID-19 Vaccination Rates." *Journal of Rural Health* 38 (4): 916–922.

Swendener, Alexis, Katie Rydberg, Mariana Tuttle, Hawking Yam, and Carrie Henning-Smith. 2023. "Crowded Housing and Housing Cost Burden by Disability, Race, Ethnicity, and Rural-Urban Location." UMN Rural Health Research Center Policy Brief. Accessed March 17, 2023. https://rhrc.umn.edu/publication/crowded-housing-and-housing -cost-burden-by-disability-race-ethnicity-and-rural-urban-location/.

Tate, Eric, Md Asif Rahman, Christopher T. Emrich, and Christopher C. Sampson. 2021. "Flood Exposure and Social Vulnerability in the United States," *Natural Hazards* 106 (1): 435–457.

Taylor, Charles A., Christopher Boulos, and Douglas Almond. 2020. "Livestock Plants and COVID-19 Transmission." *Proceedings of the National Academy of Sciences of the United States of America* 117 (50): 31706–31715.

Taylor, Jonathan, and Joseph Kalt. 2005. *American Indians on Reservations: A Databook of Socioeconomic Change between the 1990 and 2000 Censuses.* Cambridge, MA: The Harvard Project on American Indian Economic Development.

Thiede, Brian C., David L. Brown, Scott R. Sanders, Nina Glasgow, and Laszlo J. Kulcsar. 2017. "A Demographic Deficit? Local Population Aging and Access to Services in Rural America, 1990–2010." *Rural Sociology* 82 (1): 44–74.

Thiede, Brian C., Daniel T. Lichter, and Tim Slack. 2018. "Working, but Poor: The Good Life in Rural America?" *Journal of Rural Studies* 59: 183–193.

Thiede, Brian C., and Tim Slack. 2017. "The *Old* versus *New* Economies and their Impacts." In *Rural Poverty in the United States*, edited by Ann R. Tickamyer, Jennifer Sherman, and Jennifer Warlick, 231–256. New York: Columbia University Press.

Tickamyer, Ann R., Jennifer Sherman, and Jennifer Warlick. 2017. *Rural Poverty in the United States.* New York: Columbia University Press.

Tönnies, Ferdinand. [1887] 1940. *Fundamental Concepts of Sociology (Gemeinschaft und Gesellschaft).* Translated by Charles P. Loomis. New York: American Book.

Towers, Frank. 2019. "Urban and Rural America in the Civil War." In *The Cambridge History of the Civil War*, edited by Aaron Sheehan-Dean, 264–284. New York: Cambridge University Press.

Truesdell, Leon E. 1949. "The Development of the Urban-Rural Classification in the United States: 1874–1949." *Current Population Report*, Series P-23, No. 1. U.S. Census Bureau.

Ulrich-Schad, Jessica D. 2018. "'We Didn't Move Here to Move to Aspen': Community Making and Community Development in an Emerging Rural Amenity Destination." *Journal of Rural and Community Development* 13 (4): 43–65.

Ulrich-Schad, Jessica D., and Cynthia M. Duncan. 2018. "People and Places Left Behind: Work, Culture, and Politics in the Rural United States." *Journal of Peasant Studies* 45 (1): 59–79.

REFERENCES

Ulrich-Schad, Jessica D., Jennifer E. Givens, and Mitchell Beacham. 2022. "Preventive Behaviors along the Rural-Urban Continuum in Utah during the COVID-19 Pandemic." *Journal of Rural Social Science* 37 (2).

Ulrich-Schad, Jessica D., and Hua Qin. 2018. "Culture Clash? Predictors of Views on Amenity-Led Development and Community Involvement in Rural Recreation Counties." *Rural Sociology* 83 (1): 81–108.

Umberson, Debra, and Jennifer Karas Montez. 2010. "Social Relationships and Health: A Flashpoint for Health Policy." *Journal of Health and Social Behavior* 51 (Supp. 1): S54–S66.

U.S. Bureau of Economic Analysis. 2022. "Regional GDP and Personal Income, Interactive Data Tables, CAINC5." Accessed June 30, 2022. https://www.bea.gov/itable/regional-gdp-and-personal-income.

U.S. Bureau of Labor Statistics. 2021. "Employment by Major Industry Sector." Accessed October 11, 2021. https://www.bls.gov/emp/tables/employment-by-major-industry-sector.htm.

U.S. Census Bureau. 2011. *2006–2010 American Community Survey.* Accessed October 11, 2021. https://www.socialexplorer.com/explore-tables.

U.S. Census Bureau. 2016. *2011–2015 American Community Survey.* Accessed October 11, 2021. https://www.socialexplorer.com/explore-tables.

U.S. Census Bureau. 2017. "One in Five Americans Live in Rural Areas." Accessed December 5, 2022. https://www.census.gov/library/stories/2017/08/rural-america.html.

U.S. Census Bureau. 2021a. "Rural America: How Does the Census Bureau Define Rural?" Accessed July 27, 2021. https://mtgis-portal.geo.census.gov/arcgis/apps/MapSeries/.index.html?appid=49cd4bc9c8eb444ab51218c1d5001ef6.

U.S. Census Bureau. 2021b. *Supplementary Tables on Race and Hispanic Origin: 2020 Redistricting Data (P.L. 94-171).* Accessed July 1, 2022. https://www.census.gov/data/tables/2020/dec/2020-redistricting-supplementary-tables.html.

U.S. Census Bureau. 2021c. *American Community Survey 2021 (1-Year Estimate): SE:A03001:Race and ACS21:B02010, American Indian and Alaska Native Alone or in Combination with One or More Other Races.* Accessed October 11, 2021. https://www.socialexplorer.com/explore-tables.

U.S. Census Bureau. 2021d. *2016–2020 American Community Surveys.* Accessed October 11, 2021. https://www.socialexplorer.com/explore-tables.

U.S. Census Bureau. 2022a. "Nation's Urban and Rural Populations Shift Following 2020 Census." Accessed June 28, 2023. https://www.census .gov/newsroom/press-releases/2022/urban-rural-populations.html.

U.S. Census Bureau. 2022b. "Census Bureau Releases Estimates of Undercount and Overcount in the 2020 Census." Accessed May 10, 2023. https://www.census.gov/newsroom/press-releases/2022/2020 -census-estimates-of-undercount-and-overcount.html#.

U.S. Census Bureau. 2022c. "2020 Decennial Census." Accessed November 1, 2022. https://data.census.gov/cedsci/all?q=Scioto%20County, %20Ohio&g=0100000US.

U.S. Census Bureau. 2023a. "List of 2020 Census Urban Areas." Accessed July 25, 2023. https://www.census.gov/programs-surveys/geography /guidance/geo-areas/urban-rural.html.

U.S. Census Bureau. 2023. "Core Based Statistical Areas (CBSAs), Metropolitan Divisions, and Combined Statistical Areas (CSAs)." Accessed July 25, 2023. https://www.census.gov/geographies/reference -files/time-series/demo/metro-micro/delineation-files.html.

U.S. Centers for Disease Control and Prevention. 2020. "First Travel-Related Case of 2019 Novel Coronavirus Detected in the United States." *CDC Newsroom.* Accessed October 20, 2022. https://www.cdc .gov/media/releases/2020/p0121-novel-coronavirus-travel-case.html.

U.S. Centers for Disease Control and Prevention. 2022a. "National Vital Statistics System, Mortality 1968–1988." *CDC WONDER Online Database.* Accessed October 27, 2022. http://wonder.cdc.gov/cmf-icd9.html.

U.S. Centers for Disease Control and Prevention. 2022b. "National Vital Statistics System, Mortality 1999–2020." *CDC WONDER Online Database.* Accessed October 27, 2022. http://wonder.cdc.gov/ucd-icd10.html.

U.S. Centers for Disease Control and Prevention. 2022c. "National Vital Statistics System, Detailed Mortality, All Counties, 2017–2019. Accessed via a restricted data use agreement with the National Center for Health Statistics.

U.S. Department of Agriculture, Economic Research Service. 2017. "Immigration and the Rural Workforce." Accessed October 31, 2022. https://www.ers.usda.gov/data-products/chart-gallery/chart-detail /?chartId=77726.

U.S. Department of Agriculture, Economic Research Service. 2019a. "What Is Rural?" Accessed July 27, 2021. https://www.ers.usda.gov /topics/rural-economy-population/rural-classifications/what-is-rural/.

U.S. Department of Agriculture, Economic Research Service. 2019b. "County Typology Codes.' Accessed October 11, 2021. https://www.ers

.usda.gov/data-products/county-typology-codes/descriptions-and -maps/.

U.S. Department of Agriculture, Economic Research Service. 2020a. "Nonmetro Population Change Has Remained Near Zero in Recent Years." Accessed December 5, 2022. https://www.ers.usda.gov/data -products/chart-gallery/gallery/chart-detail/?chartId=99693.

U.S. Department of Agriculture, Economic Research Service. 2020b. "Rural-Urban Continuum Codes (RUCCs)." Accessed July 27, 2021. https://www.ers.usda.gov/data-products/rural-urban-continuum-codes/.

U.S. Department of Agriculture, Economic Research Service. 2022a. "Natural Amenities." Accessed April 7, 2023. https://www.ers.usda.gov /topics/rural-economy-population/natural-amenities/.

U.S. Department of Agriculture, Economic Research Service. 2022b. "Rural Poverty & Well-Being." Accessed May 26, 2023. https://www.ers .usda.gov/topics/rural-economy-population/rural-poverty-well-being/.

U.S. Department of Agriculture, Economic Research Service. 2022c. "Food Security in the U.S." Accessed November 1, 2022. https://www .ers.usda.gov/topics/food-nutrition-assistance/food-security-in-the-us /measurement/.

U.S. Department of Agriculture, Economic Research Service. 2024. "Rural-Urban Continuum Codes." Accessed January 28, 2024. https:// www.ers.usda.gov/data-products/rural-urban-continuum-codes/.

U.S. Department of Health and Human Services. 2022. "Profile: American Indian/Alaska Native." Accessed December 23, 2022. https://minority health.hhs.gov/omh/browse.aspx?lvl=3&lvlid=62.

U.S. Department of State, Office of the Historian. n.d. "Chinese Immigration and the Chinese Exclusion Acts." Accessed May 10, 2023. https://history.state.gov/milestones/1866-1898/chinese-immigration.

U.S. Department of the Interior. 2022. *Federal Indian Boarding School Initiative Investigative Report*. Washington, DC. Accessed December 27, 2022. https://www.bia.gov/sites/default/files/dup/inline-files /bsi_investigative_report_may_2022_508.pdf.

U.S. Office of Management and Budget. 2023. "Initial Proposals For Updating OMB's Race and Ethnicity Statistical Standards." *Federal Register*. January 27. https://www.federalregister.gov/documents/2023 /01/27/2023-01635/initial-proposals-for-updating-ombs-race-and -ethnicity-statistical-standards.

USA Facts. 2023. "US COVID-19 Cases and Deaths by State." Accessed May 5, 2023. https://usafacts.org/visualizations/coronavirus-covid-19 -spread-map/.

Van Dam, Andrew. 2019. "The Real (Surprisingly Comforting) Reason Rural America Is Doomed to Decline." *Washington Post*, March 24.

Van Vlaanderen, Zoe. 2018. "What's behind the Addiction Crisis in Rural America?" National Council on Alcoholism and Drug Dependence. Accessed January 5, 2022. https://www.ncadd.org/ blogs/addiction-update/what-s-behind-the-addiction-crisis-in-rural-america.

Vargas, Clemencia M., Bruce A. Dye, and Kathy L. Hayes. 2002. "Oral Health Status of Rural Adults in the United States." *Journal of the American Dental Association* 133 (12): 1672–1681.

Vierboom, Yana C., Samuel H. Preston, and Arun S. Hendi. 2019. "Rising Geographic Inequality in Mortality in the United States." *SSM-Population Health* 9: 100478.

von Reichert, Christiane, and E. Helen Berry. 2020. "Rural–Urban Patterns of Disability: The Role of Migration." *Population, Space and Place* 26 (1): E2271.

von Reichert, Christiane, John B. Cromartie, and Ryan O. Arthun. 2014. "Reasons for Returning and Not Returning to Rural U.S. Communities." *The Professional Geographer* 66 (1): 58–72.

Vrijheid, M., H. Dolk, B. Armstrong, L. Abramsky, F. Bianchi, I. Fazarinc, E. Garne, et al. 2002. "Chromosomal Congenital Anomalies and Residence Near Hazardous Waste Landfill Sites." *Lancet* 359 (9303): 320–322.

Warlick, Jennifer. 2017. "The Safety Net in Rural America." In *Rural Poverty in the United States*, edited by Ann R. Tickamyer, Jennifer Sherman, and Jennifer Warlick, 389–415. New York: Columbia University Press.

Warner, Mildred E., George C. Homsy, and Lydia J. Morken. 2017. "Planning for Aging in Place: Stimulating a Market and Government Response." *Journal of Planning Education and Research* 37 (1): 29–42.

Weber, Bruce, and Kathleen Miller. 2017. "Poverty in Rural America Then and Now." In *Rural Poverty in the United States*, edited by Ann R. Tickamyer, Jennifer Sherman, and Jennifer Warlick, 28–64. New York: Columbia University Press.

Wiener, R. Constance, and Richard J. Jurevic. 2016. "Association of Blood Lead Levels in Children 0–72 Months with Living in Mid-Appalachia: A Semi-Ecologic Study." *Rural and Remote Health* 16: 3597.

Williams, Colin C., and Jan Windebank. 1998. *Informal Employment in the Advanced Economies: Implications for Work and Welfare*. London: Routledge.

Winkler, Richelle. 2013. "Living on Lakes: Segregated Communities and Inequality in a Natural Amenity Destination." *The Sociological Quarterly* 54 (1): 105–129.

Winkler, Richelle, Donald R. Field, A. E. Luloff, Richard S. Krannich, and Tracy Williams. "Social Landscapes of the Inter-Mountain West: A Comparison of 'Old West' and 'New West' Communities." 2007. *Rural Sociology* 72 (3): 478–501.

Wright, Earl, II. 2020. *Jim Crow Sociology: The Black and Southern Roots of American Sociology.* Cincinnati, OH: University of Cincinnati Press.

Wuthnow, Robert. 2018. *The Left Behind: Decline and Rage in Rural America.* Princeton, NJ: Princeton University Press.

Yueng, Malcolm, and Evelyn Hu-DeHart. 2004. "Asian Americans" In *Encyclopedia of the Great Plains,* edited by David J. Wishart, 133–48. Lincoln, NE: Center for Great Plains Studies.

Zabek, Mike. 2019. *Local Ties in Spatial Equilibrium.* Finance and Economics Discussion Series 2019-080. Washington, DC: Board of Governors of the Federal Reserve System.

Zhao, Guixiang, Catherine A. Okoro, Jason Hsia, William S. Garvin, and Machell Town. 2019. "Prevalence of Disability and Disability Types by Urban-Rural Classification—U.S., 2016." *American Journal of Preventive Medicine* 57 (6): 749–756.

Index

abortion, rural-urban divide on, 131
adequately employed, 46
adverse childhood experiences (ACEs), 109
Affordable Care Act (ACA), 114–115
age: changes in population structure and composition, 31–33, 147; mortality trends, metro and nonmetro areas compared, 99, 100*fig*, 155n14; net migration data, 24; older adults, 109; rural population data, 23; safety net programs, 57–59
Agencies on Aging (AAA), 59
agriculture: farm, definition of, 38–39, 38*fig*; farm policy as synonymous with rural policy, 141, 144; health effects of employment, 105; history of rurality in America, 3; mechanization of, 37–38; Midwest farm foreclosures in 1980s, 38; natural disasters and climate change, 112–113; as one part of rural economy, 6–7; rural depopulation, 26–28, 26*fig*, 27*fig*; toxin exposure from, 111–112; transition in rural America, 36–39, 38*fig*, 147–148

Aid to Families with Dependent Children (AFDC), 58
Alabama, disability benefits paid in, 57–58
Alaska Natives: ethnoracial inequality, 87–92, 88*tab*; mortality rates, 101–105, 102*fig*, 103*fig*; population data, 76; rural ethnoracial population trends, 65–70, 66*fig*, 68*fig*, 69*fig*, 73*fig*; U.S. Census Bureau categories, 64
amenity destinations. *See* natural amenity destinations
American Indian people: boarding schools, 76; Dawes Act (1887), 76; economies on tribal lands, 50, 77–78; ethnoracial inequality, 62, 87–92, 88*tab*; generational trauma, health effects of, 104–105; geographic variation in rural populations, 71–74, 72*fig*, 73*fig*; hazardous waste facilities, locations of, 111–112; history of ethnoracial settlement, 75–78, 86; history of rurality in America, 3; mortality rates, 101–107, 102*fig*, 103*fig*, 106*fig*; poverty

205

206   INDEX

American Indian people (*continued*)
and, 50, 89–90; rural ethnoracial
population trends, 65–70, 66*fig*, 68*fig*,
69*fig*; terminology for, 64; U.S. Census Bureau categories, 64; U.S. population data, 2, 76; voting behavior, 7,
138–139
Appalachia: coal extraction, health effects
of, 111, 149; drug overdose epidemic,
115–119, 123; ethnoracial diversity in,
74, 78–79, 92; history of settlement in
rural America, 78; mortality rates,
106–107, 106*fig*; poverty in, 36,
49–50, 49*fig*, 89, 92, 106; rural
depopulation, 26–28, 26*fig*, 27*fig*;
rural economies and livelihoods, 43,
44*fig*, 50, 111; rural mortality trends,
22, 155n14; SNAP benefits paid in, 58
Arkansas, 19, 50, 57–58, 83
Asian people: Chinese Exclusion Act
(1882) and anti-Chinese sentiment,
84–85; education levels, 89; ethnoracial inequality, 87–92, 88*tab*; health
outcomes, ethnoracial groups compared, 105; history of settlement in
rural America, 8, 84–87; homeownership rates, 90; mortality rates, 101–
105, 102*fig*, 103*fig*; poverty rates, 89;
rural ethnoracial population trends,
32, 65–70, 66*fig*, 68*fig*, 69*fig*, 73*fig*,
74; terminology for, 64; U.S. Census
Bureau categories, 63, 64; U.S. population data, 2, 73*fig*, 74

Baechtel, Mark, 27–28
barter, 53
Bartik, Timothy, 140
Biden, Joseph (Joe), 126, 138–139
Black Belt region: defined, 50; ethnoracial diversity and inequities, 62; history of settlement in rural America,
62, 71, 81–82; poverty in, 49–50,
49*fig*, 89; voting behavior in, 138
Black people: civil rights movement,
80–81, 86; ethnoracial inequality, 62,
87–92, 88*tab*; geographic variation in
rural populations, 70–74, 72*fig*, 73*fig*;
Great Migration, 5, 80, 139; hazardous waste facilities, locations of, 111–

112; health outcomes, ethnoracial
groups compared, 103–105; Historic
Black Colleges and Universities
(HBCUs), 86; history of enslavement,
effects of, 5, 50, 75, 86; history of
ethnoracial settlement, 5, 74–75,
78–81; homeownership rates, 90–91;
Jim Crow era, 80, 86, 128; mortality
rates, 91, 101–105, 102*fig*, 103*fig*;
poverty rates, 89–90; racialization
processes, effects of, 74–75; Reconstruction (1865–1877), 79–80; rural
economies and livelihoods, 52, 90;
rural ethnoracial population trends,
32, 65–71, 66*fig*, 68*fig*, 69*fig*, 72*fig*, 74;
segregation, 91; "sundown towns," 80;
U.S. Census Bureau categories, 63, 64;
U.S. population data, 2; voting behavior, 7, 79, 128, 138; W. E. B. Du Bois,
5, 86
Bozeman, Montana, 19
Bracero Program, 81–82
"brain drain," 24
broadband access, 142, 151
Brown v. Board of Education (1954), 81
built environment, health and well-being,
109–113
Bush, George H., 130

cardiovascular health, 101
Carter, Jimmy, 130
casinos, income from, 77
categorization, challenges with, 14–15
childcare: access to, 52; costs of, 52; informal economy and, 53
Child Tax Credit, 57
Chinese Exclusion Act (1882), 84–85
Chinese immigrants, 84–85. *See also*
Asian people
Civil Rights Act (1964), 81, 128
civil rights movement, 80–81
climate change, 112–113; low-carbon
economy, transition to, 142–143,
150–151
Clinton, Hillary, 125, 137
Clinton, William (Bill), 58
coal production: economies and livelihoods, 43, 44*fig*, 50, 116; health
effects, 111–112; job losses, effect on

population, 17, 116–117; rural settlement history, 79
cocaine, 118
colonization: generational trauma of American Indians, 104–105; history of ethnoracial settlement, 75–78, 81–82; history of rurality in America, 2–3; history of settlement in rural America, 78–79
congressional elections: rural-urban party divide, 130–131; structural forces for rural-urban divide, 133–136, 135*fig*
conservatism: state policy orientations, 134–136, 135*fig*. *See also* politics and policymaking
contingent work, 41
cost of living, poverty measures and, 51–52
counties: metropolitan-nonmetropolitan designation and, 11–13, 12*map*; Rural-Urban Continuum Codes (RUCC), 13–15, 14*tab*
COVID-19 pandemic, 22, 25, 57; Great Resignation and, 139; mortality rates during, 97, 98*fig*, 99, 100*fig*, 104; natural amenity destinations, popularity of, 29–30, 29*fig*; rural health inequalities and, 119–122, 120*fig*, 123–124
cracking, gerrymandering methods, 133–134
Cramer, Katherine, 132–133
creative destruction, 36, 43; informal economy, growth of, 54
criminal economy, defined, 53
culture clash, in natural amenity destinations, 30
Curtis, Katherine, 43

Dawes Act (1887), 76
death, causes of, 22–23; mortality trends, metro and nonmetro areas compared, 99, 100*fig*, 155n14; rural mortality penalty, 8, 22–23, 95–96, 113–115, 155n14. *See also* health and health disparities, rural populations; mortality rates
Deep South, rural depopulation, 26–28, 26*fig*, 27*fig*
deindustrialization, 7; drug overdose epidemic in rural regions, 116–119,

123; health inequalities, structural factors of, 113–115; transition in rural America, 39–40, 40*fig*. *See also* manufacturing
Delta region: poverty in, 49–50, 49*fig*; SNAP benefits paid in, 58
Democratic Party: congressional elections, rural-urban party divide, 130–131; gerrymandering, 133–134; New Deal and, 128; New Deal coalition, splintering of, 128–129, 129*fig*; "Reagan Democrats," 129; rural America as political monolith, 138–139; "rural consciousness" and voter sentiment, 132–133; rural voting behavior (1980s to present), 129–131. *See also* politics and policymaking
demographic cycle, 33
demographic paradox, 28, 34, 147
demographics: age, 23; categorization, challenges with, 14–15; changes in population structure and composition, 31–33; education level, 21; federal definitions used for rural and urban spaces, 9–15, 11*map*, 12*map*, 14*tab*; geographic variation in rural populations, 70–74, 72*fig*, 73*fig*; history of rurality in America, 2–3; income level, 21; net migration, 23–25, 26*fig*; rural ethnoracial population trends, 65–70, 66*fig*, 68*fig*, 69*fig*; rural mortality penalty, 22–23, 155n14; Rural-Urban Continuum Codes (RUCCs), 13–15, 14*tab*; U.S. population data, 1–2
depopulation, rural, 25–28, 26*fig*, 27*fig*
deserving poor, 47
digital divide, 142, 151
disability benefits, 57–58
discouraged workers, 46–47, 47*fig*
diversity. *See* ethnoracial diversity and inequities; ethnoracial groups
diversity categorization, challenges with, 14–15
Division of Farm Population and Rural Life, USDA, 5
Dreamland: The True Tale of America's Opiate Epidemic (Quinones), 117
drought, 112–113
drug overdose epidemic, 115–119, 123

208 INDEX

Du Bois, W. E. B. (1868–1963), 5, 86
Durkheim, Émile (1858–1917), 4
Dust Bowl, 112

Earned Income Tax Credit, 57
economic diversity, 42–45, 44*fig*; farm policy as synonymous with rural policy, myth of, 141, 144
economic issues: in Colonial America, 3; creative destruction, 36; education level, rural and metro areas, 21; embeddedness, 54–55; gentrification, 30; health inequalities, macroeconomic factors, 113–115; income level, rural and metro areas, 21; metropolitan-nonmetropolitan designations, 11–13, 12*map*; in natural amenity destinations, 30; rural depopulation and, 28; rural labor force, 6–7; rural-urban continuum and, 2. *See also* economies and livelihoods
economies and livelihoods, rural, 35–36, 59–60, 147–148; agricultural transition in rural America, 36–39, 38*fig*; deindustrialization and drug overdose epidemic, 116–119, 123; economic development, local government and, 140–141; economic diversity and dependence, 42–45, 44*fig*; ethnoracial inequality, 87–92, 88*tab*; formal, criminal, and informal economies, defined, 53; future-facing rural policy, 141–143, 150–151; during Gilded Age, 127–128; health effects, structural factors, 113–115; health effects of employment, 105, 111; informal work, 52–57, 56*tab*; labor force, defined, 157n27; landscapes of despair, 137; manufacturing and deindustrialization, 39–40, 40*fig*; nonstandard employment (temporary and contingent work), 41; person- *versus* place-based policies, 139–141; poverty, 47–52, 48*fig*, 49*fig*; safety net programs, 57–59; service sector, 40–42; toxic exposure from industry and agriculture, 111–112; on tribal lands, 77–78; underemployment, 45–47, 47*fig*; U.S. Civil War (1861–1865) and Northern and Southern economies, 127

education level: "brain drain," 24; ethnoracial inequality, 87–92, 88*tab*; health behaviors and, 108; health inequalities, structural factors of, 113–115; mortality rates, 105–107, 106*fig*; population data on, 21; underemployment, 45–47, 47*fig*
elections, 125–126; gerrymandering, 133–134; rural America as political monolith, 138–139; rural revolt for Donald Trump, 136–137; rural-urban political divide, 126–136, 129*fig*, 135*fig*; structural forces for rural-urban divide, 133–136, 135*fig*; winner-take-all districts, 134. *See also* politics and policymaking
Electoral College, 125–126, 133, 137
emancipatory empiricism, 86
embeddedness, 54–55
employment: in agriculture, 38–39, 38*fig*; Asian population, recruitment during labor shortages, 84–87; "good" *vs.* "bad" jobs, 41; health effects of, 105, 111; health inequalities, structural factors of, 113–115; Hispanic population, recruitment during labor shortages, 81–82; informal work, 52–57, 56*tab*; labor force, defined, 157n27; in manufacturing, 39–40, 40*fig*; nonstandard employment (temporary and contingent work), 41; person- *versus* place-based policies, 139–141; in service sector, 40–42; underemployment, 45–47, 47*fig*. *See also* economies and livelihoods, rural
energy resource development, toxic exposure from, 111–112
environmental issues, 9; built, employment, and physical environments, health effects of, 109–113; health outcomes, ethnoracial groups compared, 104; locally undesirable land uses (LULUs), 111–112; natural disasters and climate change, 112–113; toxic exposures, employment and, 111
environmental racism, 104
ethnicity: U.S. Census Bureau categories, 63–64, 153n2, 158n7. *See also* ethnoracial diversity and inequities; ethnoracial groups

INDEX   209

ethnoracial diversity and inequities, 61–62, 92–94, 148–149; Asian populations, 84–87; Black populations, 79–81; geographic variation in rural populations, 70–74, 72*fig*, 73*fig*; health inequities, 91–92, 101–105, 102*fig*, 103*fig*; Hispanic populations, 81–84; history of ethnoracial settlement, 74–87; in housing, 90–91; immigration and, 69–70, 69*fig*; Indigenous populations, 75–78; mortality rates, 101–105, 102*fig*, 103*fig*; rural inequalities, 87–92, 88*tab*; rural population trends, 65–70, 66*fig*, 68*fig*, 69*fig*; White populations, 78–79
ethnoracial groups: changes in population structure and composition, 31–33, 148–149; gerrymandering methods, 133–134; New Deal, politics of, 128; social construction of race, ethnoracial terminology, 62–64; U.S. Census Bureau categories of, 63–64, 153n2, 158n7; U.S. population data, 2. *See also* specific group names
Extension Act (1902), 84–85

family environment, health and well-being, 109
farm, definition of, 38–39, 38*fig*
Farm Belt, rural depopulation, 26–28, 26*fig*, 27*fig*
Farmer-Labor Party, 138
farming. *See* agriculture
farming-dependent counties, USDA, 42–45, 44*fig*
Federalism, 126–127
federal/state government-dependent counties, USDA, 43–45, 44*fig*
females: life expectancy data, 22–23, 155n14; mortality trends, 97, 98*fig*, 155n14
fentanyl, 116, 117, 118
fertility, natural population change, 20–21
floods, 112–113
food insecurity, 110–111
food production, 2
Ford, Gerald, 130
formal economy, defined, 53

Gallatin County, Montana, 19
Galpin, Charles (1864–1947), 5

Garcilazo, Jose Enrique, 141–143
Geary Act (1892), 84–85
gemeinschaft, 4–5, 55
gentrification, 30
gerrymandering, 133–134
gesellschaft, 4–5
Gilded Age, 127–128
globalization: deindustrialization and, 39–40, 40*fig*; deindustrialization and drug overdose epidemic, 116–119, 123; informal economy, growth of, 54; low-carbon economy, transition to, 143
government, role of: public opinion, rural-urban divide, 131; rural politics as anti-statist, 132–133. *See also* politics and policymaking
Granovetter, Mark, 54–55
Great Depression, 128
Great Migration, 5, 80
Great Plains: Dust Bowl, 112; economies and livelihoods, rural, 43, 44*fig*; ethnoracial diversity in, 74; mortality rates, 106–107, 106*fig*; rural depopulation, 26–28, 26*fig*, 27*fig*
Great Recession, 58
Great Resignation, 139
gun laws: gun ownership and, 131; public opinion, rural-urban divide, 131

Hamilton, Alexander, 126
Harvey, Mark, 74–75
hazardous waste facilities, 111–112
health and health disparities, rural populations, 95–96, 122–124, 149; American Indian population, effects of generational trauma on, 104–105; built, employment, and physical environments, effects of, 109–113; COVID-19 pandemic response, 119–122, 120*fig*, 123–124; drug overdose epidemic, 115–119, 123; ethnoracial groups compared, 101–105, 102*fig*, 103*fig*; health behaviors, metro and nonmetro comparisons, 107–108; health-care infrastructure, 109–110; health outcomes, explanations for rural disadvantage, 107–115; healthy migrant effect, 105; immigrant health paradox, 105; patterns and trends in nonmetro health and mortality,

210   INDEX

health and health disparities (*continued*) 96–101, 98*fig*, 100*fig*, 155n14; rural mortality penalty, 8, 22–23, 95–96, 113–115, 155n14; social relationships and, 108–109; structural factors, 113–115
health-care infrastructure, 109–110
health insurance, 91–92
health outcomes, 91–92
healthy migrant effect, 105
heroin, 117
Hispanic people: Bracero Program, 81–82; economies and livelihoods, 61, 83, 90; education levels, 87; ethnoracial composition of rural areas, 32, 34, 71–74, 72*fig*, 73*fig*, 93, 148–149; ethnoracial inequality, 87–92, 88*tab*; food insecurity, 111; health outcomes, ethnoracial groups compared, 91–92, 105, 111; Hispanic paradox, mortality and, 91; history of settlement in rural America, 8, 61, 81–84; homeownership, 90; hostility and stigma faced by, 84; immigration policies and, 82, 83; mortality rates, 91, 101–105, 102*fig*, 103*fig*; Operation Wetback, 82; poverty rates, 89; rural ethnoracial population trends, 65–70, 66*fig*, 68*fig*, 69*fig*; segregation and, 91; terminology for, 64; U.S. Census Bureau categories, 63–64; voting behavior, 7, 139
historical perspective, rurality in America, 2–6
home attachment, labor mobility and, 140
hospitals, access to, 109–110
housing: built environment and health effects, 110; health inequalities, structural factors of, 113–115; homeownership rates, ethnoracial inequality, 90–91; mobile homes, 112–113; segregation, 91
housing costs: gentrification, 30, 52; in natural amenity destinations, 30; as percent of income, 52; supplemental poverty measure (SPM), 51

immigrant destinations, rural areas as, 25, 90, 93
immigrant health paradox, 105

immigrants and immigration: Asian population, history of settlement, 84–87; health outcomes, ethnoracial groups compared, 105; Hispanics, history of settlement, 81–84; New Deal, politics of, 128; public opinion, rural-urban divide, 131; rural ethnoracial population trends, 69–70, 69*fig*
Immigration and Naturalization Act (1965), 82
Immigration Reform and Control Act (1986) (IRCA), 82, 85–86
income: health behaviors and socioeconomic status, 107–108; health inequalities, structural factors of, 113–115; population data, 21; poverty threshold, 51; supplemental poverty measure (SPM), 51. *See also* poverty
Indigenous people: Hispanics as, 81–82; history of ethnoracial settlement, 75–78; U.S. Census Bureau categories, 64. *See also* American Indian people
Industrial Revolution, 3–4, 37. *See also* deindustrialization; manufacturing
inequality: COVID-19 pandemic response, 119–122, 120*fig*, 123–124; digital divide, 142, 151; ethnoracial inequality, 87–92, 88*tab*; health-care infrastructure, 109–110; health outcomes, ethnoracial differences, 91–92; health outcomes, explanations for rural disadvantage, 107–115; in natural amenity destinations, 30; natural disasters and climate change, effects of, 112–113. *See also* poverty
infant mortality rates, 99, 100*fig*
informal economy, defined, 53
informal work, 52–57, 56*tab*; embeddedness, 54–55; by household, metro and nonmetro data, 55–57, 56*tab*
"Informal Work in Rural America" (Slack and Jensen), 53
information technology, 142, 150–151
internet access, 110
Iowa, 61

Japanese immigrants, 85–86. *See also* Asian people
Jefferson, Thomas, 126–127

INDEX   211

Jefferson County, Arkansas, 19
Jensen, Leif, 53
Jim Crow era, 80
jobs. *See* economies and livelihoods, rural; employment

Kansas, 27–28
Kelly, Paige, 140

labor force, 157n27. *See also* employment
labor mobility, 139–141
labor unions, New Deal and, 128
Labor Utilization Framework, 45–47, 47*fig*
Land Grant Universities, 86
landscapes of despair, 137
Latinos, U.S. Census Bureau categories, 63–64. *See also* Hispanic people
lead poisoning, 112
Lebanon, Kansas, 27–28
Lefebvre, Henri, 1
liberalism: state policy orientations, 134–136, 135*fig*. *See also* politics and policymaking
life expectancy, 22–23, 155n14
Link, Bruce, 108
livelihood. *See* economies and livelihoods, rural
Lobao, Linda, 140
local government, economic development and, 140–141
locally undesirable land uses (LULUs), 111–112
local policy environments, health inequalities, structural factors of, 113–115
low-carbon economy, 142–143, 150–151
Lower Rio Grande Valley, 49, 50, 58, 138
low-hour workers, 46–47, 47*fig*
low-income workers, 46–47, 47*fig*

males: life expectancy data, 22–23, 155n14; mortality trends, 97, 98*fig*, 155n14
manufacturing: globalization, effects of, 39–40, 40*fig*; rural labor force and deindustrialization, 6–7; transition in rural America, 39–40, 40*fig*. *See also* deindustrialization
manufacturing-dependent counties, USDA, 43–45, 44*fig*
maternal mortality rates, 99, 100*fig*

McDowell County, West Virginia, 116–119
mechanical solidarity, 4
mechanization of farming, 37–38
Medicaid, 114–115
"Megatrends and Implications for Rural Development Policy" (Garcilazo), 141–143
mental health, 101; family environment and, 109; substance use disorders, access to care, 118, 123
methamphetamine, 117, 118
metropolitan, definitions of, 9–15, 11*map*, 12*map*, 14*tab*
metropolitan areas: COVID-19 pandemic response, 119–122, 120*fig*, 123–124; drug overdose epidemic, 115–119, 123; ethnoracial inequality, 87–92, 88*tab*; health and mortality trends, 96–101, 98*fig*, 100*fig*, 155n14; health behaviors, metro and nonmetro comparisons, 107–108; health outcomes, ethnoracial groups compared, 103–105; health outcomes, explanations for rural disadvantage, 107–115; informal work by household, 55–57, 56*tab*; net migration, 23–25, 26*fig*; poverty in, 48–52, 48*fig*; supplemental poverty measure (SPM), 51; underemployment, rates of, 46–47, 47*fig*; urbanization and classification of rural communities, 17–20. *See also* politics and policymaking
micro-credit programs, 55, 57
micro-enterprise programs, 55, 57
micropolitan (micro) areas, 13
Mid-Atlantic states, rural mortality trends, 22
Midwest: ethnoracial diversity in, 74, 85; farm foreclosures in 1980s, 38; Great Migration and, 80; history of settlement in rural America, 78; majority-minority populations in, 71; "sundown towns" in, 80; voting in 2016 election, 137
migrant farm labor, 50; health and, 105; living conditions, 91
migration, international, 25; ethnoracial composition of rural areas, 32–33; healthy migrant effect, 105. *See also* immigrants and immigration

212 INDEX

migration, net, 23–25, 26*fig*; defined, 23
mining-dependent counties, USDA,
42–45, 44*fig*
mining industry: toxic exposures from,
111–112. *See also* coal production
Minnesota, 138
minoritized populations. *See* ethnoracial
diversity and inequities; ethnoracial
groups
Mississippi: disability benefits paid in,
57–58; state policy orientation, 136
mixed race, rural ethnoracial population,
32, 66–67, 66*fig*, 68*fig*, 74
mobile homes, 112–113
Montana, 19
morbidity: health behaviors, metro and
nonmetro comparisons, 107–108. *See
also* health and health disparities,
rural populations
mortality rates, 22–23, 91–92, 155n14;
ethnoracial groups compared, 101–
105, 102*fig*, 103*fig*; health outcomes,
explanations for rural disadvantage,
107–115; males and females compared,
97, 98*fig*; patterns and trends in nonmetro populations, 96–101, 98*fig*,
100*fig*; by region, 105–107, 106*fig*;
rural mortality penalty, 8, 22–23,
95–96, 113–115, 155n14; socioeconomic status and, 107–108
Mountain West: natural amenity destinations, 28–30, 29*fig*; rural economies
and livelihoods, 43
multiracial identity, rural ethnoracial
population, 32, 66–67, 66*fig*, 74
myths and misunderstandings about rural
America: ethnoracial composition of
rural areas, 32–33, 61–62, 92–94;
examples of, 6–7; farm policy as synonymous with rural policy, 141, 144; as
narrative tool, 6–7; population change
and classification of rural communities, 19–20; poverty as exclusive to
inner city, 47–49, 48*fig*, 49*fig*, 92;
rural as synonymous with farming,
35–36, 41–42, 147–148; rural depopulation, 34, 147

national policy environments, health
inequalities, 113–115

Native American people: boarding
schools, 76; Dawes Act (1887), 76;
economies on tribal lands, 50, 77–78;
ethnoracial inequality, 62, 87–92,
88*tab*; generational trauma, health
effects of, 104–105; geographic variation in rural populations, 71–74, 72*fig*,
73*fig*; hazardous waste facilities, locations of, 111–112; history of ethnoracial
settlement, 75–78, 86; history of rurality in America, 3; mortality rates, 101–
107, 102*fig*, 103*fig*, 106*fig*; poverty
and, 50, 89–90; rural ethnoracial
population trends, 65–70, 66*fig*, 68*fig*,
69*fig*; terminology for, 64; U.S. Census Bureau categories, 64; U.S. population data, 2, 76; voting behavior, 7,
138–139
natural amenities, 2; scale for measuring,
28–30, 29*fig*
natural amenity destinations, 28–30,
29*fig*; housing costs and gentrification,
52; rural areas as, 24–25
natural change, population, 20–23
natural environment: health effects,
111–112; natural disasters and climate
change, 112–113
natural resources, 2; early history of rural
economy, 3, 37; population growth,
effect on, 30; rural areas and the low-
carbon economy, 142–143; rural economies and livelihoods, 43–45, 44*fig*,
50, 55; tribal lands, economies of, 77
net migration, 23–25, 26*fig*; age and, 24;
changes in population structure and
composition, 31–33; defined, 23
New Deal coalition, 128–129, 129*fig*
New Deal policies, 37, 128
New England states, 22, 26, 74
New York, state policy orientation, 136
noncore areas, 13
nonmetropolitan, definitions of, 9–15,
11*map*, 12*map*, 14*tab*
nonmetropolitan areas: COVID-19
pandemic response, 119–122, 120*fig*,
123–124; drug overdose epidemic,
115–119, 123; ethnoracial inequality,
87–92, 88*tab*; health and mortality
patterns and trends, 96–101, 98*fig*,
100*fig*, 155n14; health behaviors,

INDEX   213

metro and nonmetro comparisons, 107–108; health outcomes, explanations for rural disadvantage, 107–115; informal work by household, 55–57, 56*tab*; natural disasters and climate change, risks of, 112–113; net migration, 23–25, 26*fig*; poverty in, 48–52, 48*fig*; rural ethnoracial population trends, 65–70, 66*fig*, 68*fig*, 69*fig*; supplemental poverty measure (SPM), 51; underemployment, rates of, 46–47, 47*fig*; urbanization and classification of rural communities, 17–20. *See also* politics and policymaking; rural-urban continuum

nonspecialized counties, USDA, 43–45, 44*fig*

nonstandard employment (temporary and contingent work), 41

Northeast, 74, 80, 83, 106*fig*, 107

Northern region: New Deal policies, voting blocks in, 128; U.S. Civil War (1861–1865) and, 127, 128

not in the labor force, defined, 46

obesity, 101

official poverty measure (OPM), 48–49, 48*fig*; short-comings of, 51–52

Ohio, drug overdose epidemic, 116–119, 123

Older Americans Act (OAA), 59

Operation Wetback, 82

opioid epidemic, 115–119, 123

organic solidarity, 4

Organisation for Economic Co-operation and Development (OECD), 141–142

Pacific Islander population: mortality rates, 101–105, 102*fig*, 103*fig*; rural ethnoracial population trends, 65–70, 66*fig*, 68*fig*, 69*fig*; U.S. Census Bureau categories, 64. *See also* Asian people

Pacific region, mortality rates, 22, 106*fig*, 107

packing, gerrymandering methods, 133–134

Palin, Sarah, 129

Pandemic Politics: The Deadly Toll of Partisanship in the Age of COVID-19, 121–122

The People Left Behind, 48

Perry, Iowa, 61

Personal Responsibility and Work Opportunity Reconciliation Act (PRWORA), 58–59

person- *versus* place-based policies, 139–141

pesticides, 111–112

Pew Research Center, 131

Phelan, Jo, 108

The Philadelphia Negro (Du Bois), 5

physical environment, health and well-being, 109–113

Pine Bluff, Arkansas, 19

Plessy v. Ferguson (1896), 80

politics and policymaking, 125–126, 143–144, 149–150; abortion, public opinion polling, 131; COVID-19 pandemic response, 121–124; economic development and local government, 140–141; farm policy as synonymous with rural policy, myth of, 141, 144; future-facing rural policy, 141–143, 150–151; gerrymandering, 133–134; gun laws, public opinion polling, 131; health inequalities, structural factors of, 113–115; immigration, public opinion polling, 131; New Deal and the Great Depression, 128; New Deal coalition, 128–129, 129*fig*; person- *versus* place-based policies, 139–141; populism and the Gilded Age, 127–128; "Reagan Democrats," 129; role of government, public opinion polling, 131, 132–133; rural America as political monolith, 138–139; "rural consciousness," 132–133; rural revolt for Donald Trump, 7, 136–137; rural-urban political divide, 126–136, 129*fig*, 135*fig*; rural voting behavior (1980s to present), 7, 129–131; same-sex marriage, public opinion polling, 131; social processes and conservative values in rural areas, 131–132; Southern Strategy, 129, 129*fig*; state policy orientations, 134–136, 135*fig*; state preemption laws, 141; structural forces for rural-urban divide, 133–136, 135*fig*; during U.S. Civil War (1861–1865), 127; winner-take-all districts, 134

214 INDEX

population data: California, 2; ethnoracial groups in U.S., 2; federal definitions used for rural and urban spaces, 9–15, 11*map*, 12*map*, 14*tab*; history of rurality in America, 2–6; natural change in, 20–23; rural areas in U.S., 1–2; rural depopulation, 25–28, 26*fig*, 27*fig*; Rural-Urban Continuum Codes (RUCCs), 13–15, 14*tab*. *See also* rural population change
populism, Donald Trump and, 137
Populist Party, 127–128
Portsmouth, Ohio, 117
poverty: common images of, 36; deserving and undeserving poor, 47; ethnoracial inequality, 87–92, 88*tab*; government threshold for, 51; health behaviors, socioeconomic status and, 107–108; health effects of, 105–107, 106*fig*; measuring, challenges of, 51–52; natural disasters, effects of, 112–113; as persistent challenge in rural America, 47–52, 48*fig*, 49*fig*, 148; persistent poverty counties, USDA, 49–50, 49*fig*; safety net programs, 57–59; stereotypes about geography and, 36; supplemental poverty measure (SPM), 51
Powhatan tribe, 78
prosperity, common images of, 36
public health: COVID-19 pandemic response, 119–122, 120*fig*, 123–124; patterns and trends in health and mortality, 96–101, 98*fig*, 100*fig*, 155n14; substance use disorders, access to care, 118, 123. *See also* health and health disparities, rural populations
public services, economic development and local government, 140–141

Quinones, Sam, 117

race, gerrymandering methods, 133–134
race, social construction of, 62–64; racialization and racialized social structures, 74–75. *See also* ethnoracial diversity and inequities; ethnoracial groups

racism: environmental, 104; structural, 74–75, 104
Reagan, Ronald, 129
"Reagan Democrats," 129
Reconstruction (1865–1877), 79–80, 128
recreation-dependent counties, USDA, 43–45, 44*fig*
Regional and Rural Unit, OECD, 141–142
religion, social processes and conservative values in rural areas, 5, 21, 132–133
republicanism, 126–127
Republican Party: congressional elections, rural-urban party divide, 130–131; gerrymandering, 133–134; New Deal and, 128; New Deal coalition, splintering of, 128–129, 129*fig*; "Reagan Democrats," 129; rural America as political monolith, 138–139; rural voting behavior (1980s to present), 129–131. *See also* politics and policymaking
retirement destinations, rural areas as, 24–25
Rio Grande Valley (Texas Borderland), 138; ethnoracial diversity and inequities, 62; poverty in, 49–50, 49*fig*; SNAP benefits paid in, 58
Roosevelt, Franklin D., 128
rootedness, labor mobility and, 140
rural, definitions of, 9–15, 11*map*, 12*map*, 14*tab*
rural ghettos, 91
rurality in America: historical perspective of, 2–6; myths and misunderstandings, examples of, 6–7. *See also* economies and livelihoods, rural
rural mortality penalty, 8, 22–23, 95–96, 155n14; health inequalities, structural factors of, 113–115
rural politics and policymaking. *See* politics and policymaking
rural population change, 33–34, 146–147; depopulation, 25–28, 26*fig*, 27*fig*; ethnoracial inequality, 87–92, 88*tab*; fertility rate, total, 20–21; geographic variation in rural populations, 70–74, 72*fig*, 73*fig*; history of ethnoracial settlement, 74–87; mortality, 22–23; natural amenity destinations, 28–30,

INDEX   215

29*fig*; natural change, 20–23; net migration, 23–25, 26*fig*; population gain and loss, 20–30, 26*fig*, 27*fig*, 29*tab*; population structure and composition, 31–33; rural ethnoracial population trends, 65–70, 66*fig*, 68*fig*, 69*fig*; urbanization and classification of rural communities, 17–20; in Wyoming, 17–18. *See also* ethnoracial diversity and inequities
Rural Poverty in the United States (Lay), 61
rural rebound, 7
rural-urban continuum, population change and classification of rural communities, 17–20
Rural-Urban Continuum Codes (RUCCs), 13–15, 14*tab*
Rust Belt: drug overdose epidemic, 116–119, 123; voting behavior in, 7

safety net programs, 57–59
same-sex marriage, public opinion, rural-urban divide, 131
Sanders, Bernie, 138
Scioto County, Ohio, 116–119
selective deconcentration, rural population, 26–28, 26*fig*, 27*fig*
service sector, employment in, 40–42
severe weather, 112–113
Sherman, Jennifer, 35, 36
slavery, 3, 78, 127; history of ethnoracial settlement, 74–75, 79–81; W. E. B. Du Bois on, 5
smoking, health effects, 105, 108, 114
Snipp, C. Matthew, 85–86
social construction of race, 62–64, 75
Social Security benefits, 57, 59
social ties and networks: embeddedness, 54–55; health and well-being, 108–109; person- *versus* place-based policies, 140; in rural areas, 55
socioeconomic status (SES), health behaviors and, 107–108
Sorokin, Pitirim (1889–1968), 5
South Atlantic states: mortality rates, 106*fig*, 107; rural mortality trends, 22
South-Central United States, rural mortality trends, 22

Southern region: mortality rates, 106–107, 106*fig*; New Deal policies, voting blocks in, 128; U.S. Civil War (1861–1865) and, 127, 128
Southern Strategy, 129, 129*fig*
Southwest, history of settlement in rural America, 81–82
SPM (supplemental poverty measure), 51, 57–59
state policy environments, health inequalities and, 113–115. *See also* politics and policymaking
states rights, 126–127
structural factors, health disparities, 113–115
structural racism, 104
substance use and abuse: drug overdose epidemic, 115–119, 123; health outcomes, ethnoracial groups compared, 104
suicide, ethnoracial groups compared, 104
"sundown towns," 80
Supplemental Nutrition Assistance Program (SNAP), 58
supplemental poverty measure (SPM), 51, 57–59

tax base, rural depopulation and, 28
tax policy, health inequalities and, 114
Taylor, Carl (1884–1975), 5
telehealth, 109–110
Temporary Assistance for Needy Families (TANF), 58–59
temporary work, 41
Texas Borderland (Rio Grande Valley): ethnoracial diversity and inequities, 62; mortality rates, 106*fig*, 107; poverty in, 49–50, 49*fig*
Those Who Work, Those Who Don't (Sherman), 35, 36
Tönnies, Ferdinand (1855–1936), 4–5
tornadoes, 112–113
total fertility rate (TFR), 20–21
toxins: employment exposures to, 111; from industrial production and agriculture, 111–112; locally undesirable land uses (LULUs), 111
tribal sovereignty, 76–77

216 INDEX

Trump, Donald: anti-immigration stance of, 84; COVID-19 response, 7, 121–122; Electoral College system and, 125–126; nonmetro vote for, 130; rural revolt for, 136–137

Ulrich-Schad, Jessica, 30
underemployment, 45–47, 47*fig*; ethnoracial inequality, 87–92, 88*tab*
undeserving poor, 47
unemployed workers, 46–47, 47*fig*; ethnoracial inequality, 87–92, 88*tab*
urbanization, classification of rural communities, 17–20
urban-rural, definitions of, 9–15, 11*map*, 12*map*, 14*tab*
urban sprawl, 17–20
U.S. Census Bureau: American Indian population data, 76; population change and classification of rural communities, 19–20; racial and ethnic categories, 63–64, 153n2, 158n7; urban-rural definition, 10–11, 11*map*
U.S. Civil War (1861-1865), 127
U.S. Department of Agriculture (USDA): Division of Farm Population and Rural Life, 5; Economic Research Service, economic typology, 42–45, 44*fig*; persistent poverty counties, 49–50, 49*fig*; Rural-Urban Continuum Codes (RUCC), 13–15, 14*tab*
U.S. House of Representatives: structural forces for rural-urban divide, 133–136, 135*fig. See also* politics and policymaking
U.S. Office of Management and Budget (OMB): metropolitan-nonmetropolitan definitions, 11–13, 12*map*
U.S. Senate, 133–136, 135*fig. See also* politics and policymaking

Vermont, 138
Vietnam War, 85
Virginia Company, 78
voting behavior: gerrymandering, 133–134; rural America as political monolith, 138–139; rural revolt for Donald Trump, 136–137; structural forces for

rural-urban divide, 133–136, 135*fig. See also* politics and policymaking
Voting Rights Act (1965), 81, 128

wages: health inequalities, structural factors of, 113–115; manufacturing in rural areas, 39–40, 40*fig*; nonstandard employment (temporary and contingent work), 41
War on Poverty, 48, 51
Washington, Booker T., 86
Washington Post, 17, 27–28
weather, climate change and natural disasters, 112–113
Weaver, James, 127
welfare programs, 57–59
welfare state, retrenchment of, 54, 58–59
Western states: Asian immigrants, history of settlement, 84–85; natural amenity destinations, 28–30, 29*fig*; populist movements in, 127–128; voting behavior, 131
West Virginia: disability benefits paid in, 57–58; drug overdose epidemic, 116–119, 123
White people: ethnoracial composition of rural areas, 32–33; geographic variation in rural populations, 70–74, 72*fig*, 73*fig*; health outcomes, ethnoracial groups compared, 103–105; history of settlement in rural America, 78–79; mortality rates, ethnoracial groups compared to, 101–105, 102*fig*, 103*fig*, 155n14; rural ethnoracial population trends, 65–70, 66*fig*, 68*fig*, 69*fig*; U.S. Census Bureau categories, 64, 158n7
wildfires, 112–113
winner-take-all districts, voting and, 134
work: Asian population, recruitment during labor shortages, 84–87; employment in agriculture, 38–39, 38*fig*; "good" *vs.* "bad" jobs, 41; health effects of employment, 105, 111; health inequalities, structural factors of, 113–115; Hispanic population, recruitment during labor shortages, 81–82; informal work, 52–57, 56*tab*; labor force, defined, 157n27; in manufacturing,

39–40, 40*fig*; nonstandard employment (temporary and contingent work), 41; person- *versus* place-based policies, 139–141; in service sector, 40–42; underemployment, 45–47, 47*fig*. *See also* economies and livelihoods, rural

working class: landscapes of despair, voting behavior and, 137; New Deal and, 128; as "Reagan Democrats," 129

Wyoming, population change in, 17–18

Zoom-towns, 29–30, 29*fig*

Founded in 1893,
UNIVERSITY OF CALIFORNIA PRESS
publishes bold, progressive books and journals
on topics in the arts, humanities, social sciences,
and natural sciences—with a focus on social
justice issues—that inspire thought and action
among readers worldwide.

The UC PRESS FOUNDATION
raises funds to uphold the press's vital role
as an independent, nonprofit publisher, and
receives philanthropic support from a wide
range of individuals and institutions—and from
committed readers like you. To learn more, visit
ucpress.edu/supportus.

Milton Keynes UK
Ingram Content Group UK Ltd.
UKHW040027180824
447066UK00002B/3